CompTIA
Network+®
Review Guide

Bill Ferguson

WILEY

Wiley Publishing, Inc.

Acquisitions Editor: Jeff Kellum
Development Editor: Gary Schwartz
Technical Editor: Quentin Docter
Production Editor: Christine O'Connor
Copy Editor: Kim Wimpsett
Production Manager: Tim Tate
Vice President and Executive Group Publisher: Richard Swadley
Vice President and Publisher: Neil Edde
Project Manager 1: Laura Moss-Hollister
Associate Producer: Shawn Patrick
Media Quality Assurance: Angie Denny
Book Designer: Judy Fung, Bill Gibson
Compositor: James D. Kramer, Happenstance Type-O-Rama
Proofreader: Sheilah Ledwidge, Word One New York
Cover Designer: Ryan Sneed

Copyright © 2009 by Wiley Publishing, Inc., Indianapolis, Indiana

Published simultaneously in Canada

ISBN: 978-0-470-43099-6

For general information on our other products and services or to obtain technical support, please contact our Customer Care Department within the U.S. at (877) 762-2974, outside the U.S. at (317) 572-3993 or fax (317) 572-4002.

Wiley also publishes its books in a variety of electronic formats. Some content that appears in print may not be available in electronic books.

Library of Congress Cataloging-in-Publication Data is available from the publisher.

10 9 8 7 6 5 4

Dear Reader,

Thank you for choosing *CompTIA Network+ Review Guide*. This book is part of a family of premium-quality Sybex books, all of which are written by outstanding authors who combine practical experience with a gift for teaching.

Sybex was founded in 1976. More than thirty years later, we're still committed to producing consistently exceptional books. With each of our titles we're working hard to set a new standard for the industry. From the paper we print on, to the authors we work with, our goal is to bring you the best books available.

I hope you see all that reflected in these pages. I'd be very interested to hear your comments and get your feedback on how we're doing. Feel free to let me know what you think about this or any other Sybex book by sending me an email at nedde@wiley.com, or if you think you've found a technical error in this book, please visit http://sybex.custhelp.com. Customer feedback is critical to our efforts at Sybex.

Best regards,

Neil Edde
Vice President and Publisher
Sybex, an Imprint of Wiley

To my father, who in the 1980s told me to learn as much about computers as I could and to buy and hold Microsoft stock. Unfortunately, I took only part of his good advice. Seriously, his purchase of an IBM PC XT computer in 1983 has made all the difference in my life and in my IT career. He still helps me keep my skills sharp by "allowing" me to troubleshoot his computers now and then!
Thanks, Dad!

To my mother, who has always been and continues to be a source of inspiration for me. She taught me to pursue my goals and never give up. She provides a great example for me as an entrepreneur and an author in her own right.
Thanks, Mom!

Acknowledgments

First I'd like to thank Jeff Kellum for giving me the opportunity to write this important book. Several people have assisted me in many ways, so I'd like to acknowledge their contributions and offer my sincere appreciation. Specifically, I'd like to thank Quentin Docter, Gary Schwartz, and Pete Gaughan for technical and developmental editing and support and for keeping me on track throughout the process. My thanks also goes to Christine O'Connor for helping me put all the final, professional touches on the book. To the many people involved in this effort with whom I never worked with one-on-one — thanks! It takes a great team to put together a great book.

Finally, I'd like to acknowledge the encouragement and prayers of my family and friends and the students in my technical classes and Sunday school classes. In Him, all things are possible!

About the Author

Bill Ferguson   MCT, MCSE, MCP+I, CCSI, CCNA, A+, Network+, Server+, Security+, VCP, VCI has been in the computer industry for over 15 years. Originally in technical sales and sales management with Sprint, Bill made his transition to Certified Technical Trainer in 1997 with ExecuTrain. Bill now runs his own company (Parallel Connections) as an independent contractor/author in Birmingham, Alabama, teaching classes for most of the national training companies and some regional training companies as well as international classes and virtual (online) classes. In addition, Bill writes and produces technical training videos for Quickcert, VTC, and Palaestra Training Company. He has written video titles including *A+, Network+, Windows 2000 Management, Windows XP Management, Windows MCDST,* and *Interconnecting Cisco Network Devices.* In addition, he wrote the *Microsoft Certified Desktop Support Technician (MCDST) Study Guide* and *Network+ Fastpass* books for Sybex/Wiley Press. Bill says, "My job is to understand the material so well that I can make it easier for my students to learn than it was for me to learn."

Contents at a Glance

Contents

Introduction

The Computer Technology Industry Association (CompTIA) developed the Network+ certification to provide an industry-wide means of certifying the competency of computer service technicians in the basics of computer networking. The Network+ certification is granted to those individuals who have attained a level of knowledge and networking skills that show a basic competency with the networking needs of both personal and corporate computing environments.

CompTIA's exam objectives are periodically updated to keep its exams applicable to the most recent technological developments. The foundational elements, however, remain constant even as higher-end technology advances. The Network+ objectives have recently been changed to a small degree to reflect the very latest changes in technology. At the time of this writing, this book is current for the 2009 objectives as stated by CompTIA (www.comptia.org).

What Is Network+ Certification?

The Network+ certification offers an introductory step into the complex world of IT networking. You need to pass only a single exam to become Network+ certified. This is often the first step toward true networking knowledge and experience. By obtaining Network+ certification, you will be able to obtain more networking experience and gain an interest in networks in order to pursue more complex and in-depth network knowledge and certifications.

For the latest pricing on the exam and updates to the registration procedures, go to either www.vue.com or www.prometric.com. You can register online for the exam. If you have further questions about the scope of the exam or related CompTIA programs, refer to the CompTIA website at www.comptia.org.

Is This Book for You?

CompTIA Network+ Review Guide is designed to be a succinct, portable exam review guide that can be used either in conjunction with a more complete study program (such as Wiley's *CompTIA Network+ Study Guide*, computer-based training courseware, or a classroom/lab environment) or as an exam review for those who don't need more extensive test preparation. It isn't my goal to give the answers away but rather to identify those topics on which you can expect to be tested and to provide sufficient coverage of these topics.

Perhaps you've been working with information technologies for many years. The thought of paying lots of money for a specialized IT exam preparation course probably doesn't sound too appealing. What can they teach you that you don't already know, right? Be careful, though. Many experienced network administrators have walked confidently into the test center only to walk sheepishly out of it after failing an IT exam. After you've finished reading this book, you should have a clear idea of how your understanding of networking technologies matches up with the expectations of the Network+ test makers.

Perhaps you're relatively new to the world of IT — drawn to it by the promise of challenging work at a higher salary? You've just waded through an 800-page study guide, or you've taken a class at a local training center. Lots of information to keep in your head, isn't it? Well, by organizing this book according to CompTIA's exam objectives and by breaking up the information into concise, manageable pieces, I've created what I think is the handiest exam review guide available. Throw it in your laptop bag and carry it to work with you. As you read the book, you'll be able to identify quickly those areas you know best and those that require a more in-depth review.

The goal of the Review Guide series is to help Network+ candidates brush up on the subjects on which they can expect to be tested on the Network+ exam. For complete in-depth coverage of the technologies and topics involved, we recommend *CompTIA Network+ Study Guide*, from Wiley.

How Is This Book Organized?

This book is organized according to the official objectives list prepared by CompTIA for the Network+ exam. The chapters correspond to the six major domains of objective and topic groupings. In fact, the exam itself is weighted across these six domains as follows:

- Domain 1.0 Network Technologies (20 percent)
- Domain 2.0 Network Media and Topologies (20 percent)
- Domain 3.0 Network Devices (17 percent)
- Domain 4.0 Network Management (20 percent)
- Domain 5.0 Network Tools (12 percent)
- Domain 6.0 Network Security (11 percent)

Within each chapter, the top-level exam objective from each domain is addressed in turn. This discussion of each objective also contains an "Exam Essentials" section. Here you are given a short list of topics that you should explore fully before taking the test. Included in the "Exam Essentials" areas are notations on key pieces of information you should have taken out of *CompTIA Network+ Study Guide*.

At the end of each chapter you'll find the "Review Questions" section. These questions are designed to help you gauge your mastery of the content in the chapter.

The Exam Objectives

The following are the areas (referred to as *domains*, according to CompTIA) in which you must be proficient in order to pass the Network+ exam:

Domain 1.0 Network Technologies   This content area deals with the functions of common network protocols, ports, addressing technologies, and addressing schemes. I will also discuss routing and routing protocols used primarily with TCP/IP.

Domain 2.0 Network Media and Topologies This area includes the basics of the logical and physical shapes of various networks and how the topology of the network affects the technologies used in the network. I will also discuss common network devices and the connectors that you can use to form various types of networks.

Domain 3.0 Network Devices This area covers specific devices that can be used in today's networks. I will discuss the similarities and differences among these devices and their impact on the network in which they are used. I will also discuss basic router and switch configuration.

Domain 4.0 Network Management This domain illustrates the OSI model of communication and how all the network devices and network protocols are organized based on this model. I will focus on the TCP/IP suite of protocols and differentiate between all the protocols in the suite. In addition, I will discuss network monitoring and methods of network performance optimization and troubleshooting.

Domain 5.0 Network Tools This domain includes the use of various tools to examine a network. I will discuss the appropriate use of the command-line interface as well as other software and hardware tools you can use to receive and interpret output from your network.

Domain 6.0 Network Security This area includes recognizing and defending against common network threats. I will discuss the proper use of firewalls, IDS, VPN concentrators, and other network hardware and software that can help you combat network attacks. I will also discuss common authentication and encryption techniques used by network administrators.

How to Contact the Publisher

Wiley welcomes feedback about all its books. Visit the Wiley website at www.wiley.com for book updates and additional certification information. You'll also find forms you can use to submit comments or suggestions regarding this or any other Wiley book.

The Network+ Exam Objectives

At the beginning of each chapter, I have included a complete listing of the topics that will be covered in that chapter. These topic selections are deeloped straight from the test objectives listed on CompTIA's website. These are provided for easy reference and to assure you that you are on track with learning the objectives. Note that exam objectives are subject to change at any time without prior notice and at CompTIA's sole discretion. Please visit the Network+ Certification page of CompTIA's website (http://certification.comptia.org/network/default.aspx) for the most current listing of exam objectives.

Domain 1.0 Network Technologies

1.1 Explain the function of common networking protocols

- TCP
- FTP
- UDP
- TCP/IP suite
- DHCP
- TFTP
- DNS
- HTTP(S)
- ARP
- SIP (VoIP)
- RTP (VoIP)
- SSH
- POP3
- NTP
- IMAP4
- Telnet
- SMTP
- SNMP2/3
- ICMP
- IGMP
- TLS

1.2 Identify commonly used TCP and UDP default ports

TCP ports:
- FTP – 20, 21
- SSH – 22
- TELNET – 23
- SMTP – 25
- DNS – 53
- HTTP – 80
- POP3 – 110
- NTP – 123

- IMAP4 – 143
- HTTPS – 443

UDP ports:

- TFTP – 69
- DNS – 53
- BOOTPS/DHCP – 67
- SNMP – 161

1.3 Identify the following address formats

- IPv6
- IPv4
- MAC addressing

1.4 Given a scenario, evaluate the proper use of the following addressing technologies and addressing schemes

Addressing Technologies:

- Subnetting
- Classful vs. classless (e.g. CIDR, Supernetting)
- NAT
- PAT
- SNAT
- Public vs. private
- DHCP (static, dynamic, APIPA)

Addressing Schemes:

- Unicast
- Multicast
- Broadcast

1.5 Identify common IPv4 and IPv6 routing protocols

Link state:

- OSPF
- IS-IS

Distance vector:

- RIP
- RIPv2
- BGP

Hybrid:

- EIGRP

1.6 Explain the purpose and properties of routing

- IGP vs. EGP
- Static vs. dynamic
- Next hop
- Understanding routing tables and how they pertain to path selection
- Explain convergence (steady state)

1.7 Compare the characteristics of wireless communication standards

802.11 a/b/g/n:

- Speeds
- Distance
- Channels
- Frequency

Authentication and encryption:

- WPA
- WEP
- RADIUS
- TKIP

Domain 2.0 Network Media and Topologies

2.1 Categorize standard cable types and their properties

Type:

- CAT3, CAT5, CAT5e, CAT6
- STP, UTP
- Multimode fiber, single-mode fiber
- Coaxial
    - RG-59
    - RG-6
- Serial
- Plenum vs. Non-plenum

Properties:

- Transmission speeds
- Distance

- Duplex
- Noise immunity (security, EMI)
- Frequency

2.2 Identify common connector types

- RJ-11
- RJ-45
- BNC
- SC
- ST
- LC
- RS-232

2.3 Identify common physical network topologies

- Star
- Mesh
- Bus
- Ring
- Point to point
- Point to multipoint
- Hybrid

2.4 Given a scenario, differentiate and implement appropriate wiring standards

- 586A
- 586B
- Straight vs. cross-over
- Rollover
- Loopback

2.5 Categorize WAN technology types and properties:

Type:
- Frame relay
- E1/T1
- ADSL
- SDSL

- VDSL
- Cable modem
- Satellite
- E3/T3
- OC-x
- Wireless
- ATM
- SONET
- MPLS
- ISDN BRI
- ISDN PRI
- POTS
- PSTN

Properties:

- Circuit switch
- Packet switch
- Speed
- Transmission media
- Distance

2.6 Categorize LAN technology types and properties:

Types:

- Ethernet
- 10BaseT
- 100BaseTX
- 100BaseFX
- 1000BaseT
- 1000BaseX
- 10GBaseSR
- 10GBaseLR
- 10GBaseER
- 10GBaseSW
- 10GBaseLW
- 10GBaseEW
- 10GBaseT

Properties:

- CSMA/CD
- Broadcast
- Collision
- Bonding
- Speed
- Distance

2.7 Explain common logical network topologies and their characteristics

- Peer to peer
- Client/server
- VPN
- VLAN

2.8 Install components of wiring distribution

- Vertical and horizontal cross connects
- Patch panels
- 66 block
- MDFs
- IDFs
- 25 pair
- 100 pair
- 110 block
- Demarc
- Demarc extension
- Smart jack
- Verify wiring installation
- Verify wiring termination

Domain 3.0 Network Devices

3.1 Install, configure, and differentiate between common network devices

- Hub
- Repeater
- Modem

- NIC
- Media converters
- Basic Switch
- Bridge
- Wireless access point
- Basic router
- Basic firewall
- Basic DHCP server

3.2 Identify the functions of specialized network devices

- Multilayer switch
- Content switch
- IDS/IPS
- Load balancer
- Multifunction network devices
- DNS Server
- Bandwidth shaper
- Proxy server
- CSU/DSU

3.3 Explain the advanced features of a switch

- PoE
- Spanning tree
- VLAN
- Trunking
- Port mirroring
- Port authentication

3.4 Implement a basic wireless network

- Install client
- Access point placement
- Install access point
  - Configure appropriate encryption
  - Configure channels and frequencies
  - Set ESSID and beacon
- Verify installation

Domain 4.0 Network Management

4.1 Explain the function at each layer of the OSI model

- Layer 1 – physical
- Layer 2 – data link
- Layer 3 – network
- Layer 4 – transport
- Layer 5 – session
- Layer 6 – presentation
- Layer 7 – application

4.2 Identify types of configuration management documentation

- Wiring schematics
- Physical and logical network diagrams
- Baselines
- Policies, procedures, and configurations
- Regulations

4.3 Given a scenario, evaluate the network based on configuration management documentation

- Compare wiring schematics, physical and logical network diagrams, baselines, policies and procedures, and configurations to network devices and infrastructure
- Update wiring schematics, physical and logical network diagrams, configurations, and job logs as needed

4.4 Conduct network monitoring to identify performance and connectivity issues using the following

- Network monitoring utilities (e.g., packet sniffers, connectivity software, load testing, throughput testers)
- System logs, history logs, event logs

4.5 Explain different methods and rationales for network performance optimization

Methods:

- QoS
- Traffic shaping
- Load balancing
- High availability

- Caching engines
- Fault tolerance

Reasons:

- Latency sensitivity
- High bandwidth applications
  - VoIP
  - Video applications
- Uptime

4.6 Given a scenario, implement the following network troubleshooting methodology

- Information gathering — identify symptoms and problems
- Identify the affected areas of the network
- Determine if anything has changed
- Establish the most probable cause
- Determine if escalation is necessary
- Create an action plan and solution identifying potential effects
- Implement and test the solution
- Identify the results and effects of the solution
- Document the solution and the entire process

4.7 Given a scenario, troubleshoot common connectivity issues and select an appropriate solution

Physical issues:

- Cross talk
- Nearing cross talk
- Near end cross talk
- Attenuation
- Collisions
- Shorts
- Open impedance mismatch (echo)
- Interference

Logical issues:

- Port speed
- Port duplex mismatch
- Incorrect VLAN

- Incorrect IP address
- Wrong gateway
- Wrong DNS
- Wrong subnet mask
    - Issues that should be identified but escalated:
        - Switching loop
        - Routing loop
        - Route problems
        - Proxy arp
        - Broadcast storms
    - Wireless issues:
        - Interference (bleed, environmental factors)
        - Incorrect encryption
        - Incorrect channel
        - Incorrect frequency
        - ESSID mismatch
        - Standard mismatch (802.11 a/b/g/n)
        - Distance
        - Bounce
        - Incorrect antenna placement

Domain 5.0 Network Tools

5.1 Given a scenario, select the appropriate command line interface tool and interpret the output to verify functionality

- Traceroute
- Ipconfig
- Ifconfig
- Ping
- Arp Ping
- Arp
- Nslookup
- Hostname
- Dig
- Mtr

- Route
- Nbtstat
- Netstat

5.2 Explain the purpose of network scanners

- Packet sniffers
- Intrusion detection software
- Intrusion prevention software
- Port scanners

5.3 Given a scenario, utilize the appropriate hardware tools

- Cable testers
- Protocol analyzer
- Certifiers
- TDR
- OTDR
- Multimeter
- Toner probe
- Butt set
- Punch down tool
- Cable stripper
- Snips
- Voltage event recorder
- Temperature monitor

Domain 6.0 Network Security

6.1 Explain the function of hardware and software security devices

- Network based firewall
- Host based firewall
- IDS
- IPS
- VPN concentrator

6.2 Explain common features of a firewall

- Application layer vs. network layer

- Stateful vs. stateless
- Scanning services
- Content filtering
- Signature identification
- Zones

6.3 Explain the methods of network access security

Filtering:

- ACL
    - MAC filtering
    - IP filtering
- Tunneling and encryption
    - SSL VPN
    - VPN
    - L2TP
    - PPTP
    - IPSEC
- Remote access
    - RAS
    - RDP
    - PPPoE
    - PPP
    - VNC
    - ICA

6.4 Explain methods of user authentication

- PKI
- Kerberos
- AAA
    - RADIUS
    - TACACS+
- Network access control
    - 802.1x
- CHAP
- MS-CHAP
- EAP

6.5 Explain issues that affect device security

- Physical security
- Restricting local and remote access
- Secure methods vs. unsecure methods
    - SSH, HTTPS, SNMPv3, SFTP, SCP
    - TELNET, HTTP, FTP, RSH, RCP, SNMPv1/2

6.6 Identify common security threats and mitigation techniques

Security threats:

- DoS
- Viruses
- Worms
- Attackers
- Man in the middle
- Smurf
- Rogue access points
- Social engineering (phishing)

Mitigation techniques:

- Policies and procedures
- User training
- Patches and updates

Chapter

1

Domain 1 Network Technologies

COMPTIA NETWORK+ EXAM OBJECTIVES COVERED IN THIS CHAPTER:

✓ **1.1 Explain the function of common networking protocols**

- TCP
- FTP
- UDP
- TCP/IP suite
- DHCP
- TFTP
- DNS
- HTTP(S)
- ARP
- SIP (VoIP)
- RTP (VoIP)
- SSH
- POP3
- NTP
- IMAP4
- TELNET
- SMTP
- SMNPv2/3
- ICMP
- IGMP
- TLS

✓ **1.2 Identify commonly used TCP and UDP default ports**

- TCP ports
- FTP – 20, 21
- SSH – 22
- TELNET – 23
- SMTP – 25
- DNS – 53
- HTTP – 80
- POP3 – 110
- NTP – 123
- IMAP4 – 143
- HTTPS – 443
- UDP ports
- TFTP – 69
- DNS – 53
- BOOTPS/DHCP – 67
- SNMP – 161

✓ **1.3 Identify the following address formats**

- IPv6
- IPv4
- MAC addressing

✓ **1.4 Given a scenario, evaluate the proper use of the following addressing technologies and addressing schemes**

- Subnetting
- Classful vs. classless (e.g., CIDR, Supernetting)
- NAT
- PAT
- SNAT
- Public vs. Private
- DHCP (static, dynamic, APIPA)
- Unicast
- Multicast
- Broadcast

✓ **1.5 Identify common IPv4 and IPv6 routing protocols**

- Link state
- OSPF
- IS-IS
- Distance vector
- RIP
- RIPv2
- BGP
- Hybrid
- EIGRP

✓ **1.6 Explain the purpose and properties of routing**

- IGP vs. EGP
- Static vs. dynamic
- Next hop
- Understanding routing tables and how they pertain to path selection
- Explain convergence (steady state)

✓ **1.7 Compare the characteristics of wireless communication standards**

- 802.11 a/b/g/n
- Speeds
- Distance
- Channels
- Frequency
- Authentication and encryption
- WPA
- WEP
- RADIUS
- TKIP

In every network, three components are essential in order for computers to be able to communicate: a common protocol, a common network media, and a common network client or service. In this chapter, I'll discuss the first component — the protocol. Although many types of protocols are in use today, all protocols have one element in common: they are a set of rules by which a network or a group of components behave in order to communicate.

The types of protocols you utilize will depend largely on the type of network you are using. Some protocols are much more common than others. Many protocols can stand on their own, whereas other protocols are part of a larger suite of protocols. You can use protocols to facilitate as well as to secure communication, but ultimately you must understand protocols in order to make effective use of them. You should be aware of the many different protocols in use today and understand how they work together and, in some cases, how they don't work together.

In this chapter, I'll start by discussing the factors that protocols have in common and how you can identify different types of protocols. I will also identify the types of network components that are most likely to use each type of protocol. After I have discussed the commonalities of protocols, you will then turn your attention to the differences in various protocols. Later, I will also define each of the protocols as it relates to the entire model of communication, namely, the Open Systems Interconnect (OSI) model. You should understand protocols in general terms as well as the many specific protocols in various protocol suites.

For more detailed information on these topics, please see *Network+ Study Guide*, published by Wiley.

1.1 Explain the function of common networking protocols

As I've discussed, protocols are sets of rules that determine how communication will take place. In regard to networks, you might think of them as a language that computers use to "talk" to one another. If two devices speak the same language, then they can understand each other. In addition, groups of protocols are combined to create protocol suites. One of the most important protocol suites in today's networks is Transmission Control Protocol/Internet Protocol (TCP/IP).

The TCP/IP protocol suite contains many protocols. These protocols work together to provide communication, management, diagnostics, and troubleshooting for a network that uses the TCP/IP protocol. To understand TCP/IP, it is essential that you understand all the protocols in the suite.

In the following sections, I will define the purpose, function, and use of each of the protocols in the TCP/IP protocol suite. In addition, I will discuss the TCP/IP protocol layers and define the layer at which each of the protocols operates. I will also discuss how the TCP/IP protocol loosely aligns with the OSI model of communication. Table 1.1 summarizes the essential elements of each of these protocols, which are covered next.

TABLE 1.1   Characteristics of Protocols in the TCP/IP Protocol Suite

Protocol	Purpose	Function	Use
IP	Addresses and transports data from one network node to another.	A Network layer connectionless protocol, it "fires and forgets." Performs fragmenting and assembling of packets.	IP addresses are assigned to computers and to router interfaces. These addresses are used to transfer a packet into the proper network so it can be delivered to a host.
TCP	Responsible for flow control and error recovery.	Waits for receipt of acknowledgments from the destination that packets have been delivered without errors. Resends packets that are not acknowledged within a specified time frame. Works at the Transport layer of the TCP/IP suite.	Used with protocols that require a guaranteed delivery such as FTP, HTTP, SMTP, and others.
UDP	Broadcasts packets through a network making a "best effort" to deliver them to the destination.	Connectionless protocol. Works at the Transport layer of the TCP/IP suite.	Used for applications that can provide their own acknowledgments or can be monitored, such as multimedia over the internet.
FTP	Provides the rules of behavior for transferring files through an intranet or over the Internet.	Works at the Application layer of the TCP/IP suite. Provides a protocol as well as an application for transferring files.	Used to browse file structures on a remote computer and to transfer files between computers within intranets and on the Internet.

TABLE 1.1   Characteristics of Protocols in the TCP/IP Protocol Suite *(continued)*

Protocol	Purpose	Function	Use
TFTP	Provides for transferring files within a network.	Connectionless protocol that works at the Application layer. Uses UDP for low overhead without a guarantee of delivery.	Typically used for simple file transfers such as those between a computer and a router or a switch for management purposes.
SMTP	Provides for the delivery of mail messages within a network or between networks.	Works at the Application layer and uses TCP to guarantee delivery of mail to remote hosts.	Typically used to transfer email messages within a network and between networks.
HTTP	Provides for browsing services for the World Wide Web.	Works at the Application layer and provides access to files on web servers through the use of URLs to pages that are formatted web languages such as HTML.	Typically used to browse information on the many servers that interconnect the World Wide Web.
HTTPS	Provides for access to resources on the Internet in a secure fashion.	Works at the Application layer and uses SSL to encrypt data traffic so communications on the Internet can remain secure.	Used for Internet communications that must remain secure, such as banking, e-commerce, and medical transactions.
POP3	Allows the storage and retrieval of user email on servers. Allows users to access and download email from servers.	Works at the Application layer. Users can connect to the server and download messages to a client. The messages can then be read of the client.	Used for many email applications. User can check their email boxes and download messages that have been placed in them.
IMAPv4	Allows the storage and retrieval of user email on servers. Allows users to access email on servers and either read the email on the server or download the email to the client to read it.	Works at the Application layer of the TCP/IP suite. Allows a user to read messages on an email server without the need to download the messages off the server.	Typically, this method of email retrieval is convenient for users who travel and therefore might access their email from more than one location. The mail remains on the server until they delete it, so they can gain access to it from multiple locations.

TABLE 1.1   Characteristics of Protocols in the TCP/IP Protocol Suite *(continued)*

Protocol	Purpose	Function	Use
Telnet	Provides a virtual terminal protocol for connecting to a managing server.	Works at the Application layer of the TCP/IP suite. Provides a connection using an authentication method that is performed in clear text. This protocol and application are not considered secure.	Has been used in the past for "dumb terminals" that connected to main-frame computers. Is now used to connect comput-ers to servers, routers, switches, and so on, for remote management.
SSH	Provides the capability to log onto a computer remotely, execute commands, and move files in a secure and encrypted environment.	Works at the Application layer of the TCP/IP suite. Provides for a secure logon and a secure environment in which to execute commands.	Typically used to manage servers from clients and to move sensitive files from one server to another within the same network or between networks.
ICMP	Provides error checking and reporting functionality.	Works at the Internet layer of the TCP/IP suite. Provides background services that can be used to provide information to an administrator and to request a "quench" of the information flow in the network.	Typically used as part of the ping tool to test net-work connectivity. Can send back an echo reply when an echo request message is sent to it. Can also send back a mes-sage such as "Destina-tion Host Unreachable" and "Time Exceeded" when the connection to the "pinged" host is not possible.
ARP	Resolves IP addresses to MAC addresses.	Works at the Internet layer of the TCP/IP suite. Includes a cache that is checked first. If the entry is not found in the cache, then ARP uses a broadcast to determine the MAC address of the client.	Typically used by the system as a background service but also includes a utility that can be used for troubleshooting.
RARP	Resolves IP addresses to MAC addresses.	Works at the Internet layer of the TCP/IP suite. It assigns an IP address when presented with a MAC address.	Used with diskless work-stations to assign an IP address automatically. Also sometimes used as very rudimentary security for computer authentication.

TABLE 1.1   Characteristics of Protocols in the TCP/IP Protocol Suite *(continued)*

Protocol	Purpose	Function	Use
NTP	Synchronizes time between computers in a network.	Works at the Application layer of TCP/IP suite. Can synchronize time between clients and servers.	Used to synchronize time to assure that authentication protocols such as the Kerberos protocol work properly and that applications that require collaboration operate properly.
NNTP	Provides access to the USENET newsgroups on news servers.	Works at the Application layer of the TCP/IP suite. Provides a set of standards for accessing and opening news articles on a USENET-based news server.	Typically used by individuals and organizations to research information about a variety of topics. News servers do not provide for "browsing" but instead provide lists of articles for specified topics.
SIP	Sets up and tears down voice and video calls over the Internet.	Works at the Session layer of the OSI model and the Application layer of the TCP/IP suite.	Typically used for Voice over IP (VoIP) and video communications.
RTP	Defines a standardized packet format for delivering audio and video over the Internet.	Works at the Session layer of the OSI model and the Application layer of the TCP/IP suite.	Used to enhance multimedia communications for streaming, video conferencing, and push-to-talk applications.
IGMP	Provides a standard for multicasting on an intranet.	Allows a host to inform its local router, using Host Membership Reports that it wants to receive messages addressed to a specific multicast group.	Used to establish host memberships in multicast groups on a single network.
TLS	A network security protocol that provides for data confidentiality and integrity.	Works through active peer negotiation of authentication and encryption protocols.	Used for secure transmission of data between servers and clients within a network and between networks.

Note: The OSI layer names and numbers will be covered in more detail in Chapter 4, "Network Management."

It's important to understand that TCP/IP is not just one protocol, or even two protocols, but it is instead an entire group of protocols that work together to support network communication. Although the OSI model is just a model, the TCP/IP suite represents the continual development of protocols, each of which loosely aligns itself to a portion of the OSI model. The Department of Defense (DOD) defines the TCP/IP suite of protocols as having four layers, as shown in Figure 1.1. Each of the protocols in the TCP/IP suite can be said to function in one or more of these layers. In the following sections, I'll discuss the most common of these protocols.

FIGURE 1.1   The TCP/IP protocol suite

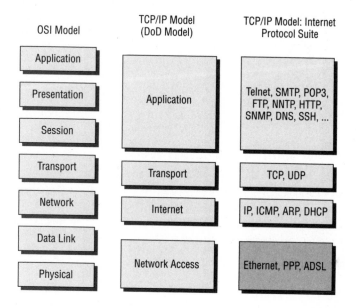

Internet Protocol (IP)

IP is a protocol that is used to transport data from one node on a network to another node. A node can be a computer or a router interface. IP is considered to be a *connectionless* protocol, which works at the Network layer of the OSI model. Because it is connectionless, it does not establish a session with another computer and does not guarantee the delivery of packets; it only makes an effort to deliver them. To guarantee the delivery of packets, a higher-level protocol such as TCP is required.

IP also performs the task of fragmenting and reassembling packets when needed. *Fragmentation* is sometimes necessary because devices that make up the network have a maximum transmission unit (MTU) size that is smaller than the packet to be delivered. In this case, the packet must be "broken up" into smaller pieces and then reassembled on the other side of the transmission. This is an important role that IP provides for the network.

Probably the most widely known role that IP provides is the addressing of packets. IP marks each packet with a source address and a destination address. IP addressing is essential to the success of network communications. For example, when you see a number assigned to a computer's location in a network, such as 192.168.0.1, you are looking at an IP address for this device. I will discuss more IP addressing functions later in this chapter.

Transmission Control Protocol (TCP)

TCP is a connection-oriented protocol that works at the Transport layer (layer 4) of the OSI model. It uses IP as its transport protocol and assists IP by providing a guaranteed mechanism for delivery. TCP requires that a session first be established between two computers before communication can take place. TCP also adds features such as flow control, sequencing, and error detection and correction. This guaranteed delivery mechanism is a requirement in order for TCP to operate at all. For this reason, you should understand how TCP operates.

TCP works by a process referred to as a *three-way handshake*. The TCP three-way handshake works as follows:

1. TCP sends a short message called a SYN to the target host.

2. The target hosts opens a connection for the request and sends back an acknowledgment message called a SYN ACK.

3. The host that originated the request sends back another acknowledgment called an ACK, confirming that it has received the SYN ACK message and that the session is ready to be used to transfer data.

A similar process is used to close the session when the data exchange is complete. The entire process provides a reliable protocol. TCP extends its reliability by making sure that every packet it sends is acknowledged. If a packet is not acknowledged within the timeout period, the packet is resent automatically by TCP. The only disadvantage of a connection-oriented protocol is that the overhead associated with the acknowledgments tends to slow it down.

User Datagram Protocol (UDP)

UDP also operates at the Transport layer of the OSI model and uses IP as its transport protocol, but it does not guarantee the delivery of packets. It doesn't guarantee the delivery of packets because UDP does not establish a session. UDP is instead known as a "fire and forget" protocol because it assumes that the data sent will reach its destination and does not require acknowledgments. Because of this, UDP is also referred to as a *connectionless protocol*.

Now you might be wondering why anyone would want to use UDP instead of TCP. The advantage of UDP is its low overhead in regard to bandwidth and processing effort. Whereas a TCP header has 11 fields of information that have to be processed, a UDP header has only 4 fields. Applications that can handle their own acknowledgments and that do not require the additional features of the TCP protocol might use the UDP protocol to take advantage of the lower overhead. Multimedia presentations that are broadcast or multicast onto the network often use UDP since they can be monitored to make sure that the packets are being received. Services such as the Domain Name System (DNS) service also take advantage of the lower overhead provided by UDP.

Dynamic Host Configuration Protocol (DHCP)

DHCP is actually more of a service than a protocol. When a client comes on to a network, it needs an IP address. You could statically assign every computer in your network, but that would be doing it the hard way. The easier and smarter way would be to use the DHCP protocol (service) to make automatic assignments for you. You can even configure a DHCP server to give a client other information, such as the address of the DNS server.

All Microsoft clients since Windows 98 have their default installation configurations set to obtain an IP address automatically. They are already looking for a DHCP server when they start up. When you include a properly configured DHCP server on your network, you avoid a great number of IP misconfigurations and save yourself a lot of manual labor.

Domain Name System (DNS)

DNS is a service and a protocol. It uses relational databases to resolve hostnames of computers and other network clients to their assigned IP addresses. DNS facilitates "friendly naming" of resources on a network and on the Internet so you don't have to remember, for example, the IP address for MSNBC.com. Clients can be statically configured with the addresses of the DNS servers that host the DNS database, or the DHCP server can provide that information to the client.

File Transfer Protocol (FTP)

FTP, as its name indicates, provides for the transfer of files through a network environment. It can be used within an intranet or through the Internet. FTP is actually more than just a protocol; it is an application as well, and thus FTP works at the Application layer of the OSI model and uses the TCP protocol as a transport mechanism. FTP allows a user to browse a folder structure on another computer (assuming they have been given the permissions to authenticate to the computer) and then to download files from the folders or to upload additional files.

Many organizations use FTP to make files available to the general public and therefore allow users to log on to the FTP server anonymously. In other words, the users do not have to utilize a username and password to authenticate to the server. Since the files are there for the public, the users are allowed to access them without authenticating. Organizations also use FTP to transfer files within an organization. Typically, these servers require authentication by the user, either by supplying an additional username and password or by using a pass-through authentication provided by a previous logon, such as to Active Directory.

You can use FTP through most browsers and even from a command line, but it is quite common for users to purchase third-party software such CuteFTP or SmartFTP instead. Using FTP to transfer files allows you to transfer much larger files than are generally allowed as attachments by most ISPs. Using the third-party tool allows you to see that the file was actually transferred to the intended location. Figure 1.2 shows a connection to the FTP server at Wiley. This is one of the servers to which authors send completed work.

FIGURE 1.2   A connection to an FTP server at Wiley

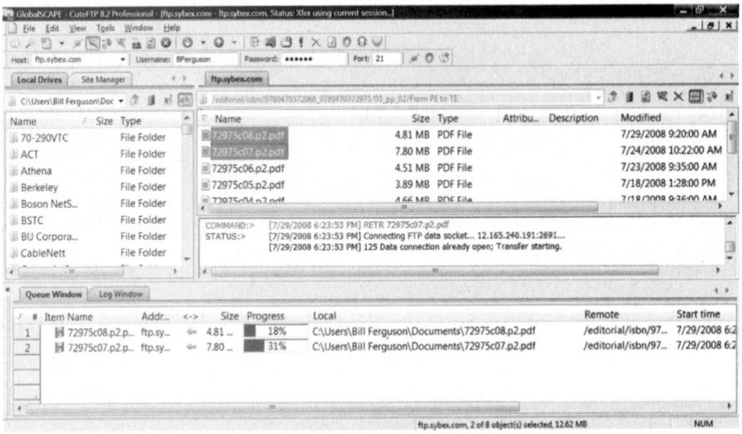

Trivial File Transfer Protocol (TFTP)

TFTP is similar to FTP in that it allows the transfer of files within a network, but that's where the similarity stops. Whereas FTP allows for the browsing of files and folders on a server, TFTP requires that you know the exact name of the file you want to transfer and the exact location where to find the file. Also, whereas FTP uses the connection-oriented TCP protocol, TFTP uses the connectionless UDP protocol. TFTP is most often used for simple downloads such as transferring firmware to a network device, for example, a router or a switch.

Simple Mail Transfer Protocol (SMTP)

SMTP defines how email messages are sent between hosts on a network. You can remember SMTP as "sending mail to people." SMTP works at the Application layer of the OSI model and uses TCP to guarantee error-free delivery of messages to hosts. Since SMTP actually requires that the destination host always be available, mail systems spool the incoming mail into a user's mailbox so that the user can read it at another time. How users read the mail is determined by what protocol they use to access the SMTP server.

Hypertext Transfer Protocol (HTTP)

HTTP is the protocol that users utilize to browse the World Wide Web. HTTP clients use a browser to make special requests from an HTTP server (web server) that contains the files they need. The files on the HTTP server are formatted in web languages such as Hypertext Markup Language (HTML) and are located using a uniform resource locator (URL). The URL contains the type of request being generated (http://, for example), the DNS name of the server to which the request is being made, and, optionally, the path to the file on the server. For example, if you type `http://support.microsoft.com/` in a browser, you will be directed to the Support pages on Microsoft's servers.

Hypertext Transfer Protocol Secure (HTTPS)

One of the disadvantages of using HTTP is that all the requests are sent in clear text. This means the communication is not secure and therefore unsuited for web applications such as e-commerce or exchanging sensitive or personal information through the Web. For these applications, HTTPS provides a more secure solution that uses a Secure Sockets Layer (SSL) to encrypt information that is sent between the client and the server. For HTTPS to operate, both the client and the server must support it. All the most popular browsers now support HTTPS, as do web server products such as Microsoft Internet Information Services (IIS), Apache, and most other web server applications. The URL to access a website using HTTPS and SSL starts with `https://` instead of `http://`. For example, `https://partnering.one` `.microsoft.com/mcp` is the page that is used to authenticate Microsoft Certified Professionals to Microsoft's private website.

Post Office Protocol Version 3 (POP3)

POP3 is one of the protocols that is used to retrieve email from SMTP servers. Using POP3, clients connect to the server, authenticate, and then download their email. Once they have downloaded their email, they can then read it. Typically, the email is then deleted from the server, although some systems hold a copy of the email for a period of time specified by an administrator. One of the drawbacks of POP3 authentication is that it is generally performed in clear text. This means that an attacker could sniff your POP3 password from the network as you enter it.

Internet Message Access Protocol Version 4 (IMAPv4)

IMAPv4 is another protocol that is used to retrieve email from SMTP servers, but IMAPv4 offers some advantages over POP3. To begin with, IMAPv4 provides a more flexible method of handling email. You can read your email on the email server and then determine what you want to download to your own PC. Since the email can stay in the mailbox on the server, you can retrieve it from any computer that you want to use, provided that the computer has the software installed to allow you to access the server. Microsoft Hotmail is a good example of an IMAPv4 type of service. You can access your Hotmail mail from any browser. You can then read, answer, and forward email without downloading the messages to the computer that you are using. This can be very convenient for users who travel.

Telnet

Telnet is a virtual terminal protocol that has been used for many years. Originally, Telnet was used to connect "dumb terminals" to mainframe computers. It was also the connection method used by earlier Unix systems. Telnet is still in use today to access and control network devices such as routers and switches.

The main problem with Telnet for today's environment is that it is not a secure protocol; everything is transmitted in plain text. For this reason, Telnet is being replaced by more secure methods such as Secure Shell and Microsoft's Remote Desktop Connection, which provide encrypted communication.

Secure Shell (SSH)

First developed by SSH Communications Security Ltd., Secure Shell is a program used to log into another computer over a network, execute commands, and move files from one computer to another. SSH provides strong authentication and secure communications over unsecure channels. It protects networks from attacks such as IP spoofing, IP source routing, and DNS spoofing. The entire login session is encrypted; therefore, it is almost impossible for an outsider to collect passwords. SSH is available for Windows, Unix, Macintosh, and Linux, and it also works with RSA authentication.

Internet Control Message Protocol (ICMP)

The ICMP protocol works at the Network layer of the OSI model and the Internet layer of the TCP/IP protocol suite. ICMP provides error checking and reporting functionality. Although ICMP provides many functions, the most commonly known is its ping utility. The ping utility is most often used for troubleshooting. In a typical "ping scenario," an administrator uses a host's command line and the ping utility to send a stream of packets called an *echo request* to another host. When the destination host receives the packets, ICMP sends back a stream of packets referred to as an *echo reply*. This confirms that the connection between the two hosts is configured properly and that the TCP/IP protocol is operational.

ICMP can also send back messages such as "Destination Host Unreachable" or "Time Exceeded." The former is sent when the host cannot be located on the network, and the latter is sent when the packets have exceeded the timeout period specified by TCP. Still another function of ICMP is the sending of source quench messages. These messages are sent by ICMP when the flow of data from the source is larger than that which can be processed properly and quickly by the destination. A source quench message tells the system to slow down and therefore prevents the resending of many data packets.

Address Resolution Protocol (ARP)

The ARP protocol works at the Network layer of the OSI model and the Internet layer of the TCP/IP suite. It is used to resolve IP addresses to MAC addresses. This is an extremely important function, since the only real physical address that a computer has is its MAC address; therefore, all communication will have to contain a MAC address before it can be delivered to the host. This is accomplished in a series of steps:

1. A computer addresses a packet to another host using an IP address.

2. Routers use the IP address to determine whether the destination address is in their network or on another network.

3.   If a router determines that the address is on another network, it forwards the packet to another router based on the information that is contained in its routing table.

4.   When the router that is responsible for the network that contains the destination address receives the packet, it checks the ARP cache to determine whether there is an entry that resolves the IP address to a MAC address. If there is an entry, it uses the MAC address contained in the entry to address the packet to its final destination.

5.   If there is no entry in the ARP cache, the router resolves the IP address to a MAC address for the destination by using ARP to broadcast onto the local network. It asks the computer with the IP address contained in the destination address of the packet to respond with its MAC address. The router also gives the computer its own MAC address to use for the response.

6.   The broadcast is "heard" by all the computers in the local network, but it will be responded to only by the computer that has the correct IP address. All other computers will process the request only to the point that they determine it is not for them.

7.   The computer that is configured with the IP address in question responds with its MAC address.

8.   The router addresses the packet with the MAC address and delivers it to its final destination.

Reverse Address Resolution Protocol (RARP)

RARP, as its name implies, is the opposite of ARP. RARP resolves a MAC address to an IP address. RARP was first used by diskless workstations to obtain an IP address from a server before DHCP servers were available. It simply presented its MAC address and was given an IP address based on its MAC address. RARP is sometimes used as a rudimentary form of security on applications.

Network Time Protocol (NTP)

NTP is a protocol that works at the Application layer of the OSI model and synchronizes time between computers in a network. In today's distributed networks, ensuring that the time is synchronized between clients and servers is essential. Authentication protocols, such as the Kerberos protocol used with Microsoft's Active Directory, use keys that are valid only for about five minutes. If a client and a server are not synchronized, the keys could be invalid the very second they are issued. In many of today's networks, an authoritative time source such as the Internet is first used and configured onto a time server (perhaps a domain controller). Then that server uses NTP to synchronize time with other computers in the network. Some computers may be a receiver of the correct time as well as a sender of the time to other computers in the network.

Internet Group Multicast Protocol (IGMP)

IGMP is the standard for IP multicasting on intranets. It is used to establish host memberships in multicast groups on a single network. The mechanisms of the protocol allow a host to inform its local router, using Host Membership Reports indicating that it wants to receive messages addressed to a specific multicast group.

Session Initiation Protocol (SIP)

SIP is a Session layer protocol that is primarily responsible for setting up and tearing down voice and video calls over the Internet. It also enables IP telephony networks to utilize advanced call features such as SS7.

Real-Time Transport Protocol (RTP)

RTP defines a standardized packet format for delivering audio and video over the Internet. It can also be used with other protocols, such as RTSP, to enhance the field of multimedia applications. It is frequently used in streaming, video conferencing, and push-to-talk applications.

Simple Network Management Protocol (SNMP)

The SNMP protocol is used to monitor devices on a network. A software component (called an *agent*) runs on the remote device and reports information via SNMP traps to the management systems. These management systems can be configured to record information such as errors on a network or resource information of the computers on a network.

SNMPv2 is an enhancement to the original SNMP (SNMPv1). The management information databases used in SNMPv1 are cumbersome and confusing to an administrator. SNMPv2 provides more user-friendly input and output options for data. SNMPv3 adds security measures for message integrity, authentication, and encryption. The enhancements of SNMPv3 have made the previous two versions obsolete. The RFC that defines SNMPv3 (RFC-3411) refers to the previous versions as "historic."

Transport Layer Security (TLS)

TLS allows network devices to communicate across a network while avoiding eavesdropping, tampering, and message forgery. It is designed to allow end users to be sure with whom they are communicating. Clients can negotiate the keys that will be used to secure the data to be transferred. TLS is set to supersede its predecessor SSL.

Exam Essentials

Know the purpose of each protocol in the TCP/IP protocol suite.   You should understand the general purpose for each protocol in the TCP/IP protocol suite. In addition, you should understand how the protocols work together.

Know the function and use of each protocol in the TCP/IP protocol suite.   You should know the function for each protocol in the TCP/IP protocol suite. In addition, you should know the level of the OSI model at which each protocol functions.

1.2 Identify commonly used TCP and UDP default ports

If people performed only one task at a time with each computer, there might not be a need for ports, but we all know that computers can perform many tasks at one time. Because this is the case, you need a way to identify packets so that they will be processed by the computer in the correct manner. By identifying each packet with a port number, you assure that the computer will direct the packet to the right area within it where the appropriate processes can be performed.

TCP and UDP port numbers are used to identify packets in regard to the services that they require. You can also filter traffic using these port numbers to restrict only specific types of traffic from a network. You should understand how TCP and UDP ports can be used to facilitate and control traffic. In the following sections, I will discuss the various types of TCP and UDP ports and describe their general use. You should be able to identify the port number that each of the most common network protocols, services, and applications use. You should know the port number when given a service as well as the service when given a port number.

Port Designations

TCP/IP has 65,536 ports available. As you can imagine, some ports are used much more than others. Ports are divided into three main groups, or designations:

Well-known ports   These port numbers range from 0 to 1023. These are the most commonly used ports and have been used for the longest period of time. When CompTIA states that you should know the definition of well-known ports, it's referring to the ports in this group.

Registered ports   These port numbers range from 1024 to 49151. Registered ports are used by applications or services that need to have consistent port assignments. These ports, like the well-known ports, are agreed upon by most organizations for standardization of use.

Dynamic or private ports   These port addresses range from 49152 to 65535. These ports are not assigned to any particular protocol or service and can therefore be used for any service or application.

It is common for applications to establish a connection on a well-known port and then move to a dynamic port for the rest of the conversation. It's important that you understand port numbers, because you may be configuring them for communication purposes as well as to provide filtering and therefore prevent the communication of specified applications or

n the next section, you will examine the most common specific port assignments
 ly.

Now that I have discussed the general nature of ports, I'll get much more specific in regard to well-known ports. Although there are 1,024 well-known ports, only a handful of these are commonly used on networks. The ones that are used most frequently are not arranged in any logical order in regard to their use, so unfortunately the only way to remember most of them is just to memorize them. In the following sections, I will pair up each of the most commonly used well-known ports with its protocol, service, or application.

Well-Known Port Numbers

As I said earlier, *well-known* is the name given for the port designation, but not all of the numbers between 0 and 1023 have a well-known service assigned to them. The good news is that you don't have to memorize 1,024 port assignments! Aren't you relieved? The bad news, however, is that you do have to memorize the port assignments in Table 1.2. Sorry!

TABLE 1.2 The Most Common Well-Known Port Numbers and Associated Services

Service, Protocol, or Application	Port Assignment	TCP, UDP, or Both
File Transfer Protocol (FTP)	20, 21	TCP
Secure Shell (SSH)	22	TCP
Telnet	23	TCP
Simple Mail Transfer Protocol (SMTP)	25	TCP
Domain Name System (DNS)	53	UDP
Trivial File Transfer Protocol (TFTP)	69	UDP
Hypertext Transfer Protocol (HTTP)	80	TCP/UDP
Post Office Protocol version 3 (POP3)	110	TCP
Network Time Protocol (NTP)	123	TCP
Internet Message Access Protocol version 4 (IMAP4)	143	TCP
Simple Network Management Protocol (SNMP)	161	UDP
HTTPS	443	TCP

You should memorize the port numbers in the Table 1.2 so that you can recognize them in the configuration of servers, routers, switches, and other network equipment. You might use them to configure a service or protocol. In addition, you might use them to filter a protocol or service on a firewall. In either case, a familiarity with the port numbers will assist you in configuration as well as in communication about the services and applications themselves.

Exam Essentials

Know the three port types and their ranges.   You should know the three main types of ports: well-known, registered, and dynamic. In addition, you should be able to identify the ranges of each type of port. You should know when and where each port type might be used.

Know the most common well-known ports.   The well-known ports should be very well known to you! You should be able to identify the most common well-known ports. You should understand the purpose of each type of port and the application or service that uses it.

1.3 Identify the following address formats: IPv6, IPv4, MAC addressing

In the end, all network devices find each other by their MAC addresses. When it comes to delivering a frame from one host to another, the next MAC address of a computer or a router interface in the path toward the client must be known. Essentially overlaid on top of the MAC address is a logical address that assists you in building complex networks. In the past, we have used primarily one protocol for this logical addressing, IPv4. In the last few years a new type of addressing, IPv6, has emerged that will allow for the growth of our industry and provide the security and control mechanisms that are needed with today's networks. You should be able to recognize IPv6, IPv4, and MAC addresses, and you should be able to differentiate between the different types of addresses. You should understand the format of each type of address and the difference between how network engineers interpret it and how network devices read it.

IPv6

You probably wouldn't think you would ever be in danger of running out of a group of things if you had 4 billion of them to start! Well, that is what happened with IPv4 addresses. Later, I will discuss the structure of IPv4 addresses, and then you can see what happened. First, I'll talk about what the world is going to do next in regard to logical addressing.

IPv6 is the latest logical addressing scheme for networks. Each IPv6 address is a 128-bit binary address represented in hexadecimal numbers. Most companies are not being "forced" into IPv6 as of yet. The latest server and client operating systems (Windows XP, Windows Vista, Windows Server 2003, Windows Server 2008, and so forth) support the protocol, but you don't necessarily have a compelling reason to change as of yet. When you do change, you will need to know a little about hexadecimal addresses to be able to interpret what you are seeing in an IPv6 address.

The following is an IPv6 address on my laptop:

fe80::218:deff:fe08:6e14

That looks pretty weird, doesn't it?

Now I'll talk about what this really says and how you should interpret it.

Each hexadecimal character in the address is actually seen by the network device as a binary number with 4 bits. Table 1.3 illustrates the relationship of each decimal, binary, and hexadecimal number and/or character.

TABLE 1.3   Decimal Binary and Hexadecimal Conversion

Decimal	Binary	Hexadecimal
0	0000	0x0
1	0001	0x1
2	0010	0x2
3	0011	0x3
4	0100	0x4
5	0101	0x5
6	0110	0x6
7	0111	0x7
8	1000	0x8
9	1001	0x9
10	1010	0xA
11	1011	0xB
12	1100	0xC
13	1101	0xD

TABLE 1.3   Decimal Binary and Hexidecimal Cionversion *(continued)*

Decimal	Binary	Hexadecimal
14	1110	0xE
15	1111	0xF

As you can see from the table, if you were first to convert each of the characters you see in your address into its binary equivalent, the result would be as follows:

1111 1110 1000 0000 :: 0010 0001 1000 : 1101 1110 1111 1111 : 1111 1110 0000 1000 : 0110 1110 0001 0100

Not so fast, though! Equally important as what you see is what you do not see but you still know must be there. For example, you know that there are a total of 128 bits in this address. Also, you know that each section between a set of colons should actually have 16 bits on its own, so what are you missing?

Well, to begin with, any "leading zeros" can be interpreted by the device easily and can therefore be left out, as you can see in the second section of the previous address. In addition, successive fields of zeros can be represented as ::, but this can be done only once in an address, because otherwise the device wouldn't know how many successive zeros were represented by each ::. If you do a quick count, you will find that you are missing 52 zeros! In other words, although you can represent the IPv6 address in this case as the following hexadecimal number:

fe80::218:deff:fe08:6e14

what the device will use is a 128-bit number that looks like the following:

1111 1110 1000 0000 : 0000 0000 0000 0000 : 0000 0000 0000 0000 : 0000 0000 0000 0000 : 0000 0010 0001 1000 : 1101 1110 1111 1111 : 1111 1110 0000 1000 : 0110 1110 0001 0100

As you can see, this is a huge addressing system that should allow for an almost limitless supply of addresses. Of course, the last time someone said that, we soon began to run out of addresses!

IPv4

Now that you have seen the wildness of an IPv6 address, you should be glad to talk about the mundane IPv4 address again. An IPv4 address is a 32-bit binary address represented in what we call *dotted decimal format*. The following is an example of an IPv4 address:

192.168.1.1

In addition to the IP address, a subnet mask is also used with IPv4, which has the effect of "measuring" the address to determine which parts of it are the network portion and which parts are the host portion. You can think of the network portion as the street on which you live and the host portion as the specific address of your house or apartment. Simply put, where there are 1s in the binary of the subnet mask, the corresponding bits in the IPv4 address are network bits; and where there are 0s in the binary of the subnet mask, the corresponding bits in the IPv4 address are host bits.

Now you may be thinking that IPv4 isn't in the binary form — IPv4 is in the dotted decimal format. Well, the network devices "see" the IPv4 addresses as binary numbers. In fact, 192.168.1.1 ends up looking like the following:

11000000 10101000 00000001 00000001

"How does that happen?" you may ask. Well, I'm glad you asked. The dotted decimal form uses the first 8 bits of binary over and over four times. The bits of the address are then valued based on the following template of values:

128 64 32 16 8 4 2 1 . 128 64 32 16 8 4 2 1 . 128 64 32 16 8 4 2 1 . 128 64 32 16 8 4 2 1

The address would then line up with the template as follows:

1 1   1   1   1   1   1

Everywhere there is not a 1 is a 0.

Later, I will discuss how the subnet mask combines with the IP address to determine which bits will be network bits and which will be host bits. I will also discuss how you can use a custom subnet mask to subnet a network further for more efficient and effective use of IP addresses.

MAC Addressing

Every device in a network must learn the MAC address of another device in order to communicate with it. Since we represent MAC addresses as hexadecimal numbers, it only makes sense to assume that network addresses must be able to read hexadecimal code — but you know what happens when you assume! In reality, network devices can only read binary, so the hexadecimal representation of the MAC address is in fact interpreted by the device as a binary number. The following is a MAC address on my computer:

00-18-DE-08-6E-14

If you examine this address closely against Table 1.3, you will note that its binary equivalent is the following:

0000 0000 – 0001 1000 – 1101 1110 – 0000 1000 – 0110 1110 – 0001 0100

In other words, the MAC address is actually a 48-bit binary address that is represented as hexadecimal. Figure 1.3 illustrates the structure of a MAC address. The first two bits on the left (high order) represent whether the address is broadcast and whether it is local or remote. The next 22 bits are assigned to vendors that manufacture network devices, such as routers and network interface cards (NICs). This is called the *organizational unique identifier* (OUI). The next 24 bits should be uniquely assigned in regard to the OUI. In other words, if I am 3COM and I have already used a specific hexadecimal number with one of my OUIs, then I should not use it again. In this way, each NIC has an address that is as unique as a person's fingerprint.

FIGURE 1.3   The structure of a MAC address

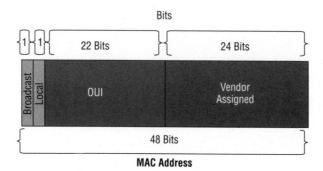

The main point to remember about MAC addresses is that they should be unique within the network in which they are to be used. This means that if one is assigned to a NIC, it should be unique within the whole world; but if a MAC addresses is functioning only on an interface within your LAN, then you should just ensure that it's unique within your LAN. Sometimes administrators may change the MAC address on a router interface, for example, to facilitate a behavior of another protocol. These types of changes are beyond the scope of this book.

Exam Essentials

Know how to identify an IPv6 address.   You should know that an IPv6 address is a 128-bit binary address represented in hexadecimal. In addition, you should understand that leading 0s and successive fields of 0s may be omitted when representing an IPv6 address.

Know how to identify an IPv4 address.   You should know that an IPv4 address is a 32-bit binary address that is represented in dotted decimal format. You should understand that the address is divided into four sections, which each contain 8 bits and are therefore called *octets*. In addition, you should understand how a subnet mask combines with an IP address to determine which bits are network and which are host.

Know how to identify a MAC address.   Understand that a MAC address is a 48-bit binary address that is represented in hexadecimal code. You should know that MAC addresses are assigned to NICs, routers, switches, and other network equipment and should be unique in the network in which they are to be used. In addition, you should realize a MAC address must always be determined in order for communication to move from any host on a network to any other host.

1.4 Given a scenario, evaluate the proper use of the following addressing technologies and addressing schemes: Classful vs. classless, NAT, PAT, SNAT, Public vs. Private, DHCP, Unicast, Multicast, Broadcast

Today's networks are not "your father's network." Networks continue to evolve, and what we want to do on them continues to evolve. We are placing very fast computers on our networks now and expecting to receive reports, email, chat, music, videos, games, and so forth — often all at once! Because of these challenges, network administrators have to rely on newer and better technologies to both control traffic and to provide security for a network. In addition, you have to rethink some of the schemes used to push data around a network. In the following sections, I'll discuss both of these important topics. You should be able to evaluate the proper use of many different network technologies such as subnetting, supernetting, NAT, PAT, DHCP, and others. In addition, you should be able to evaluate the difference between and the proper use of unicast, broadcast, and multicast traffic.

Addressing Technologies

Today's networks use IP addressing in many creative ways based on the needs of the administrator and ultimately the needs of the users on the network. Some methods that administrators use to customize their networks include subnetting, classful addressing, classless addressing, NAT, PAT, SNAT, public addressing, private addressing, DHCP assigned addresses, static assigned addresses, and APIPA addresses. I will discuss each of the concepts in detail.

Subnetting

Subnetting is a method used to create additional broadcast domains. You may wonder why you want additional broadcast domains when broadcasts are typically considered bad; that is, they are something to be avoided whenever possible. Look at it this way: if you have a fixed number of hosts in a network, you can reduce the number of hosts per broadcast domain and therefore reduce the effect of broadcasts on the hosts by increasing the number of broadcast domains. This is because there will be fewer hosts in each of the broadcast domains.

In addition to reducing the effect of broadcasts, subnetting also allows you to apply security policies in an easy and efficient manner. Each subnet can represent a location, role, job, and so on. By applying access control lists and other types of network filtering rules, you can control who gets access to what on a network. This job would be made much more difficult if you could not use subnets.

Now that you know the "why" of subnetting, I'll cover the "how" of subnetting. In plain terms, when you subnet IPv4, you are just reapplying the same sets of rules that were used to create the classful system of IP addressing in the first place. Because of this, it's only fitting that I begin there.

The early developers of IPv4 established a classful system of IP addresses that defined five classes of addresses. The engineers wanted to identify the type of class as quickly as possible in the addressing, so they actually did it in the first three bits of the address. Table 1.4 references how this was done and the effect it has on the number of networks and hosts per network.

TABLE 1.4 IPv4 Classful Addressing System

Class	First Octet Range	Subnet Mask	Number of Networks	Number of Hosts/ Networks
A	00000001–01111111 1–126 (127 is reserved)	255.0.0.0	126	16,777,214
B	10000000–10111111 128–191	255.255.0.0	16,384	65,534
C	11000000–11011111 192–223	255.255.255.0	2,097,152	254

As you can see in the table, when the first bit of the address was a 0 and the subnet mask was 255.0.0.0, then the address was a Class A address. There were many more Class B addresses, but they could not have a lot of hosts! These were generally assigned to the military, government, and very large corporations.

When the first bit was a 1, the second bit was a 0, and the subnet mask was 255.255.0.0, then the address was a Class B address. There were many more Class B addresses, but they can't have the tremendous number of hosts as Class A. These were generally assigned to medium-sized to large corporations and smaller governmental entities.

When the first bit was a 1, the second bit was also a 1, the third bit was a 0, and the subnet mask was 255.255.255.0, then the address was a Class C address. There were a great number of Class C addresses, but each one could contain only 254 hosts. These were originally used for small companies and very small government entities.

Now, you may have noticed that I've been speaking in the past tense. That's because we don't follow this classful system anymore, but that doesn't mean you don't need to know it! What we *do* follow is based on the classful system, but we have customized it to fit our needs using logical addressing methods and new technologies such as NAT, PAT, and proxies, which I will discuss later.

In today's networks, you need to make the most efficient use possible of the IP addressing space that you have been given by the Internet Corporation for Assigned Names and Numbers (ICANN) or that you have created for yourself with private IP addressing. To do this, you use custom subnet masks that define the appropriate number of networks and the appropriate number of hosts per network for your particular situation.

You generally start with a classful address that has the capacity to be subnetted further to meet the needs of your network. For example, let's say I have one network defined as 192.168.1.0 with a subnet mask of 255.255.255.0. As I discussed before, this subnet mask identifies the network bits and host bits in the network. If you were to convert the dotted decimal subnet mask to binary, you would find twenty-four 1s in a row followed by eight 0s in a row. This means that the network portion of the address is 192.168.1. The 0 identifies the beginning of new network, and the addresses after it would be 1 to 254. The last address would be 255; this is not a host address but rather a broadcast address. "What's the difference?" you may ask. Well, if another host wanted to address a packet in such a way that it would be received by all 254 hosts (in this case), then the host would use 192.168.1.255, which is the broadcast address. The broadcast address should be set aside for broadcasts and never be used as a host address.

Now that you have established what you already have, let's say what you have is not what you want. Let's say you want to have 8 subnets with as many hosts as possible in them instead of just one network with 254 hosts. What would you do then? You guessed it — you would subnet the classful network to create the custom networks you need. How would you do this?

You would begin by understanding that you have 8 host bits with which to work. The network bits will not be changed, and you will always be moving from the left to the right on your template. The question now is "How many of those 8 host bits do you need to change into subnet bits to create the eight subnets that you need?" (Some people refer to this part as *borrowing*, which is a term I never really liked because I'm not really planning on "giving them back.") The answer to this question lies in the formula $2^s \geq$ # of subnets. In this formula, s is the number of host bits that will be turned into subnet bits and # *of subnets* is the number of subnets you need to create.

In this case, $2^s \geq 8$. Solving for s, you find that it must be at least 3. You want the lowest s that works because you also want to maximize the number of host bits that you still have remaining, so $s = 3$. Now the next question is "Which three?" Well, you are always going to move from the left to the right, so you will start at the left of the remaining 8 bits and take the first 3 bits from the left toward the right. This means that the subnet bits will be the 128, 64, and 32 bits. To make these host bits into subnet bits, you will simply change the corresponding bits in the subnet mask from 0 to 1. When you make this change, the subnet mask will then change to 255.255.255.224 since 128 + 64 + 32 = 224.

The next question on your mind might be "Then what are my 8 subnets?" You can answer this question by determining the increment of the subnets and therefore their numbers and ranges of hosts. The increment is always 256 — the last number in the subnet mask that is not a 0. In this case, it's 256 – 224, which equals 32. The first network is always the same as what you started with, but with a new subnet mask. You can express the new subnet mask as 255.255.255.224, or you can express it by using a forward slash at the end of

the IP address followed by a number indicating the number of 1s in the subnet mask. In t[
case, you could express your subnet mask as a /27. This is referred to as *CIDR notation.*

Since all the other networks are determined by the increment, your networks will be as follows:

192.168.1.0/27

192.168.1.32/27

192.168.1.64/27

192.168.1.96/27

192.168.1.128/27

192.168.1.160/27

192.168.1.192/27

192.168.1.224/27

The host ranges and broadcast addresses can then be determined without any further use of the binary. For example, the 0 network will have 30 hosts in it ranging from 1 to 30, and it will have a broadcast address of 31. The 32 network hosts will range from 33 to 62 with a broadcast address of 63, and so on, through the networks.

You can also check your math by understanding that the number of hosts will always be $2^h - 2$, where h is the number of remaining host bits after the subnet bits are determined. In this example, there are five remaining host bits, so the formula will be $2^5 - 2 = 30$. Since this matches the number of hosts as determined by the increment, you know you are on the right track!

Now let's try one that is a little more complicated. Don't worry, I'll walk you right through it, and then you will be able to do it yourself. Let's say you have an IP network of 172.16.0.0 with a subnet mask of 255.255.0.0 and you want to have 60 subnets with as many hosts per subnet as possible. What would the new subnet mask be? How many hosts would you have? What would your networks look like?

You start solving this problem in the same way as the last by noticing where you are beginning in the address, based on the subnet mask. In other words, my first question is always "Where am I?" Since you have a subnet mask here of 255.255.0.0, you are halfway through the address. In other words, you have sixteen 1s followed by sixteen 0s in the subnet mask. The fact that you have sixteen 0s means you have 16 host bits, some of which will be used for subnet bits. The next question is "How many host bits do you need to convert to subnet bits to create the 60 subnets that you need?"

You can answer this question with the same formula as before, $2^s \geq$ # of subnets. In this case, $2^s \geq 60$. Solving for s, you determine that $s = 6$, since $2^6 = 64$, and that's the first number that is higher than 60. Now the question is "Which six?" Remember that you are always moving from left to right, so the six bits that you will use will be the first six in the third octet starting from the left. This means you will change the corresponding bits in the subnet mask from 0s to 1s. This in turn means that the subnet mask number will change to 255.255.252.0, since 128 + 64 + 32 + 16 + 8 + 4 = 252. In other words, when you change the subnet bits to 1s, the values count and change the subnet mask accordingly.

The next question is "How many hosts could you have per network?" A close look at the template should show you that you have 2 host bits left in the third octet and 8 host bits left in the fourth octet. That's a total of 10 host bits. This means you can have $2^{10} - 2$ hosts per subnet, or 1,022.

Now you might be wondering how you are going to do that and what the addresses are going to look like when you get done. Just as before, the first network is always the same network you started with, but it has the new subnet mask, and the rest of the networks are determined by the increment. In this case, your first network is 172.16.0.0 with a subnet mask of 255.255.252.0. The increment is always 256 — the last number in the subnet mask that is not a 0. In this case, the increment is $256 - 252 = 4$. This means that the first three networks will be as follows:

172.16.0.0/22

172.16.4.0/22

172.16.8.0/22

Notice that I left some blank space between the network addresses. I like to call that space "thinking room," because you are going to do a lot of thinking in there. It's rather straightforward to see that the first host in the 172.16.0.0 network will be 172.16.0.1, but where do you go from there to get 1,022 hosts? Imagine an old odometer that actually spins out the 10ths of miles. Do you have that in your mind? Now when it gets to nine 10ths, think about what happens. The 10ths will then go back to 0, the number on the left will increment by 1, and then it all starts over again. Right? That's the same thing that happens with the IP addresses, except that it's not 0 to 9 but rather 0 to 255. In this case, when the addresses get to 172.16.0.255, the next number is then 172.16.1.0. Now, here's the kicker: both of those addresses are valid hosts! In fact, there will be a lot of weird-looking numbers that will be valid hosts as well. So, what is the last host in the 172.16.0.0/22 network? The last host is 172.16.3.254, and the broadcast is 172.16.3.255. After that, the 172.16.4.0/22 network starts, which has a broadcast address of 172.16.7.255. Use the "thinking room," and you will see it.

It's extremely important with today's networks that you understand IP addressing and subnetting. The quicker you can determine the subnet on which a host resides, the better you will be at network troubleshooting. I hope this has helped you to see IP addresses for what they are without having to convert them to binary numbers. With practice, you will be able to "see" the answers instead of always having to figure them out. I highly recommend you spend some time working on IP address subnetting. One tool that I've found invaluable is the website: http://subnetttingquestions.com. It was created in part by Todd Lammle, a fellow Wiley author. This site is free and offers hundreds of questions and answers. Your challenge is to get the same answer as the site has and to do it as quickly as possible.

Classful vs. Classless

Now that you know about the subnet mask, I can talk about classful addressing vs. classless addressing. The first thing to remember is that the names for these can throw you off track if you aren't careful. Logically, it might seem that classful would be better than classless. However, this is not true in this case, and it isn't true that classless is always better than classful. It depends on what you are trying to accomplish in your network.

Classful addressing takes its name because the first octet of the address determines the subnet mask that will be used, and therefore the subnet mask does not have to be, and is not, advertised by the routers in the routing protocols. In other words, referring to the information in Table 1.5, you will notice that an address that has 1 to 126 in the first octet would be considered a Class A address if it had a subnet mask of 255.0.0.0. With classful addressing, that's its only choice. In other words, with classful addressing, the subnet mask is always assumed to be the one that corresponds with its first octet address. This has the affect of limiting some network designs that otherwise could have used, for example, networks 172.16.1.0 and 172.16.2.0 with other networks between them. This cannot be done because the classful routing protocols will assume both of the networks to be 172.16.0.0, because of the assumed mask of 255.255.0.0. This will result in a network scheme that will not function properly.

Now let's say you have a routing protocol that actually takes into account the address and subnet mask you assigned to the interface. Wouldn't that be nice? In that case, you could specify the networks 172.16.1.0/24 and 172.16.2.0/24 by assigning the subnet mask of 255.255.255.0 to each, rather than the classful subnet mask of 255.255.0.0. If the protocol could advertise the address along with the subnet mask, then you could use these two networks even if you had other networks between them because they would be seen as two unique networks. This type of addressing is used in today's networks because it allows for more complex networking schemes that can make more efficient use of the available IP addresses.

Network Address Translation (NAT)

NAT is a service that translates one set of IP addresses to another set of IP addresses. NAT is most often used between a private network and the Internet, but it can also be used in other ways such as to translate a group of global internal addresses to a group of global external addresses. NAT is a service that can be run on a computer, a router, or a specialized device that provides only network address translation.

Port Address Translation (PAT)

PAT is a service that most people actually think of as NAT. When you have two or more computers on the inside of a network that share one address as represented on the outside of the network (usually the outside interface address of the router), the only way to keep their network communication channels separate and organized is by port designation on each packet. PAT changes the source address of a packet as it passes through the router or other device using PAT, appending it with a specific port number. It then keeps a record of the port numbers to which it has assigned packets and the true inside local address of the computers that generated them. In this way, PAT uses ports to provide address translation for many inside source addresses to one outside source address.

Secure Network Address Translation (SNAT)

SNAT is the simplest form of NAT and is often used in conjunction with other more sophisticated forms such as PAT. It provides for a one to one translation of an inside local address (on the inside of a network) to an inside global address (on the outside of a network). One of the advantages of SNAT is that the address that will be used on the outside is completely configured and therefore very easy to determine and to troubleshoot. SNAT is often used when specialized equipment attached to a network requires a specified IP address range that is different than the organization has available.

Public vs. Private Addresses

Unique IP address assignment on the Internet was originally the responsibility of the Internet Assigned Numbers Authority (IANA), but it has been handed over to other organizations that coordinate with each other to make sure that addresses are unique. The current three major organizations for the entire world are divided geographically as follows:

- *American Registry for Internet Numbers (ARIN)*: Serves the North American continent and parts of the Caribbean
- *Asia Pacific Network Information Centre (APNIC)*: Serves the Asia Pacific Region
- *Réseaux IP Européens Network Coordination Centre (RIPE NCC)*: Serves Europe, the Middle East, and parts of Africa

Addresses that are assigned by these authorities are referred to as registered, or *public*, addresses. If you are connecting a computer to the Internet, then you must use an address that has been assigned by one of these authorities. Now I know what you are thinking: "I'm connected to the Internet, and I never contacted any of those organizations." That's probably because you use an address that is provided by your Internet service provider (ISP) that obtained the address from one of these authorities. ISPs have large blocks of IP addresses that they can assign to their clients, thereby giving them a valid and unique IP address to use on the Internet. Some large organizations still go through the process of registering for their own address blocks, but most individuals and smaller organizations simply get whatever addresses they need from their ISP.

Private IP addresses are completely different. To understand a network diagram, you have to be able to see the difference between public and private addresses. Public addresses are said to be routable, whereas private addresses are said to be nonroutable. What does this really mean? Is there something wrong with the bits in the private IP addresses that prevent them from being routed? No, the private addresses are actually nonroutable because they are filtered by the routers that would take you from one network to another on the Internet.

But now you may be asking "How do they know which addresses to filter?" Well, the original designers of the Internet set aside some groups of IP addresses to be used for private addressing. That way, even if two companies were to choose the same addresses, and even if neither of them used a firewall, there still could be no conflict because the addresses would never "see" each other. Table 1.5 lists the addresses that are automatically filtered by routers leading onto the Internet.

TABLE 1.5   Private IP Address Ranges

Class	Address Range	Default Subnet Mask
A	10.0.0.0–10.255.255.255	255.0.0.0
B	172.16.0.0–172.31.255.255	255.255.0.0
C	192.168.0.0–192.168.255.255	255.255.255.0

You may have noticed that 127 is missing. This is because the 127 network is reserved for diagnostics and testing. The most notable address on this network is the loopback address 127.0.0.1, which I will discuss in later chapters. Also, note that Class D addresses are reserved for multicasts and that Class E addresses are reserved for experimentation and future development.

As always, the full address is indicated by the IP address combined with the subnet mask. The important point to remember here is that these are the addresses that are filtered. In reality, you could use any address that you chose for the private IP addressing schemes of your network. However, if we both decided to use a public address on the inside, for example 14.1.1.1 for a router, then we could possibly see each other and have an address conflict if everything went wrong with the firewalls and other network protection. In other words, we would not be able to rely on the automatic filters throughout the Internet. This is why it is recommended to use the private IP addresses that I have listed, and this is why you should know them.

DHCP (Static, Dynamic, APIPA)

As discussed earlier, DHCP stands for Dynamic Host Configuration Protocol, but what exactly does that mean? It means you can offload a whole lot of work configuring IP addresses, subnet masks, default gateways, DNS server addresses, and much more to a server that is relatively easy to set up and maintain. Figure 1.4 shows the DHCP server tool in Windows Server 2003. Programs like this one can be used to configure addresses on client computers in a network.

In general, computer clients should obtain their IP addresses from a DHCP server whenever possible. In contrast, devices such as servers, network printers, plotters, and router interfaces should be statically configured so their addresses do not change. Figure 1.5 shows an example of a static configuration on a Windows Server 2003 server.

All client computers since Windows 98 are configured by default to obtain their IP address from a DHCP server. What if a DHCP server is not available? In that case, they are also configured by default to use an address in the range of 169.254.0.1 to 169.254.255.254. These addresses are called Automatic Private Internet Protocol Addressing (APIPA) addresses. The advantage of using APIPA is that the clients in the same network segment that could not obtain a true IP address from a DHCP server can still communicate with each other.

The disadvantage is that the clients can communicate with each other but not with the true network. This can lead to some wild troubleshooting for the "unseasoned" administrator. The bottom line is that when you see an address that begins with 169.254, you can rest assured that it was not obtained from any DHCP server!

FIGURE 1.4   The DHCP server tool in Windows Server 2003

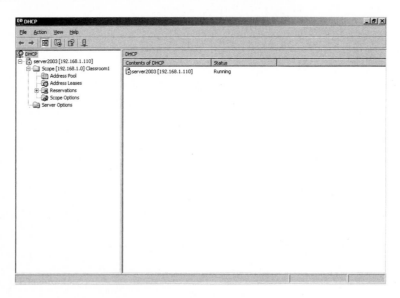

FIGURE 1.5   A static IP configuration on a DHCP server

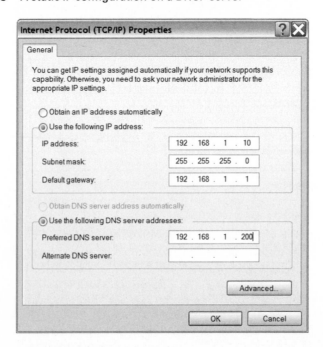

Addressing Schemes

Three major types of addressing schemes are used on IPv4 networks. These are unicast, multicast, and broadcast. Each type has its own place in the network. In the following sections, I'll discuss each of these types of network addressing schemes.

Unicast

Of the three types of addressing schemes used in IPv4, *unicast* is the most simple and straightforward. A packet (layer 3) or frame (layer 2) is said to have a unicast address if it has one source address and one destination address. If we are discussing packets, then the source and destination addresses are of a layer 3 protocol, likely IP. If we are discussing Ethernet frames, then the source and destination addresses of a layer 2 protocol are MAC addresses. In either case, the devices need to determine only the correct unique destination address to send the packet.

Multicast

Multicast addressing can be much more complex than unicast. With multicast addressing there is still only one source address; however, there can be multiple destination addresses. In other words, the frame or packet basically carries a list of destination addresses with it, and each device checks to see whether it is on the list when it sees the data. Multicasting is especially useful for applications that send voice and video through network systems. Multicast addressing uses specialized protocols such as Internet Group Multicast Protocol (IGMP) to create and carry the "list." The IP addresses carried by IGMP can be mapped to MAC addresses for Layer 2 multicasting.

Broadcast

Broadcast addressing is similar to just standing in a room yelling out a person's name or an announcement. Anyone in the room who hears you with the name you yelled would likely respond, but everyone in the room would be disturbed in the process. On the other hand, if the announcement were actually intended for everyone in the room, then you would have accomplished your goal.

Broadcasting is accomplished by using an address that directs the data to all the members of a network or subnet. Every IPv4 network or subnet has a broadcast address, which is the last numerical address before the next network. In the binary form of a broadcast address, you will notice that all the host bits are 1s. For example, the broadcast address of the network 192.168.1.0/27 is 192.168.1.31. As you can see, the host address portion is 31 in dotted decimal, which is 11111 in binary.

Some services in an IPv4 network work by broadcasts, such as DHCP and even ARP. That said, broadcasts are typically thought of as bad and to be avoided whenever possible. IPv6 uses a different form of addressing referred to as *anycast* to avoid using broadcasts. This is beyond the scope of this chapter and not listed as an objective on the current exam.

Exam Essentials

Know the most common addressing technologies.   You should know the most common addressing technologies used in today's networks, such as subnetting, NAT, PAT, DHCP, APIPA, and so on. You should understand how network engineers communicate about these technologies and how the devices use them to send data. In addition, you should understand the appropriate use of each technology in a network.

Know the most common addressing schemes.   You should know the most common addressing schemes, such as unicast, multicast, and broadcast addressing. You should understand how each may be used in a network and where each one is appropriate. In addition, you should understand the underlying addressing structure in respect to the source and destination addresses of each.

1.5 Identify common IPv4 and IPv6 routing protocols

There is a big difference between a routed protocol and a *routing protocol*. In most networks today, the only routed protocol used to transmit user data from network to network is IP. It is the underlying protocol that is used by the routers to identify and accurately deliver data packets.

Today's routers determine what do with a packet that does not belong on a network to which they are connected by using a routing table. The protocols that routers use to communicate with each other about networks, and thereby build the routing table, are referred to as *routing protocols*. In the following sections, I will identify two categories of routing protocols: link state and distance vector. I will then discuss the most common protocols in each of these categories. You should understand the basic differences in the way that each routing protocol functions.

This is only a brief discussion for the purposes of the exam, because many entire books have been written about each of these protocols and their configuration.

Link State

Link state identifies and describes one of the most common categories of routing protocols in use today. *Link* means interface, and *state* means the attributes of the interface, in other words, where it is, what is connected to it, how fast it is, and so forth. Link state routing protocols send all this interface information out in the form of link state advertisements (LSAs). From these LSAs, the routers will build a map of the network. Each router in the same area will have the same map and will therefore be able to make decisions as to how to forward a packet. The two most common link state routing protocols are OSPF and IS-IS.

Open Shortest Path First (OSPF)

OSPF is by far the most common link state routing protocol in use today. OSPF is so named because it is an "open" protocol. In other words, it's not proprietary, and it uses the Shortest Path First (SPF) algorithm developed by Dijkstra.

The principle advantages of this protocol include that it is quiet on the network — not "chatty" like some of the protocols that preceded it — and that it converges very rapidly when there is a change in the network. In other words, when the tables need to be changed to control network traffic, it makes that happen very fast — usually within a few seconds. Because of these advantages, OSPF can be used on small, medium, and large networks.

Intermediate System to Intermediate System (IS-IS)

IS-IS is another link state routing protocol that is not as popular with commercial and government networks as OSPF. Developed by the Digital Equipment Corporation, it has been used in the past mainly by large service providers. IS-IS uses Dijkstra's algorithm to make decisions about where to forward a packet, but it also uses a complex system of levels to obtain a network topology.

Distance Vector

Distance vector routing protocols are also exactly what they say they are. *Distance*, as you know, is "how far." *Vector*, as you may know, is "which direction." Distance vector routing protocols make decisions by examining these two factors against their routing tables. I will now briefly discuss each of the most common distance vector routing protocols.

Routing Information Protocol (RIP)

RIP is one of the first routing protocols. As you can imagine, being first in regard to technology does not necessarily mean being the best. In fact, RIP is now considered obsolete and is being replaced by more sophisticated routing protocols, such as RIPv2, OSPF, and IS-IS.

The principal reasons for RIP's demise are that it is a "chatty" protocol in which all information that each router knows regarding networks is broadcast every 30 seconds. In addition, RIP uses a "hop count" metric that doesn't take into account the bandwidth of a connection. Finally, RIPv1, commonly referred to as RIP, is classful, which means it does not provide the means to advertise the true subnet mask of a network. In today's varied networks, this type of routing protocol does not have the intelligence needed to route packets efficiently.

Routing Information Protocol Version 2 (RIPv2)

RIPv2 solves some of the problems associated with RIPv1, but not all of them. It does not broadcast every 30 seconds but instead uses multicast addressing for its advertisements. This provides for much more efficient use of network bandwidth. In addition, it can be ᵤred to be classless, which means it can carry the true subnet mask of a network and can therefore be used on more complex networks.

RIPv2, however, still uses only a hop count metric. Because of this limitation, it cannot be used effectively in today's networks that provide redundant and sometimes varied speed connections from point to point. It is therefore also considered by today's standards to be a legacy routing protocol.

Border Gateway Protocol (BGP)

BGP can be considered to be a distance vector routing protocol from autonomous system to autonomous system. An *autonomous system* is a group of devices that are under the same administrative domain, in other words, a group of devices that are under the same management and control, regardless of where they are physically located. When you connect to the Internet, you are moving from one autonomous system to another. BGP is the protocol that provides these logical connections or paths, and it is therefore also considered to be a path vector protocol. A detailed discussion of BGP is far beyond the scope of this book and is not an objective on the exam.

Hybrid

There is only one hybrid routing protocol with which you must be familiar, EIGRP. It is said to be a hybrid because it is actually a distance vector routing protocol that works like a link state routing protocol.

Enhanced Interior Gateway Routing Protocol (EIGRP)

EIGRP is a Cisco proprietary protocol that combines the ease of configuration of distance vector routing protocols with the advanced features and fast convergence of link state protocols. It is said to be a distance vector routing protocol with link state attributes. It can also be considered an advanced distance vector routing protocol or a hybrid routing protocol.

EIGRP uses a much more sophisticated metric than RIP or RIPv2. This metric includes the bandwidth of a connection and the delay, which is an experiential factor of how long it takes to pass traffic over the path of the network. It can also be "tweaked" by an administrator with load and reliability factors. Because of its more sophisticated metric, EIGRP is well suited for small, medium, and even large networks. The only possible disadvantage to EIGRP is that it is Cisco proprietary and therefore operates only on Cisco routers and Cisco layer 3 switches.

Exam Essentials

Know the most common link state routing protocols. You should be able to identify OSPF and IS-IS as the most common link state routing protocols. In addition, you should know the basic manner of function of a link state routing protocol and how it differs from distance vector routing protocols.

Know the most common distance vector routing protocols.   You should be able to identify RIP, RIPv2, and BGP as distance vector routing protocols. In addition, you should understand that RIP and RIPv2 are considered to be less sophisticated because of their limited metric of hop count. Finally, you should understand that BGP is a special type of distance vector routing protocol that maps autonomous systems together, as I will discuss further in the next section.

1.6 Explain the purpose and properties of routing

Generally speaking, routers are very specialized computers that do only two things. They deliver a packet to a host that is determined to be on one of their networks, or they consult their routing tables and follow the directions there. In the following sections, I'll discuss different types of routing and routing terminology used in today's networks. In addition, I'll discuss routing tables and how routers use them to make decisions.

Interior Gateway Protocol (IGP) vs. Exterior Gateway Protocol (EGP)

All the routing protocols I've discussed thus far, with the exception of BGP, have been IGPs. BGP is an EGP. Understanding the difference relies upon your knowledge of an autonomous system. As I mentioned earlier, an autonomous system is a group of devices under the same administrative domain. If a routing protocol works within one autonomous system, it is considered to be an IGP. If it works across autonomous systems, in effect connecting them, then it is considered to be an EGP. That's all there is to it, so don't make it any harder than it really is. The only EGP that you should be concerned with today is BGP; all of the rest are IGPs.

Static vs. Dynamic

In regard to routing configuration, the term *static* means configured by the administrator. All routers could be configured with static routes alone, but that would be the hard way. Not only would it be more work initially, but every time anything changed, every route would have to be reevaluated and possibly changed as well.

   Dynamic routing refers to letting the routers and routing protocols do the work for you. As I discussed earlier, there are many different routing protocols, but all of them have one element in common. They exchange information about possible paths through the network so that they can each make the best decision as to which way to send a data packet. Some routing protocols do this better than others, but they are all more efficient than strictly static routing.

Next Hop

Generally speaking, routers couldn't care less where a packet comes from when they make a routing decision. What they care about is where the packet wants to go. In other words, they are concerned with the destination address in the header of the packet. Based on the destination address, they can determine whether they can deliver the packet themselves or whether they need to send it to another router. If they cannot deliver the packet themselves, then they will consult their routing table to determine the next step. As I mentioned earlier, the routing table will give them the information as to the next interface that they can get to, which would be the appropriate place to send the packet. This interface is referred to as the *next hop* interface. This is because going from one network to another is like hopping over a router in the network diagram. It's really just going through two consecutive interfaces, but it's a lot more fun to say *hop*!

Understanding Routing Tables and How They Pertain to Path Selection

While I'm discussing routing tables anyway, I may as well show you a close-up look so you can see how it functions and how the router makes the decision by consulting it. Table 1.6 is a simple illustration of a RIPv2 route using hop count. This is actually a *Reader's Digest* version of what you might see in a Cisco router, but you get the point. As you can see, the router that contains this table knows how to get to other networks by virtue of the table. In other words, a packet that comes into this router that is destined for the 10.1.0.0 network will be sent out of a different interface from one that is destined for the 192.16.1.0 network.

TABLE 1.6   RIPv2 Hop Count

Destination Network	Subnet Mask	Interface	Metric (Hop Count)
10.1.0.0	255.255.0.0	S0	1
192.16.1.0	255.255.255.0	S1	1
172.16.0.0	255.255.0.0	S1	2

Convergence

Simply put, *convergence* means that everything is in agreement again after change has taken place. In other words, let's say you have a network that is all settled and in a *steady state*. All routers know the best interface to send a packet out based on the destination address of the packet. Now let's say you add a new interface to a router and thereby create a new path on which traffic could flow. This would cause the routing protocols to acknowledge and examine the new path and determine whether it is a more efficient path than the one they are currently using. In fact, each router would need to examine the new path against its current path for each network in its table. It would then make a decision as to whether to make a change. This can temporarily create quite a flurry of activity on a network in regard to routing protocol information exchange.

Once all the options are considered and the decisions are made, then the activity will settle down again. A network that has settled back down is said to be have *converged*, so the process of moving through this unsettled state to the settled state is referred to as *convergence*. Some routing protocols offer much faster convergence than others. As I discussed earlier, routing protocols such as EIGRP and OSPF are "smarter" and thus are not normally chatty, but they become very chatty for a short burst of time when something changes on the network. Their ability to move very quickly from an unsettled state to a settled state is referred to as *fast convergence*. This means that a change on an interface that affects the routing tables will have minimal effect on the user data that is traversing the network.

Exam Essentials

Know the difference between IGP and EGP.   You should know most routing protocols are IGP and that they work within one autonomous system. In addition, you should understand that BGP is the only EGP in common use today and that it works between autonomous systems, connecting the Internet.

Know the difference between static and dynamic routing.   You should understand that static routes are those configured manually by a network administrator. In addition, you should know that static routes have their limitations because all routes might have to be reevaluated based on any change to any router interface. You should also realize that dynamic routes are preferable to static routes because the routers do the work, and it can be done very quickly.

Know the concepts of routing tables, next hop, and convergence.   You should know that routers use routing tables to make decisions as to the interface to use for each network. In addition, you should understand that routers are simply looking for the next hop for any traffic that is not destined to one of their directly connected networks. You should also comprehend the concept of convergence in a network and the value of using a routing protocol with fast convergence.

1.7 Compare the characteristics of wireless communication standards

Over the past 10 years or so, wireless communication has continued to grow in business as well as in home networks. Teams of engineers have developed many standards, identified by the IEEE number 802.11 and a letter (such as *g*), to make wireless communications faster and more secure. In the following sections, I'll discuss the most common of these standards and how they are used in today's networks.

802.11 a/b/g/n

802.11 is the IEEE specification that is used for wireless LAN technology. 802.11 specifies an over-the-air interface between a wireless client and a base station or between two wireless clients. The IEEE accepted the specification in 1997. The original 802.11 standard used a frequency hopping spread spectrum radio (FHSS) signal. There have been many revisions to the standard since then. The following are the major 802.11 standards in use today:

802.11a   Uses orthogonal frequency division multiplexing to increase bandwidth. This standard uses the 5GHz radio band and can transmit at up to 54Mbps. It is not widely used today.

802.11b   Uses direct sequence spread spectrum (DSSS) in the 2.4GHz radio band. This standard can transmit at up to 11Mbps with fallback rates of 5.5Mbps, 2Mbps, and 1Mbps. It is one of the most commonly used standards today.

802.11g   Uses DSSS and the 2.4GHz radio band. This standard enhances the 802.11b standard and can transmit at speeds up to 54Mbps. It is one of the most commonly used standards and is backward compatible to 802.11b, since they both can use DSSS.

802.11n   Uses DSSS and the 2.4GHz radio band. This standard enhances the 802.11g standard and can transmit at speeds up to 600Mbps, although most devices in use today support speeds only up to about 300Mbps. This is not commonly used yet but is available and is backward compatible to 802.11g and 802.11b.

Authentication and Encryption

In the past, it was hard to say *wireless* and *security* in the same sentence without smiling a little at the irony. Gradually, newer technologies have surfaced that are slowly making these two concepts compatible with each other. In the next sections, I'll first discuss the earlier protocols that were not very secure in regard to authentication and encryption and then move on to the latest protocols that do offer some security for wireless communications.

Wired Equivalent Privacy (WEP)

One of the first attempts at wireless security was Wired Equivalent Privacy (WEP), which attempted to secure wireless connections on 802.11b-based networks. WEP attempted to secure the connections by encrypting the data transfer, but WEP was found not to be equivalent to wired security because the security mechanisms that were used to establish the encryption were not encrypted. WEP also operates only at the lower layers of the OSI model and therefore cannot offer end-to-end security for applications. Because of these shortcomings, many people have chosen newer and more sophisticated methods of securing wireless communications.

Wi-Fi Protected Access (WPA)

Wi-Fi Protected Access (WPA) was designed to improve upon WEP as a means of securing wireless communications. It can usually be installed as an upgrade on systems that currently use WEP. WPA offers two distinct advantages over WEP:

- Improved data encryption through the Temporal Key Integrity Protocol (TKIP), which scrambles the keys using a hashing algorithm. TKIP also provides an integrity-checking feature that ensures that the keys haven't been tampered with or altered.

- User authentication through the use of the Extensible Authentication Protocol (EAP) and user certificates. This ensures that only authorized users are given access to the network.

802.1x

The latest and most advanced form of wireless security is 802.1x, which is the name for the IEEE standard it supports. This type of wireless security is a standard feature of the latest operating systems such as Windows XP Professional. Access can be controlled per user and per port. 802.1x can use EAP to provide the following methods of authentication:

EAP Transport Level Security (EAP-TLS) This is the strongest method of encryption. EAP-TLS requires a certificate-based security environment. In other words, a form of certificate authority must be used. It provides mutual authentication, negotiation of the encryption method, and encrypted key determination between the client and the authenticator.

Protected EAP (PEAP) PEAP uses TLS to enhance the security of other authentication methods, such as CHAP and others. PEAP can be used without certificates unless it is being used in conjunction with MS-CHAP v2, which requires certificates in order to provide mutual authentication between the client and the server.

RADIUS

Using Remote Authentication Dial-In User Services (RADIUS), clients can be authenticated to use a wireless connection based on a current logon that can be authenticated by a domain controller. This method is used only when the user has an account in a domain such as a Microsoft Windows Active Directory domain.

Review Questions

1. What is name of the unique physical address that is assigned to every network interface card?

    A. IP address

    B. Hostname

    C. MAC address

    D. NetBIOS name

2. How many bits are used to create an IPv4 address?

    A. 8

    B. 6

    C. 32

    D. 64

3. If you have a Class B address with a default subnet mask and you need to create eight subnets, then which of the following subnet masks should you use?

    A. 255.255.255.240

    B. 255.255.224.0

    C. 255.255.240.0

    D. 255.240.0.0

4. Which of the following IP addresses are valid only for private IP addressing that is filtered from the Internet? (Choose two.)

    A. 10.1.1.1

    B. 172.17.255.254

    C. 11.1.2.4

    D. 193.168.2.1

5. Which information directory protocol is the standard for file transfer over the Internet?

    A. TCP

    B. UDP

    C. FTP

    D. HTTP

6. Which of the following are designated as well-known port numbers? (Choose two.)

    A. 80

    B. 49150

    C. 1011

    D. 8080

7. Which wireless protocol was designed to improve upon WEP and can be installed as an upgrade to WEP in many instances?

   A. 802.1x

   B. Kerberos

   C. WAP

   D. WPA

8. Which of the following is a Session layer protocol that is primarily responsible for setting up and tearing down voice and video calls over the Internet?

   A. SIP

   B. RTP

   C. HTTP

   D. FTP

9. Which of the following is an example of an IPv6 address?

   A. 192.168.1.1

   B. C0-FF-EE-C0-FF-EE

   C. fe80::216:deff:ee09:6d13

   D. 255.255.240.0

10. Which of the following subnet masks should you use to obtain 100 subnets from a Class B network?

    A. 255.255.254.0

    B. 255.254.0.0

    C. 255.255.255.128

    D. There isn't enough information to answer the question.

Answers to Review Questions

1. **C.** A media access control (MAC) address is a unique physical address that is assigned to each network interface card. MAC addresses are "burned in" to the card at the manufacturer.

2. **C.** An IPv4 address is a 32-bit address. It is composed of four sections of 8 bits each, called octets. Each octet is converted to decimal for configuration purposes, but the computer uses the entire 32-bit address for communication.

3. **B.** If you have a Class B address with a default subnet mask, then the current subnet mask is 255.255.0.0. This means you have 16 bits for networks and 16 bits for hosts. If you want to create eight subnets, then you need to solve for $2^s > 8$. Solving for s, you can determine that you need to use the first 3 bits from the network address to create the subnets. The values of the first 3 bits total 224 (128 + 64 + 32), so the new subnet mask is 255.255.224.0. (This is all assuming you use the new method, which uses the first and last subnets.)

4. **A, B.** The valid private address ranges include the following:

   - 192.168.0.0–192.168.255.255
   - 172.16.0.0–172.31.255.255
   - 10.0.0.0–10.255.255.255

   Only answers A and B fall into these ranges.

5. **C.** FTP is an Application layer protocol that uses TCP ports 20 and 21. It is the standard protocol used for file transfer over the Internet.

6. **A, C.** The port numbers that are designated as well-known port number are those in the range of 0 to 1023. Ports in the range of 1024 to 49151 are designated as registered ports. Ports in the range of 49152 to 65535 are designated as dynamic or private ports.

7. **D.** Wi-Fi Protected Access (WPA) was designed to improve upon WEP. It provides improved data encryption as well as improved authentication mechanisms.

8. **A.** Session Initiation Protocol (SIP) is a Session layer protocol that is primarily responsible for setting up and tearing down voice and video calls over the Internet. It also enables IP telephony networks to utilize advanced call features such as SS7.

9. **C.** An IPv6 address is a 128-bit binary address that is expressed as a hexadecimal address. Leading 0s can be omitted and successive fields of 0s can be represented as ::.

10. **A.** A Class B network will by definition have a subnet mask of 255.255.0.0. This means you have 16 host bits with which to work to create 100 subnets. To determine the number of subnets you need, you use the formula $2^s \geq 100$. Solving for s, you can determine that you need 7 host bits, since $2^6 = 64$ but $2^7 = 128$. This means that the 128, 64, 32, 16, 8, 4, and 2 values in the third octet will now count in the subnet mask. Adding these values, you get 254, so the new subnet mask is 254.

Chapter 2

Domain 2 Network Media and Topologies

COMPTIA NETWORK+ EXAM OBJECTIVES COVERED IN THIS CHAPTER:

✓ **2.1 Categorize standard cable types and their properties**

- CAT3, CAT5, CAT5e, CAT6
- STP, UDP
- COAX
- Multimode fiber, single-mode fiber
- Serial
- Plenum vs. Non-plenum
- Transmission speeds
- Distance
- Duplex
- Noise immunity (security, EMI)
- Frequency

✓ **2.2 Identify common connector types**

- RJ-11
- RJ-45
- BNC
- SC
- ST
- LC
- RS-232

✓ **2.3 Identify common physical network topologies**

- Star
- Bus
- Mesh
- Ring
- Point-to-point
- Point-to-multipoint
- Hybrid

✓ **2.4 Given a scenario, differentiate and implement appropriate wiring standards**

- 586A
- 586B
- Straight vs. crossover
- Rollover
- Loopback

✓ **2.5 Categorize WAN technology types and properties**

- Frame Relay
- E1/T1
- ADSL
- SDSL
- VDSL
- Cable Modem
- Satellite
- E3/T3
- OC-x
- Wireless
- ATM
- SONET
- MPLS
- ISDN BRI

- ISDN PRI
- POTS
- PSTN
- Circuit Switch
- Packet Switch
- Speed
- Transmission Media
- Distance

✓ **2.6 Categorize LAN technology types and properties**

- Ethernet
- 10BaseT
- 100BaseTX
- 100BaseFX
- 1000BaseT
- 1000BaseX
- 10GBaseX
- 10GBaseSR
- 10GBaseLR
- 10GBaseER
- 10GBaseSW
- 10GBaseLW
- 10GBaseEW
- 10GBaseT
- CSMA/CD
- Broadcast
- Collision
- Bonding
- Speed
- Distance

✓ **2.7 Explain common logical network topologies and their characteristics**

- ▪ Peer-to-peer

- ▪ Client/server

- ▪ VPN

- ▪ VLAN

✓ **2.8 Install components of wiring distribution**

- ▪ Vertical and horizontal cross connects

- ▪ Patch panels

- ▪ 66 block

- ▪ MDFs

- ▪ IDFs

- ▪ 25 pair

- ▪ 100 pair

- ▪ 110-block

- ▪ Demarc

- ▪ Demarc Extension

- ▪ Smart jack

- ▪ Verify wiring installation

- ▪ Verify wiring termination

Although the basic concept of connecting computers hasn't changed very much since the mid-1980s, the methods used to connect them have changed dramatically. The technologies that are in use now have evolved over the past 20 years to the point where they are today. These technologies will continue to evolve. The components we use in our networks have also evolved because of these technologies.

When you connect computers, your main goal is to provide fast communication with as few errors as possible. You should understand that the type of media and topology you use in your network will largely determine your ability to reach this goal. In addition, you should know that the components you choose for a network will also determine your capability to control network traffic. In this chapter, I will discuss several networking media and topologies and compare the features that they, and the components that use them, bring to your network design to help you control traffic within your network.

2.1 Categorize standard cable types and their properties

As networking has evolved the types of cable and their properties have dramatically changed. We have moved from using cables made from copper wire, to using cables made from glass fibers. Each of these general categories of cable has its own properties and has many options from which to select. In this section we discuss the most common types of cable and their corresponding properties.

Types of Cable

You will choose a type of cable based on the intended use in your network and the capabilities that you need from the cable. For example, you might choose a cable based on the fact that you need high bandwidth, or based on the fact that you need to run the cable for a great distance. It's important to understand the choices that you have in regard to cables and the resulting features and benefits of each choice. In this section, I'll discuss the main types of cable from which you can choose.

Category 3, 5, 5e, and 6 Twisted-Pair Cables

The category of a twisted-pair cable indicates the tightness of the twist applied to the wire pairs in the cable. The twist in wire pairs prevents an electrical interference called *crosstalk* from affecting the communication. Crosstalk occurs when a signal bleeds over from one wire to another (even through the insulation of the wire). The tighter the twist, the faster you can transmit information through a cable without suffering from crosstalk. Table 2.1 shows the maximum speed of the main cable categories. Category 5e (enhanced) is the cable type that is currently recommended as a minimum for all new installations.

TABLE 2.1 Cable Categories and Speeds

	Category 3	Category 5	Category 5e	Category 6
Maximum Speed	10Mbps	100Mbps	1000Mbps	1000Mbps

UTP

Unshielded twisted-pair (UTP) cable is the most common type of cable in use today. UTP is offered for all the categories of cable discussed in Table 2.1. UTP is used most often because it is far easier to install than STP (which I will discuss next). It is commonly used in the access and distribution areas of a network. The only protection from electrical interference provided by UTP is that the pairs of wires within the cable are twisted, which is usually enough. Figure 2.1 shows a UTP cable.

FIGURE 2.1 A UTP cable

STP

Shielded twisted-pair (STP) resembles UTP except that it includes a foil shield that covers the wires and adds another layer of protection against outside magnetic interference. For this protection to be effective, the connections have to be properly grounded. This adds to the complexity of installations, so most organizations have opted to use fiber-optic cable instead of STP when electromagnetic interference is a problem. Figure 2.2 shows an STP cable.

FIGURE 2.2   An STP cable

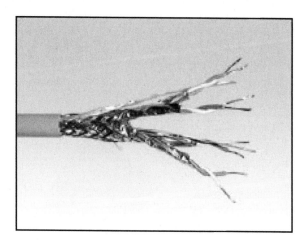

Coaxial Cable

In the late 1980s, coaxial cable was used as the backbone of network segments and to connect computers to the bus topology that made up the network. Coaxial cable is rarely used anymore for network backbones or to connect computers, but it is being used today to connect cable modems to NICs to provide computers with broadband Internet connections. Coaxial cable consists of an inner core wire and an outer braid of insulating wire. The inner core wire carries the entire signal. Figure 2.3 shows a coaxial cable.

FIGURE 2.3   A coaxial cable

Single-Mode Fiber

Single-mode fiber-optic cable (SMF) is a high-speed, high-distance media. It consists of a single strand, or sometimes two strands, of glass fiber that carries the signals. The light source that is generally used with single-mode fiber is a laser, although light-emitting diodes (LEDs) may also be used. With single-mode fiber, a single light source is transmitted from end to end and pulsed to create communication. Single-mode fiber is used for long runs because it can transmit data 50 times further than multimode fiber and at a faster rate. For example, single-mode fiber might be used on an organization's corporate campus between buildings. Since the transmission media is glass, installing single-mode fiber can be a bit tricky. Other layers are protecting the glass core, but the cable still should not be crimped or pinched around any tight corners. It is, however, completely immune to electrical interference since light is used instead of electrical signals. Figure 2.4 illustrates the layers included in single-mode fiber-optic cable.

FIGURE 2.4   Single-mode fiber-optic cable

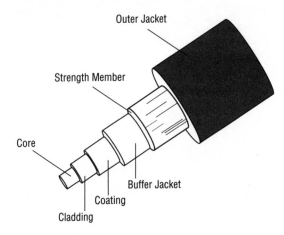

Multimode Fiber

Multimode fiber-optic cable (MMF) also uses light to communicate a signal, but the light is dispersed into numerous paths as it travels through the core and is reflected back via cladding, a special material that lines the core and focuses the light back onto it. Multimode fiber provides high bandwidth at high speeds over medium distances (up to about 3,000 feet) but can be inconsistent for very long runs. Because of this, multimode fiber is generally used within a smaller area of a building, whereas single-mode can be used between buildings. Multimode fiber is available in glass or in a plastic version that makes installation easier and increases installation flexibility. As with single-mode fiber, multimode fiber can be used when electrical interference is present, since it is completely immune to it. Figure 2.5 shows the how light is split into multiple paths in a multimode fiber-optic cable.

More specifics on data transmission distance with fiber-optic cable are discussed later in this chapter.

FIGURE 2.5   A multimode fiber-optic cable

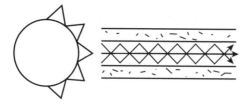

Serial Cables

I should mention here that all the cable types I've discussed, except for multimode fiber, are considered serial cable types. *Serial* means "one after the other." In regard to network communications, this means that one bit after another is sent out onto the wire or fiber to be transmitted and interpreted by a network card or other interface on the other end. Each 1 or 0 is read separately and then combined with others to form communication. This is very different from parallel communication where the bits are sent in groups that must be read together to interpret the communication properly.

Plenum vs. Nonplenum

The difference between plenum and nonplenum cable involves how each is constructed and where it is authorized for use. Many large multi-story buildings are designed to circulate air through the spaces between the ceiling of one story and the floor of the next. This area in between floors is referred to as the *plenum*. It is an area that is generally perfect for running cables to connect the many computers in the building.

However, in the event of a fire, the cables in the plenum can become a serious hazard in two ways. First, their insulation can give off a poisonous smoke that would, of course, be circulated throughout the building. Second, they can become a "wick" for the fire and actually help spread it from room to room and floor to floor. Not pretty, huh?

To prevent both of these occurrences, the National Fire Protection Association (NFPA) regulates the use of cables in the plenum to those that it has tested to be safe. A plenum cable is therefore tested to be fire retardant and to create no (or a very small amount of) smoke and poisoned gas when burned. A nonplenum cable does not meet these standards and can therefore be used anywhere except in a plenum. Nonplenum cables are typically less expensive than plenum cables. However, most organizations use plenum cable only in the plenum for obvious reasons.

Properties of Cables

The reason that many different types of cables are used in a network is that each type of cable has its own properties and therefore is best used for a specific area or purpose in the network. Different types of cables may vary in regard to many properties including transmission speeds, distance, duplex, noise immunity, and frequency. In the following sections, I'll discuss each of these properties.

Transmission Speeds

Based on the type of cable or fiber chosen and the network in which it's installed, network administrators can control the speed of a network to accommodate the network's traffic demands. Administrators will generally allow for transmission speeds of 1Gbps or faster on the core areas of their networks that connect various network segments. In the distribution and access areas, transmission speeds can often be slower because the traffic demand is not as high.

To understand this better, think about a city as you see it from the air. The large wide interstate systems are the core and allow for a tremendous amount of fast-moving traffic. The smaller highways and boulevards are the distribution areas with lower, but still relatively high, speeds. The neighborhoods are the access areas where speed is less important because there is much less demand.

Similarly, today's networks are constructed with many different types of fiber-optic and copper cable based on the needs in a particular area of the network. These all work together to provide for the communications needs of the users. Later in this chapter, we will discuss specific LAN technology types and their relevant speeds.

Distance

Often we decide what cable type to use based on the topology of a network and the distance between its components. This is because some network technologies can run much further than others without communication errors. All network communications technologies suffer from *attenuation*, which is the degradation of signal because of the medium itself. Attenuation is much more pronounced in some cable types than in others. For example, a good rule of thumb and best practice is that any network using twisted-pair cable should have a maximum segment length of only 100 meters (328 feet). Each cable type has its own limitations because of attenuation, which we will discuss in more detail later in this chapter.

Duplex

All communications can be categorized in one of two ways: half-duplex or full-duplex. The difference centers on whether the communicating parties or devices can "talk" and "listen" at the same time. I will use analogies that include both people and devices to describe these types of communication further.

In half-duplex communication, a device can either send communication or receive communication, but it cannot do both at the same time. Think "walkie-talkie" to understand this concept. Once you press the button on the walkie-talkie, the speaker is off, and you can't hear anything that the other side is saying. That's why you say "over" when you are finished talking and want a response. That way, you don't "step on" the communications of the other side...over!

In full-duplex communication, a device can send and receive communication at the same time; in fact, both devices can send and receive communication at the same time. This means that the effective throughput is doubled, and communications can be much more efficient. This is typical in most of today's switched networks.

To understand full-duplex communication, think about a telephone. You can talk into the phone and listen to what the other person is saying at the same time. At least some people can. The point is that there are two separate wires that carry the signals, one for the transmit signal and the other for the receive signal. This is the same with network devices; when you use full-duplex communication, you generally just use more wire pairs in the same cable. This type of communication can be achieved only by using a switched environment to provide point-to-point connections to the devices, which I will discuss later in this chapter.

Noise Immunity (Security, EMI)

Any time you push electrons through two wires adjacent to each other, you create a magnetic current. Similarly, if you run a magnet over the wires, you can create a current in the wires. Thank goodness for this *magnetic flux*, since the power that is surging through our computers at this very moment is a result of it. Unfortunately, it also creates two communications issues.

First, since the wire is creating a current that is based on the 1s and 0s coursing through it, it's possible with the right equipment to read the message in the wire without cutting the wire or even removing the insulation. This is generally referred to as *tapping* the wire, and it's a valid security concern. In the "old days," high-security installations such as the Pentagon would encase the communication wires in lead shielding to prevent them from being tapped. Shielded twisted-pair wires make tapping more difficult but still not impossible. Coaxial cables provide shielding but can still be tapped by actually puncturing the insulation and connecting to the core wire. This is referred to as a *vampire tap*.

As you may have guessed, the best way to get around the problem of magnetic flux caused by electricity is by not using electricity. Fiber-optic cables carry the signal as light on a glass or very pure plastic strand. The light is not susceptible to magnetic flux, thereby making fiber optics much harder to tap. Did you notice that I said "much harder" and not "impossible"? It is still possible to tap fiber optics at the equipment level, but it's nearly impossible to tap this type of cable without physically cutting and repairing the cable — not an easy thing to do unnoticed.

The second effect of magnetic flux works from the outside in instead of from the inside out. Since wires might take on an additional current if placed near any source of magnetism, you have to be careful where you run your communications cables. This property of being affected by external magnetism is referred to as *electromagnetic interference* (EMI). You can avoid EMI by taking care to keep copper cables away from all powerful magnetic sources. These may include electric motors, speakers, amplifiers, fluorescent light ballasts, and so on. Anything that could generate a magnetic field should be avoided when positioning a cable.

ncy

.. cable type has a specified maximum frequency that indicates the transmission bandwidth it can handle. As you know, bandwidth is a digital measurement of 1s and 0s. Frequency is an analog measurement that can be converted to 1s and 0s using a pulse amplitude modulation system that, thank goodness, is beyond the scope of this book! The bottom line is that you should choose the correct frequency of cable based on the needs of the part of your network in which it will be installed. Oftentimes, this is a "no-brainer" based on just using the best practice standard for the cable, but there is a reason for the standard.

For example, CAT 5e cable is tested to 100MHz maximum frequency. It can run 1Gbps signals for relatively short distances, but it is barely able to handle that type of data flow. On the other hand, CAT 6 is a 250MHz cable that can handle 1Gbps data flow "all day long without batting an eye." Although signal is measured as bandwidth, the capacity to carry the signal in a cable is measured as frequency.

Exam Essentials

Know common cable types and their uses.   You should understand that a network consists of many different cable types and that each type has its own advantages and disadvantages depending on where it is used. Copper cables such as CAT 5 and CAT 6 are commonly used in the access and distribution areas of a network. Fiber-optic cables can carry much more data and therefore will often be used in the core that connects many network segments. The areas of a building called the *plenum* require specially insulated cables that will not spread fire or poisoned gases.

Know the properties associated with cable types.   You should realize that your selection of cable type will affect the speed, distance, duplex options, and security of your network segment. Generally speaking, twisted-pair cables are very limited compared to fiber-optic cables with regard to the speed and distance of the connections. Fiber-optic cables are generally considered more secure because they are much harder to tap and they are immune to EMI. You should also select the cable that is rated for the frequency associated with the bandwidth you intend to use on it.

2.2 Identify common connector types

No matter what type of cable you are using, it won't be very effective unless it has the proper connections on each end! The type of connector you use will depend on the cable as well as the intended use for the cable. In other words, you need to have the proper connector to plug into the device you are trying to use. You should be able to recognize by sight the main types of cable connectors and describe their most common use. In the following sections, I will discuss the purpose of the major types of connectors and provide a picture of each type.

RJ-11

RJ sounds fancy, but it just stands for "registered jack." Chances are very good that you have held an RJ-11 connector in your hand, since they are used on all the telephone connections in the United States and most other countries. They can contain and connect two pairs of wires. In regard to computers, you are most likely to use an RJ-11 connector when you attach a modem to a telephone line in the unlikely event you are still using a dial-up connection. I know there are still some out there somewhere! Figure 2.6 shows an RJ-11 connector.

FIGURE 2.6   An RJ-11 connector

RJ-45

The RJ-45 connector is the most common of all network connectors. It is used to connect network interface cards (NICs) to hubs and/or switches. RJ-45s can also be used to connect network devices together for communication as well as control. The RJ-45 connector can contain and connect four pairs of wires, although they generally connect only two pairs. Figure 2.7 shows an RJ-45 connector.

FIGURE 2.7   An RJ-45 connector

BNC

Although this type of coaxial connector is rarely used in today's networks, it is still listed as an item to recognize for the exam. Who knows, you might run into one at some point if you "dig up" a very, very old network. The BNC connector is pushed in and then locked onto the connection to hold it securely in place while connecting the core wire. Figure 2.8 shows a BNC connector.

FIGURE 2.8   A BNC connector

SC

The standard connector (SC) connector is a type of fiber-optic cable connector. It uses a push-pull connector mechanism similar to common audio and video plugs. SC connectors are most often used with multimode fiber-optic cable that is providing a backbone segment for a local area network. (I will discuss single-mode and multimode fiber-optic cable later in this chapter.) Figure 2.9 shows an SC connector.

FIGURE 2.9 An SC connector

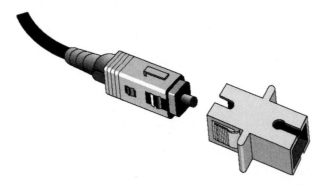

ST

The straight tip (ST) connector is a type of fiber-optic cable connector. It uses a half-twist bayonet type of lock to hold it in place securely. ST connectors are most commonly used with single-mode fiber-optic cable that runs long distances. Figure 2.10 shows an ST connector.

FIGURE 2.10 An ST connector

LC

The local connector (LC) connector is a fiber connector that is built into the body of an RJ-style jack. The LC connector is perfect for local connections in an organization's telecom room or network closet. Figure 2.11 shows an LC connector.

FIGURE 2.11   An LC connector

RS-232

Recommended standard 232 (RS-232) was a cable standard commonly used for serial data signals connecting between data terminal and data communications equipment, such as when connecting a computer's serial port to an external modem. As you can imagine, it is used much less frequently today than it was in the past. Still, you should be able to recognize a DE-9 female connector as one that might be used in an RS-232 connection. These types of connections are being superseded in today's networks by more modern connectors such as USB. Figure 2.12 shows an RS-232 connector.

FIGURE 2.12   An RS-232 connectors

Exam Essentials

Be able to recognize the main types of connectors used in networks.   You should be able to recognize a picture of the most common media connectors discussed in this chapter.

Be able to describe the use of common connectors.   For a specified connector, you should be able to describe the intended use and the type of network upon which it is used.

2.3 Identify common physical network topologies

Basically, a topology is a shape; so, a network topology is the shape of a network. There is, however, a big difference between a physical network topology and a logical network topology. The physical network topology represents how the network looks to your "naked eye." In other words, the physical network topology is the way the components are arranged. The logical network topology represents how information flows through the network, which may not be the same as how it looks to your "naked eye." You should understand the main network topologies and the difference between a physical network topology and a logical one. You should be able to recognize them given a diagram, schematic, or description. In the following paragraphs, I will discuss each network topology in greater detail.

Star

A *star* topology is a group of computers connected to a central location, such as a hub or a switch. This is the most common topology in use today. The computers may be physically located next to each other or spread throughout an entire building, but the flow of information from among computers must go through the central location. In a star topology, each computer has its own cable or connection to the hub. Since each computer has its own connection, one computer's failing will not affect the other computers in the network. However, if the hub or switch should fail, then all the computers on that hub or switch will be affected. Figure 2.13 is an illustration of a star topology.

FIGURE 2.13   A star topology

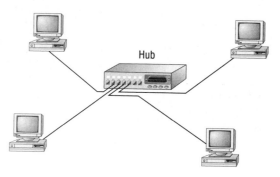

Bus

The *bus* topology was used in earlier networks but is not commonly used today. In a bus topology, all computers are connected to each other by a single cable. Coaxial cable with special connectors called *BNC connectors* (as shown earlier in Figure 2.8) and *T connectors* were used. The T connectors provided an independent connection for each computer on the bus. In addition, the bus worked only if both ends of the cable had a special resistor, called a *terminator*, installed. Figure 2.14 shows a bus topology, and Figure 2.15 shows the T connector used to connect the computers to the bus.

FIGURE 2.14   A bus topology

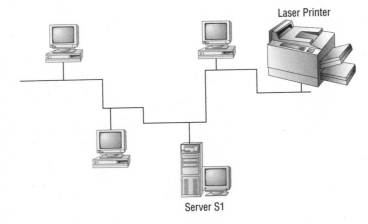

Laser Printer

Server S1

FIGURE 2.15   A T connector

Mesh

The full *mesh* topology is not often used for networks and is almost never used for individual computers. In a full mesh topology, all the components in the mesh have independent connections to all the other components in the mesh. For example, if there were four computers connected with a *full mesh*, then the number of connections could be determined by the following formula:

  [n(n–1)] / 2 = total number of connections

In this example, there would be a total of 12 connectors for 6 connections and each computer would have to contain three network interface cards:

  [4(4–1)] / 2 = 6

Any network with multiple or redundant connections to network components can be considered a mesh topology, but because of the expense involved in building this type of network, they are rarely created for individual computers. A mesh, or even a full mesh, would most likely be found connecting multiple networks in an organization. In fact, the Internet is the best and biggest example of a partial-mesh topology. Figure 2.16 shows a full-mesh topology with four computers.

FIGURE 2.16   A full mesh topology

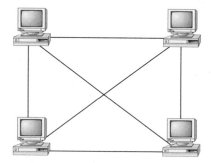

Ring

A ring topology looks exactly like a star topology to the naked eye. The real difference in a ring topology vs. a star topology is the technology that is used. Computers in a ring topology generally use IBM Token Ring technology. Other components can also be arranged in a ring topology and use different technologies. The computers in a ring topology are not generally arranged in a physical ring. In fact, just as with a star topology, they can be next to each other or spread throughout a building. The difference is that the central component that connects them contains the logical ring that facilitates communication on the network using the ring technologies. Figure 2.17 shows a ring topology.

FIGURE 2.17   A ring topology

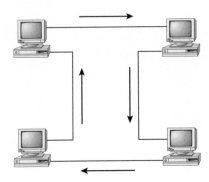

Point-to-Point

Point-to-point is not really so much of a network topology as it is a piece of one. Today's networks generally consist of many point-to-point and various other types of connections. Point-to-point just means that the connection is active only for the sender and the receiver and that there are no other computers or devices involved. In fact, point-to-point connections are said to create communication that is not shared because the only communication is between the sender and the receiver. Point-to-point connections between network devices, such as switches or routers, can provide for very efficient network communication. In fact, you may remember from the earlier discussion that full-duplex communication requires point-to-point connections. Figure 2.18 illustrates a point-to-point connection between two routers.

FIGURE 2.18:   A point-to-point connection

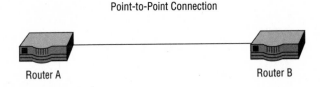

Point-to-Point Connection

Router A   Router B

Point-to-Multipoint

Point-to-multipoint connections are created when an interface is connected to two or more other interfaces. This is the general effect of a hub on a network in which the data flows into one interface and can flow out of all other interfaces. It can also be seen in router configurations, such as Frame Relay switching (which I will discuss later in the chapter), in which the point-to-multipoint connections are created using subinterfaces (virtual interfaces). Point-to-multipoint Ethernet connections cannot use full-duplex communications because the connections are shared and therefore require the use of CSMA/CD to control the traffic. Point-to-multipoint connections in Frame Relay switching might require the use of special protocols and configuration to control data traffic. Figure 2.19 illustrates point-to-multipoint configurations.

FIGURE 2.19 Point-to-multipoint configurations

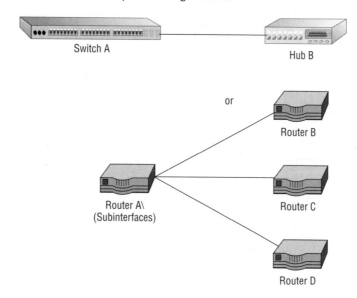

Hybrid

Actually, most networks today are a combination of many topologies. For example, a network will often use a star topology with a partial mesh consisting of some point-to-point and some multipoint connections. This type of hybrid design facilitates customization to the organization's communication needs as well as redundant connections for load balancing and fault tolerance. Figure 2.20 illustrates a hybrid network topology.

FIGURE 2.20   A hybrid configuration

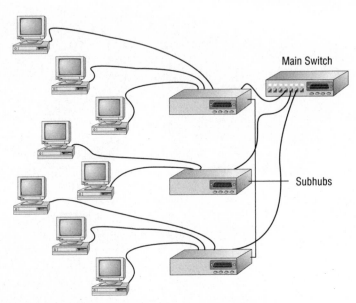

Exam Essentials

Know the difference between a physical topology and a logical topology.   You should know that the physical topology of the network is simply what it looks like or how the components are arranged. The logical topology, on the other hand, represents the flow of information in the network.

Know the main logical network topologies.   You should be able to recognize the star, bus, mesh, ring, point-to-point, point-to-multipoint, and hybrid topologies by a diagram, schematic, or description. You should be able to compare and contrast these four main topologies.

2.4 Given a scenario, differentiate and implement appropriate wiring standards

One day in the future, maybe all networks will be wireless. In the meantime, we use many wires and cables to connect our networks. Even a so-called wireless network is generally connected to a wired one if you follow it far enough. Today's networks use many types of wiring configurations to connect computers and other devices. You should understand main wiring configurations used and be able to determine which type of wiring design is appropriate in a given situation. In the following sections, I'll discuss the most often used wiring configurations and their appropriate use in a network.

568A vs. 568B

If you look inside a network cable, you will find four pairs of wires. These wire pairs are twisted together to prevent crosstalk (as I discussed earlier in this chapter). Then the pairs of twisted wires are also twisted together to help prevent EMI and tapping. You know that the same pins must be used on the same colors throughout a network for receive and transmit, but how do you decide which color wire goes with which pin? The good news is that you don't have to decide — at least not completely. Two wiring standards have surfaced that have been agreed upon by more than 60 vendors including AT&T, 3Com, and Cisco, though there isn't 100 percent agreement in the industry. In other words, over the years some network jacks have been pinned with the 568A standard, and some have used the 568B standard. This can cause confusion if you don't know what you are looking at in your network.

You may be thinking "What's the difference, and why does it matter?" Well, the difference is the position of four wires on one side of the cable — that's it! As you can see in Figure 2.21, pins 4, 5, 7, and 8 are not used at all in either standard. This leaves only the wire pairs to connect to pins 1, 2, 3, and 6. If you connect the green-white, green, orange-white, and orange wires to pins 1, 2, 3, and 6, respectively, on both sides of the cable, then you are said to be using the 568A standard and you would be creating a straight-through cable that would be used as a regular *patch cable* for most networks. If, on the other hand, you switch from pin 1 to pin 3 and from pin 2 to pin 6 on one side only, then you have created a *crossover cable* for most networks. Figures 2.22 and 2.23 further illustrate these wire pair differences.

FIGURE 2.21   EIA/TIA 568A and 568B wiring standards

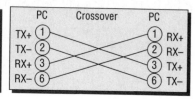

FIGURE 2.22 EIA/TIA 568A standard

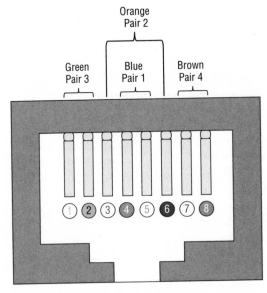

RJ-45 Jack
EIA/TIA 568A Standard

FIGURE 2.23 EIA/TIA 568B standard

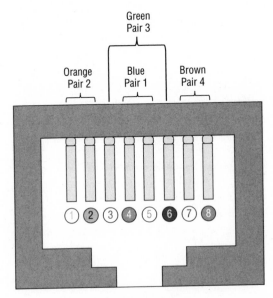

RJ-45 Jack
EIA/TIA 568A Standard

Most organizations use a specific color of cable to make their crossover cables stand out. For example, companies may use a bright yellow or a bright red for all crossover cables.

The reason that I have to say "for most networks" is that both the 568A and 568B standards will actually work as a patch cable on a network. The determining factor is how the wall jacks and patch panels are set up. Most new network installations will be 568A, but you might still encounter some that are 568B. Now you may be thinking "Why would the electrons care what color the wire is anyway?" Well, the electrons don't really care, but the wire pairs are significant. In other words, you might think that you could just connect whatever color wire to whatever pin you want and just be consistent on both ends. This won't really work, though, because the pairs of wires are significant since they are twisted together to prevent crosstalk by canceling each other out. This means that you can't just use any wire you want; you have to take the twisted-pairs into account. Now, could you use one of the other pairs instead? The answer is "yes," if you are careful in your configuration. However, why would you want to do that? It's confusing enough to have the two standards, and therefore your best move is to choose a standard for your whole organization (most likely 568A for patch cables) and stick with it.

Straight vs. Crossover

Now that I have discussed how to create a straight-through cable and a crossover cable, I'll discuss just what straight and crossover actually mean and where each type of cable is generally used. A straight (or straight-through) cable is the most common type of cable used in a network. It is typically referred to as a *patch cable*, because it is used to patch one network device to another. Straight-through cables are generally used to connect network devices that are dissimilar.

For example, in a typical network, a computer is attached to a wall jack using a straight-through cable. The wall jack is attached to a patch panel (for flexibility and redundancy), and then the patch panel is attached to a switch. In essence, a computer attached to a switch uses a straight-through cable. A computer and a switch are very different in regard to how they function on a network and therefore are considered dissimilar.

On the other hand, let's say I wanted to attach a switch to a switch. By this definition, the devices are similar, and therefore I should use a crossover cable instead. Suppose I used a straight-through cable where I should have used a crossover cable; would that work? Well, yes — most modern switches would autosense the difference and "switch the pins" for me. However, for the exam you should know that straight-through cables are used to connect dissimilar network devices, and crossover cables are used to connect similar devices. Table 2.2 illustrates the most common matchups and which cable to use.

TABLE 2.2   Cable Types and Uses

Device 1	Device 2	Cable Type
PC	Switch	Straight
PC	PC	Crossover
Switch	Router	Straight
Router	Router	Crossover
PC	Router	Crossover

Most of the time it's rather easy to see whether a straight-though or crossover cable should be used. For example, a PC-to-PC connection would obviously use a crossover cable. There is a situation that's a bit "trickier," though, and it might come up on the exam. What if you wanted to connect a PC to a network connection on a router; would you use a straight-through cable or a crossover cable? Now your first instinct might be to answer "straight-through," since a router seems very different from a PC. Well, in fact, a PC is "kind of" a router. Type **route print** on a command line, and you'll see what I mean. Because of this, the correct answer is a crossover cable.

Rollover

A *rollover cable* is so named because the wire colors would look the same if you kept one RJ-45 connection upright and rolled over the connector on the other end of the same cable. In essence, this would connect the transmit pins to the receive pins, and vice versa. Why would you want to do that? Don't you just want the information to flow through and not actually have the devices "talking" to each other? Well, you don't want to do that if you want to configure the device.

On Cisco routers and switches, a rollover cable is used to connect the transmit pins coming from a PC's serial line (usually COM1) to the receive pins on the Cisco device, and vice versa. In the past, these rollover cables were created and then attached to the console port on a Cisco device and to a connector called a *DB-9 terminal adapter*. Now you can simply use a rollover cable that is created by reversing the whole wiring diagram, and that includes a built-in terminal adapter. Figure 2.24 shows a modern rollover cable.

FIGURE 2.24 A rollover cable

Loopback

When referring to wiring, *loopback* is not so much a wiring standard as a way of redirecting data flow. Sometimes you might need a computer to "think" it has a live connection to a network even when it doesn't. This could be useful for testing purposes or to install some software that requires a live network to install. In these cases, you will need to trick the PC into seeing its own output as input. You can accomplish this using a loopback plug.

A loopback plug connects transmit to receive and receive to transmit, but it does so on the same connection. This causes the device to see its output as input from the network by "looping back" the data. Because of this, the software that needs a live network will be fooled into thinking it has found one. Loopback plugs can also be used to test whether a network interface card is sending a signal and whether an interface on a switch is actively sending data or not. Figure 2.25 shows the wiring of a typical loopback plug.

FIGURE 2.25 A loopback plug

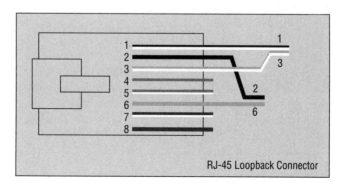

RJ-45 Loopback Connector

Exam Essentials

Know the different types of wiring standards and their uses.   You should know the difference between the 586A and 586B wiring standards and how each is used. You should understand that either will work electrically but that the determining factor is how the wall jacks and patch panels are pinned in the organization's network.

Know the main types of wiring standards and their uses.   You should understand the difference between the straight-through, crossover, rollover, and loopback wiring standards. You should also be able to differentiate the best and most appropriate use for each standard in a network.

2.5 Categorize WAN technology types and properties

Today's organizations use many different types of WAN connections. The decision to use one connection type over another will largely be dependent on the properties each connection type offers and the advantages it may provide the organization. In the following sections, I'll discuss the main WAN connection types and their properties.

Type

Most WAN connections are provided by a communications company referred to as a *service provider*. One of the main differences between a WAN and a LAN is that you generally don't own all the connections on a WAN, unless you are the service provider. Because of this, the types of network connections you will encounter in a WAN environment are very different from the connections you are used to in a LAN environment. Most network connection types have evolved over time, offering the right properties to connect a company's computers based on the needs of the company for its connections. I'll discuss WAN connection types such as Frame Relay, T1, T3, DSL, cable modem, ATM, SONET, wireless, MPLS, and ISDN.

Frame Relay

Organizations that have many locations across a wide geographic region and that want to connect each of those locations to each other have many options with today's communications networks. They could connect them all with dedicated lines. This could be very expensive, though, since they would need many dedicated lines. For example, if an organization had just five locations that it wanted to mesh fully with dedicated lines, it would require 15 dedicated lines, using the formula $[n(n-1)] / 2$, as I discussed earlier in this chapter. Dedicated lines will be discussed in more detail later in this chapter.

Instead of using dedicated lines, another option available to organizations is to use a network of switches and special routers that spans the globe and can be connected to at any point. These lines take the information from a computer or other host and relay it to its final destination. This type of networking is referred to as *Frame Relay* because the layer 2 frames are actually being relayed across the switches and special routers instead of being sent on dedicated lines. This has been an effective method of communication for many companies over the last 10 to 15 years, but it is gradually being phased out now because of even better communication options.

If you take a Cisco or other type of WAN-based class, you will no doubt learn the details, and a myriad of terminology, about Frame Relay. For the purposes of this course, you should just know that it is a method of using common (nondedicated) lines to communicate network traffic at layer 2 (the Data Link layer) so as to join two hosts together within the same subnet. The layer 2 address that it uses, referred to as a Data Link Connection Identifier (DLCI), is generally assigned by the service provider such as AT&T or Sprint. The guaranteed communication rate that the service provider agrees to is the *committed information rate* (CIR). Thus, the main reason that you might choose Frame Relay over dedicated lines is that you can get an acceptable CIR for your connections for much less money than you would pay to have dedicated lines for each one.

E1/T1

So, at this point you may be thinking "What are these dedicated lines that he keeps talking about?" Well, let's say your company has one location in New York and another in San Diego. For your communications, you would like to have a cable that connects the two locations together. You could get a very big truck and a whole lot of cable and just start driving cross-country, carefully spooling out the cable and telling everyone not to bother it. Of course, it still wouldn't work when you got to the end because of the attenuation of copper wire, but that's another story!

This ridiculous example will help you see what service providers have done for you. In essence, they have already rolled out that cable, but they will require payment to let you connect to both ends of it. Once you do, that's your connection, and nobody else is on it. The service provider will generally "condition" the line from time to time, testing it and making sure that you are getting what you are paying for, but you will be the only one authorized to use it to communicate. Sometimes this division is only logical, but often it is physical as well; in other words, it's your wire and only your wire at many points. Cool, huh?

The most common of these types of connections in the United States has been the T1. In Europe, they use a very similar connection called an E1. A T1 provides for 1.54Mbps of dedicated bandwidth for the customer. This bandwidth can be used in total or divided up into as many as 24 channels, called DS0s, which are each 64Kbps. An E1 is very similar but offers 32 DS0s instead of 24 for a total of 2.048Mbps. This is accomplished using a device called a CSU/DSU, which I will discuss further in Chapter 3. This gives the customer (you) many options in regard to the dispensation of the bandwidth to network resources. The cost of a T1 or an E1 varies based on the connection points you choose, but it's safe to say that you would pay between $500 and $1,000 a month for one T1 line in most locations today. This is why an organization will consider other options before spending the money on a dedicated T1 connection. I should also mention that a T1 is not (by far) the most expensive connection type you can choose. Later in this chapter, I will discuss WAN technologies that provide even greater benefit at an even greater cost.

ADSL

A less expensive option for small companies and home users, which provides considerable bandwidth for an economical rate, is a digital subscriber line. The most common of these is the *asymmetric digital subscriber line* (ADSL). The reason this type of connection can be economical is that the lines it uses are already in place. They are your regular telephone lines. The service provider uses the regular telephone lines and special equipment that multiplexes the signal to provide tremendous bandwidth over that which dial-up lines provide.

Now, as you may know, asymmetric means "not the same on both sides" or "not balanced." So, what is not balanced about an ADSL line? The bandwidth is not balanced; in fact, it's not even close. You may have noticed that service providers advertise ADSL using megabits per second for download speed but kilobits per second for upload speed. That's because the upload speed is so much slower that it wouldn't sound that great in megabits per second. For example, one popular carrier offers its Extreme ADSL that has a download speed of 10Mbps and an upload speed of 512Kbps. Sounds pretty good, doesn't it? Well, what if I offered it to you with 10Mbps download and only 0.5Mbps upload — how much would you buy then? As you can see, they are both the same, but many people don't catch this fact.

The upload speed of ADSL is generally about 1/20th its download speed. The reason that most people buy it anyway is that they don't really care too much about the upload speed. Most of what they do that is bandwidth intensive is downloading, such as surfing the Internet, watching movies, and pulling down files. Now, if they were building a website or transferring files to an FTP server, that would be a different story altogether. However, most people aren't doing that, so ADSL is fine for them.

SDSL

For those who want a little more upload speed, a DSL service is available in some areas that provides a balance of upload and download speed. It is referred to as *symmetric digital subscriber line* (SDSL). Typically, you won't get the fastest download speed with this option, but that is not usually what you are after anyway. If you are considering this option, you are one of the few who really does put large files back onto the Web, such as when building a website or sending files to an FTP server. The additional upload speed will save you considerable time and headaches from watching that agonizingly slow progress indicator line, if you know what I mean!

At the time of this writing, there were many areas that offered SDSL at rates of up to 1.5Mbps. You might recognize that as about the same as a T1. This is no coincidence since many small businesses consider SDSL to be a less expensive option that gives them essentially what the T1 would have, especially if they are using the bandwidth in its entirety and not dividing the DS0s. Not all areas offer SDSL, but in many areas it can be used to provide bandwidth acceptable to a business and still save money vs. leasing a dedicated T1 line.

VDSL

What if you want to "have your cake and eat it too"? In other words, what if you want very high bandwidth for both upstream and downstream so that you can watch your movies in HD and upload large files all at the same time? In that case, you will need *very high bitrate digital subscriber line* (VDSL). Currently, service providers are experimenting with new lines that will provide more than 100Mbps (that's right, I said 100Mbps) for both upstream and downstream simultaneously on regular telephone lines! As you might imagine, this is still an emerging technology, and you had better be prepared to pay for it, at least compared to what you pay now for ADSL or SDSL.

Cable Modem

Another option for Internet communications is to use that coaxial cable that currently carries your television signal. Cable companies have jumped on the bandwagon and now offer you a path to the Internet that begins with connecting your computer to a special cable modem. That modem is configured by the cable company to be recognized by its central office, also called the *headend* of the cable company. From there, the cable company becomes your Internet service provider (ISP), connecting you to the Internet.

Many small businesses and home users have chosen this option for their Internet connection. The advantages include the fact that most cable companies can provide tremendous bandwidth (10Mbps and faster) downstream and "acceptable" bandwidth (up to 1Mbps) upstream. For most users and small businesses, this is all they really need. The price for cable Internet is typically about the same as for a roughly equivalent ADSL line (depending on which company is running a special at the time). Keep in mind that, with the same downstream bandwidth choice for cable vs. DSL, you might get more upstream bandwidth with the cable option. It all depends on the individual provider.

Satellite

Earlier, when I was talking about "coaxial cable that currently carries your television signal," some of you might have been thinking "What cable? We live out in the countryside and don't have those cables out here!" If that's the case, then your best (and maybe only) option is a *satellite* hookup. You may also decide to use a satellite hookup because it is the most economical and/or dependable service in your area. In either case, you will need a dish antenna and a professional installer or instructions on how to find their satellite with your dish antenna. It always makes me laugh when I hear someone say that they put the satellite in the backyard to get the TV signal. That's not *the* "satellite." The satellite is in geostationary orbit high above the earth, and your little antenna is just going to pick up on its signal from space.

Once you do that, you can then use that signal as a download from the Internet. Now uploading is a bit trickier, since you probably won't have a high-powered transponder. Many satellite communications companies have provided the upload through your regular telephone line dial-up connections. Some now provide a DSL line to give you more bandwidth for uploads. Still others advertise a two-way satellite system that actually does send some signal back to the satellite from the antenna. These are typically more expensive and harder to install. Satellite communications companies offer data rates that rival those of their biggest competitors, cable and DSL.

E3/T3

The next couple of options are "big bucks!" What if you wanted a line like a T1 but much, much larger? Some large companies require high-bandwidth dedicated connections from one office or data center to another. One way to accomplish this is by using a T3 line in the United States or an E3 line in Europe and much of the rest of the world. This type of line provides a tremendous amount of usable bandwidth that can be divided to fit an organization's needs. A T3 provides for 672 DS0s, or the equivalent of 28 T1s! An E3 provides for the equivalent of 512 DS0s, or approximately 17 E1s.

OC-x

If you thought those were fast, you ain't seen nothin' yet! In the term *OC-x*, the OC stands for "optical carrier," and the *x* indicates the relative speed of the link. Well, the *x* just keeps getting bigger and bigger. The original speed of an OC trunk was about 50Mbps, and it was called an OC-1. OC-3 quickly followed with 150Mbps. The standard at the time of this writing is OC-3072, which offers a mind-blowing data rate of 160Gbps — that's with a *G*! As you might imagine, only very large companies have the need (or the money) for these options.

Wireless

I'll bet that you're thinking that I've already talked about wireless in great depth in Chapter 1. Well, that was wireless LANs, so now I'll discuss *wireless WANs.* You use a wireless WAN on your cell phone or your PDA and/or laptop device that connects to your cell phone provider. It's a cool way of always being able to access the Internet as long as you can "get a few bars" from your cell phone company.

I use wireless WAN on planes that I've boarded but still have an open cabin door, on military bases that will not give me an account because I'm not going to be there for long enough, and in hotel rooms that don't yet have a wireless LAN installed or don't have a strong enough signal to my floor. It's a very convenient service to have, and it has become easier and cheaper to acquire and use, a trend that I'm sure will continue.

How does it work? That depends on your carrier, which could use UMTS, GPRS, CDMA2000, GSM, CDPD, Mobitex, HSPDA, or 3G, or even a combination of some of these. Do you have to know all of the "bits and bytes" of these protocols? Thankfully, absolutely not! By the time you memorized them all, they would probably change anyway. Wireless WAN is one of the most dynamic technologies of our day. All you really need to know is that a wireless WAN differs from a wireless LAN in that a cell phone service is used to give a person access to the Internet, email, and other online services. It is not the same as the 802.11 technologies used with wireless LAN but instead is something completely different.

ATM

I like to joke that ATM is a technology that allows you to take money out of your bank! Actually, ATM does not stand for *automatic teller machine* (at least in this case) but for *asynchronous transfer mode*. Unfortunately, even knowing what the acronym means still doesn't tell you much about what this protocol does. In essence, it's a protocol that was developed after Ethernet, and it provides a much more efficient way of transferring data than does Ethernet.

ATM was originally developed in the mid-1980s to be used for voice, data, and video applications. We needed a more efficient protocol to provide movies and sound for training and for fun. It uses a fixed-length cell of 53 bytes, rather than the variable-length packets that are used by Ethernet. This allows for more efficiency, since the devices never have to fragment and reassemble large packets. The original ATM technology was already much faster than Ethernet; it was able to transfer voice, data, and video signals at up to 500Mbps. It's now even faster and is being used by some telecommunication and Internet providers as a backbone or core layer. ATM, like every other technology, will eventually be replaced by faster successors.

SONET

Speaking of faster successors, how about a protocol that will push data at 150Gbps over fiber links and has to be controlled using atomic clocks!? That's what SONET can do. SONET stands for *synchronous optical network*. It's especially useful for networks that span multiple geographic regions because the atomic clock mechanism in it keeps everyone on the same exact millisecond. As you can imagine, this protocol requires expensive equipment and expertise. It is typically used by large communication providers and very large corporations as a transfer mechanism or backbone for data traffic.

MPLS

What if you were to fast-forward from the mid-1980s into the 21st century and then look back at the protocols that you had already developed and been using for some time? You could see the advantages and disadvantages of each protocol and use that information to make the next protocol even better. For example, you could see that ATM's fixed-length cell was no longer a big deal when the newer networks can pretty much handle any size packet. You could also see that the complex mechanism of Frame Relay used to track and assure CIR was no longer a big concern with new fiber links available that carry more than 150Gbps! You could analyze what has worked in the past and how technologies have changed and then build a new protocol that takes advantage of all of the positive aspects of each. If you did that, you would build *multiprotocol label switching* (MPLS).

MPLS is similar in nature to Frame Relay and to ATM. It's similar to Frame Relay in that it is a packet-switching technology that is connection-oriented. It's similar to ATM in that it is a very organized endpoint-to-endpoint system. It is, however, also very different from either of these, because it does not require fixed-length cells (that have to be rebuilt into packet data later) as does ATM, and it does not have the overhead mechanisms of Frame Relay.

MPLS works by prefixing packets with an MPLS header containing one or more labels, called a *label stack*. These labels can be detected and managed very quickly within the switch fabric of newer devices. In other words, routers and layer 3 switches can be manufactured specifically to recognize and respond to these labels. This is much faster than using a routing table and the device's CPU. Routers and layer 3 switches that can perform routing based only on the labels are called *label switch routers* (LSRs). As you can imagine, these technologies are more expensive than their predecessors, but MPLS will probably eventually replace most ATM and Frame Relay installations.

ISDN BRI

ISDN BRI is a layer 2 protocol that allows for two communication channels and one control channel. The communication channels are referred to as B (bearer) channels, and the control channel is referred to as a D (delta) channel. Each of the B channels can carry up to 64Kbps of data (that used to be a lot), and the control channel can use 16Kbps for data control. ISDN BRI is sometimes referred to as 2B + D, but this is actually misleading because the B channels are really the only usable bandwidth for data. Thus, an ISDN line can carry a whopping 128Kbps of data! In other words, one T1 is the rough equivalent of 12 ISDN BRI lines. ISDN also employs all kinds of telephone company terminology that identifies the reference points and the devices, but the chance of you having to know that for this exam (or for real life anymore) is so remote that it hardly bears mentioning.

ISDN BRI: Then and Now

In the early 1990s, when ISDN BRI was just coming out, I was working at Sprint in Florida. We used to joke that ISDN stood for either "It Still Does Nothing" or "I Still Don't kNow." Sprint wanted about 90 bucks a month for it so that you could combine your Internet service with your telephone services. The problem was that most people at that time were saying "What's an Internet?" You see, the Internet at that point was accessible only by text commands and usually only through a university or a large corporation. It wasn't all that exciting then, except for a few of us "geeks."

By the mid-1990s, though, with the ushering in of the World Wide Web and hypertext browsing, everything had changed. We sold a lot of ISDN BRI during that time until the newer technologies of ADSL and cable modem Internet took its place. Then we still sold it as backup lines to companies that were leasing a T1 or a T3. It was no longer an expensive add-on by that time. Now ISDN BRI is all but gone, but you still need to know the historical information covered in this chapter for the exam.

ISDN PRI

ISDN PRI came out a little later, and it's a very different story than ISDN BRI. An ISDN PRI link is almost the same as a T1 line in regard to its capacity to carry data. It consists of 23 B channels (each with 64Kbps) and 1 D channel (also with 64Kbps). A little quick math should tell you that a single ISDN link will carry 1,472Kbps, which, as you can see, is very close to a T1.

So, why would a company choose an ISDN PRI link over a T1? Actually, it could come down to the availability in an area, the cost, the type of equipment that the company already owns, and the business rationale for the link. The fact is that both ISDN PRI and T1 links offer 23 DS0s for a customer's actual bandwidth use. (That's the "dirty little secret" about T1s — you don't get all 1.544Mbps for your use, but you should still know that number for the exam.) Some equipment has ISDN PRI interfaces built in, which allow flexible control of the 23 B channels, so a company can use them for special needs such as video conferences or network-based meetings. ISDN PRI also employs a myriad of telephone company jargon that, thankfully, you will not need to know. Just know that it's 23 B + D and that all channels are 64Kbps DS0s, and you will be fine.

POTS/PSTN

I'm combining the discussion of Plain Old Telephone Service (POTS) and Public Switched Telephone Network (PSTN) even though they are listed separately on the CompTIA objectives, because they are the same. Both describe those agonizingly slow (in today's terms) 56Kbps lines that we affectionately refer to as *dial-up*.

POTS is a term that telephone company employees assigned to those public switched lines when newer and more "sophisticated" links such as ISDN, T1, T3, and the like began to emerge. The point was that the normal modem-based dial-up communications ran on the same lines that everyone had been talking on for almost 100 years! What you should know about POTS are the advantages (yes, there are some) and disadvantages of it vs. the newer technologies that I've covered.

The main advantages of POTS are availability and cost. It is highly available, since almost everyone has a regular telephone line (although that is beginning to change now), and it's available at a relatively low cost when compared to other services. As you may have guessed, the major disadvantage of POTS lines is that they do not support the bandwidth that we need to do all of the "fancy stuff" that we want to do on our computers today, such as download movies and large files, surf multiple websites at the same time, and hold video conferences with our peers. Still, some people in the world still hear those screeching tones of the modem handshake when they dial up to their ISP today.

Properties

So, just how do you decide which one of these types of WAN connections is best for your situation? Well, a good place to start is to compare the properties of each type of connection against the needs of the organization in which they will be used. Some of the many properties that should be considered include whether the solution is circuit switched or packet switched, its speed relative to other solutions, the media that is used, and the distance that media can carry the data. In the following sections, I'll discuss each of these important properties of WAN communication.

Circuit Switch

The properties of WAN technology types are a description of the events that happen and/or the attributes of the communication. In the case of *circuit switch*, we are back to our POTS lines. Once you establish a connection on a circuit switched network, the entire conversation or line of data traffic is sent on those same physical connections until you terminate the connection. If you were to establish a new connection to the same place, you would likely get a very different set of connections that would also "complete your call."

Packet Switch

Packet switch networks are very different from circuit switch ones in that each data packet might take a different route to its final destination during the same transmission. The original packet switch network, called X.25, was developed to overcome the challenge of sending reliable communications through an inherently unreliable medium. The unreliable medium at that time was, you guessed it, Ma Bell!

A computer modem's "screeching" must have sounded very different from those original switches than the voice of Alexander Graham Bell saying "Come here, Watson, I need you." If one switch weren't getting the job done, X.25 would just take a different path automatically. However, because of the extensive error checking built into X.25, it was inherently very reliable and very slow.

The newer packet switched networks include some that I've already discussed in this chapter such as Frame Relay and MPLS. These networks use sophisticated virtual circuits to avoid errors and thereby improve efficiency and data throughput. They are connection oriented now, so data doesn't move from one location until it's completely cleared to "land" in the next. This makes for fast and reliable data flow.

Speed

Speed is a little deceptive in that it's a factor of available bandwidth and throughput. In other words, just because you have a T1 doesn't mean you have a fast connection. It depends on how many others are using it and on what you need to do with it. Also, your speed through a network will largely be determined by the available bandwidth on the slowest link that you encounter.

Let's say you were to take a trip all the way across the United States that was mostly on the expressways but you had to climb up and down winding mountain overpasses for the last 500 miles. That last 500 miles would likely take the bulk of your time on the trip, even though it wasn't the greatest distance. The same thing happens when user data comes from one location to another through a very fast backbone: they may have a speed of 10Gbps on the backbone, but as soon as they come into the building and hit your 100Mbps Fast Ethernet switch, their relative speed for the whole connection will be, well, 100Mbps. Maybe there is more to this speed thing than first meets the eye?

Transmission Media

This looks like a no-brainer at first glance. *Transmission media* is the stuff on which the communication is carried. This media could be copper, fiber, or even wireless. The media you choose will depend on your bandwidth needs, security needs, EMI concerns, and the distance you need to send the data before it hits another switch or router. Since I'm talking about the WAN environment, the service provider will have already made these decisions. I will categorize many types of transmission media in the next sections of this chapter.

Distance

Distance is "how far" data is sent. I don't think that's on the exam, but the relative distance of communications on various communications media might "creep in there." Generally speaking, fiber optics are capable of much greater distances because their attenuation rate is nowhere near as high as that of copper connections. This is because the signal being sent is light rather than electricity. In regard to WAN connectivity, the good news is that it's not your problem. The service provider should give you the right links to get you from point A to point B in the most efficient and effective manner. Later in this chapter, I will categorize many types of transmission media in regard to distance and speed.

Exam Essentials

Be able to categorize types of WAN technologies. You should be able to differentiate between Frame Relay, T1, T3, ADSL, SDSL, VDSL, cable, satellite, OC-x, Wireless, ATM, SONET, MPLS, ISDN, and POTS/PSTN technologies. You should know the major advantages and disadvantages of each and where they are likely to be used.

Be able to categorize WAN properties. You should understand the difference between circuit switch and packet switch. You should be able to categorize WAN properties with regard to speed, transmission media, and distance limitations.

2.6 Categorize LAN technology types and properties

Today's businesses rely on many types of LAN connections to provide for the transfer of data throughout their networks. The type of LAN connections that a network administrator chooses will depend on the properties of that specific solution and how they align with the goals of the business. In the following sections, I'll discuss the main types of LAN connections and their specific properties.

Types

Generally what users have always needed is more speed. Network administrators needed more speed but also the ability to run a link for further distances without the need for the amplification of signal. This gives them options in regard to network designs and other decisions about which most users are unaware. Over the years, LAN technology types have continued to evolve to meet the needs of users and network administrators. Table 2.3 categorizes many LAN technology types and their major properties of transmission media, speed, and distance.

TABLE 2.3 LAN Technology Types

Types	Transmission Media	Speed	Distance
Ethernet	Copper (first coax then twisted-pair)	10Mbps	100m
10BaseT	Twisted-pair copper	10Mbps	100m
100BaseTX	Twisted-pair copper	100Mbps	100m
100BaseFX	Multimode fiber	100Mbps	400m
1000BaseT	Multimode fiber	1Gbps	100m
1000BaseX		1Gbps	Overall standard for 1Gbps on fiber and copper
10GBaseSR	Multimode fiber	10Gbps	26m
10GBaseLR	Single-mode fiber	10Gbps	25km (about 16 miles)
10GBaseER	Single-mode fiber	10Gbps	40km (about 25 miles)

TABLE 2.3   LAN Technology Types *(continued)*

Types	Transmission Media	Speed	Distance
10GBaseSW	Multimode fiber	10Gbps	26m
10GBaseLW	Single-mode fiber	10Gbps	10km
10GBaseEW	Single-mode fiber	10Gbps	40km
10GBaseT	Twisted-pair cable	10Gbps	100m

Properties

The following are the properties of LAN connections.

CSMA/CD

In the past, we had networks that contained devices called *hubs*. Most of these are gone, and you would probably be hard-pressed to find a hub to buy today (maybe on eBay). These hubs created what we called a *shared network*. That meant each computer that communicated in the network had equal access to the same electrical paths as the others. Since the paths could carry only one communication at a time, the computers had to "take turns" accessing the wire.

A protocol called Carrier Sense Multiple Access with Collision Detection (CSMA/CD) was developed for this purpose. Each computer using CSMA/CD must sense the "wire" to determine whether current is fluctuating and therefore if some other computer is using it. If another computer has the wire, then the first computer must wait until the wire is not in use before it can send its data. As you can imagine, if two computers see that the wire is not busy and decide to send at the same millisecond, then the electrical signals will cancel each other out. This is referred to as a *collision*. Once the collision is detected by the protocol, each computer will be given a set time to go based on a *backoff algorithm* created by the protocol. In this way, the computers will be kept from creating subsequent collisions.

The main problem with using CSMA/CD is that it doesn't work well for networks that are large — like today's networks. Because of this, newer technologies have been developed that do not require the use of CSMA/CD. In most of today's networks, this protocol is disabled.

Broadcast

Essentially, there are three types of network communication on IPv4 networks. These are unicast, multicast, and broadcast. *Unicast* communication consists of a packet that has one source address and one destination address. Multicast communication also has one source address, but it has multiple destination addresses that have to be detected by each host to determine whether the data is for them. *Broadcast* communications are from one source but go to any destinations in the area where the data is allowed to flow.

A broadcast address at layer 2 will be flooded by switches, in other words, sent out of all the ports except for the one that it came in. Layer 3 broadcasts can be received by all the hosts on a network or subnet. Some network protocols, such as ARP and DHCP, use broadcasts as part of their normal operation. As a network administrator, one of your goals is to keep broadcast traffic to a minimum, with the exception of the broadcast traffic required by the network protocols.

Collision

Generally speaking, a *collision domain* is part of a network in which collisions could occur if more than one communication were allowed to take place at the same time. In the case of an old network that uses hubs, all the hosts connected to the hub share the same collision domain. A collision then occurs when two or more devices attempt to communicate at the same time in the same collision domain.

As I discussed in Chapter 1, the counterintuitive part is that when you have more collision domains, you will actually have fewer collisions. When you deploy a network with only switches (no hubs), each communication is contained in its own collision domain, and there is no possibility for collisions.

Bonding

Let's say you have a couple of 10Gbps interfaces, but what you really need is a 20Gbps link. Could you combine the two physical interfaces into one logical interface? You better bet you could! The process of combining more than one physical interface into one logical interface is called *bonding*. Ether channel links are one type of bonding that allows administrators flexibility and more options in regard to bandwidth allocation.

Speed

Just as with WAN links, the speed of a LAN is a product of available bandwidth. Available bandwidth is what's left over for the users after you take out your overhead to provide the network services. We tend to think that the network is there for our amusement and experimentation, but the truth is that it's really there so "Bob and Mary" can collaborate on a spreadsheet or just check their email. Bob and Mary don't know anything about the network, but they should be able to do their jobs quickly, and the network should be rather transparent for them. Speed is a relative factor, but your job is to provide as much speed as possible with the network connections and equipment available to you.

Distance

This goes full circle back to Table 2.3. Based on the type of transmission media you use, there will be distance limitations for your network segments. Anything with a *T* in it (100BaseT, for example) will have a distance limitation of 100m before it needs to hit another switch or device to amplify the signal. Fiber optics can span much greater distances because their signal does not attenuate as quickly. You should use the appropriate media to span the distance you need.

> For a troubleshooting question on the exam, you should be ready to total up the links and make sure the total is below the limit, especially in regard to the twisted-pair 100m limit.

Exam Essentials

Be able to categorize LAN technologies.   You should be able to categorize the major LAN technologies from 10BaseT through 10GBaseEW in regard to speed, transmission media, and distance.

Know the properties of LAN technologies.   You should understand the main properties of LAN technologies, including the CSMA/CD, broadcast communications, collisions, bonding connections, speed differences, and distance limitations.

2.7 Explain common logical network topologies and their characteristics

As I mentioned earlier, a topology of a network is its shape and the logical topology is the shape of the data flow. In other words, if you were the packet, the data flow is the path that you would take through the network and the devices you would encounter. In the following sections, I'll discuss the main logical network topologies and their characteristics.

Peer-to-Peer

Very small business networks and home networks are often *peer-to-peer*. This means that no server is involved at all. Each computer acts as both a client and a server. Typically, directory shares or folders are set up on each of the computers, and local accounts on the computers are used to provide some minimal security. Generally, peer-to-peer networks consist of no more than about 10 computers. A network of more than 10 computers creates tremendous confusion because the users might have to know different usernames and passwords to get to the share directories on each computer. Also, what if the other nine computers wanted to use a share directory on the 10th computer all at the same time? The 10th computer's resources would be so overwhelmed with providing the share directory for the others that you might not even be able to use it yourself!

Client/Server

In a *client/server* network, the problem of resource sharing is addressed by using specific high-capacity and high-speed computers to share resources to the client computers. Most of the resources that the clients use are centralized to the very fast server computer. The server computer is typically not used directly by a user. In the most sophisticated networks, these servers are also domain controllers that authenticate a user's access onto the network and control their access to specific resources.

VPN

If you have multiple locations to connect but do not want to pay for multiple dedicated links or even Frame Relay, you could just use the Internet. The only problem would be that the Internet isn't a very private space through which to send your business traffic. What you would really need is a way to traverse the Internet but keep your communication secure. A *virtual private network* (VPN) will do just that.

A VPN is a private connection that is going through a public network, typically the Internet but sometimes just another untrusted network. The communication is made secure by encapsulating the IP traffic within another protocol called a *tunneling protocol*. The two main tunneling protocols that are typically used are PPTP and L2TP. I will discuss each of these in detail in Chapter 6, "Network Security."

VLAN

With conventional networks using only routers for layer 3 and switches as layer 2, subnets are limited to the physical location in which they reside. This can be constricting to a network administrator if a department spans multiple locations and the administrator wants to manage and set security policies based on subnets related to departments. A *virtual local area network* (VLAN) is the solution to this problem.

In a VLAN, switches are used to create layer 3 domains, also called *subnets*. These subnets can span multiple switches regardless of the location of the switch. This gives the network administrator the flexibility to design a logical network that does not have to conform to any physical limitations, such as the actual location of the clients. Administrators can manage the security of the entire subnet as if it were all in the same location, even if it isn't. Routers or layer 3 switches can be used to connect the separate layer 3 domains while still maintaining security.

Exam Essentials

Know the characteristics network topologies.   You should know that a network topology is the shape of a network but that there is sometimes a big difference between the physical shape and the logical shape of a network. You should understand that network topologies continue to change based on the needs of the user and that some are much more secure than others.

Know the main types of network topologies.   You should be able to differentiate between peer-to-peer, client/server, VPN, and VLAN networks. You should understand the advantages and disadvantages of each type of topology. Finally, you should understand the appropriate use of each type in a network.

2.8 Install components of wiring distribution

Common computer networks have many more components than first meets the eye, that is, unless you are the involved in the initial installation of the network! In that case, you may be involved in purchasing and installing the components that will connect the computers throughout your organization's building. You might also be involved in verifying that all the network components have been installed properly and tested. In the following sections, I'll discuss each of these components and the process of verifying their proper installation.

Vertical and Horizontal Cross Connects

A *cross-connect* is a facility or a location within a cabling system that facilitates the termination of cable elements and the reconnection of those elements by jumpers, termination blocks, and/or cables to a patch panel or other cabling element. In other words, it's where all the wires come together. Cables that run from communications closets to wall outlets are known as *horizontal cables*, because they are generally used on the same floor of a building. Backbone cables that connect equipment rooms, telecommunications rooms, and other physical termination points are referred to as *vertical cables*, because they often must go from floor to floor in a building. All these cables will eventually be connected to each other to finish off the network cabling of the building. The exact pieces that are involved will depend on the size of the installation, the needs of the organization, and the structure in which they are installed.

Patch Panels

A *patch panel* is typically a rack or wall mounted structure that houses cable connections. A patch cable generally plugs into the front side, while the back holds the punched-down connection of a longer, more permanent cable. The purpose of the patch panel is to offer the administrator a way to change the path of a signal quickly when needed. For example, if a cable inside a wall becomes damaged or fails, a network administrator can "patch around" that cable by simply changing the connection on two patch panels. Figure 2.26 shows a modern patch panel.

FIGURE 2.26 A patch panel

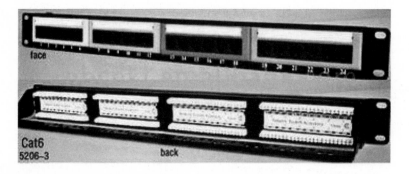

66 Block

In the past, one of the most common types of patch panels was referred to as a *66 block*. Though these are now considered legacy equipment, they are still listed as an objective on the exam. The reason they are considered legacy is that they are very large in comparison to newer wire terminating devices. Also, they have a relatively small (25-pair) capacity. Finally, they are unsuited for any network communications faster than 10Mbps. However, you may still see these used in some telephone installations. Figure 2.27 shows a 66 block connector.

FIGURE 2.27 A 66 block connector

66 Connecting Block

MDF

The *main distribution frame* (MDF) is a wiring point that is generally used as a reference point for telephone lines. It is installed in the building as part of the prewiring, and the internal lines are connected to it. Then all that's left is to connect the external (telephone company) lines to the other side, and the circuit is complete. These often have protection devices for lightening or other electrical spikes. In addition, they are often used as a central testing point.

IDF

Often another wire frame, called an *intermediate distribution frame* (IDF), is located in an equipment or telecommunications room. It is connected to the MDF and is used to provide greater flexibility in regard to the distribution of the communications lines to the building. In other words, it's just one more place where a network administrator or telephone administrator can change their mind and redirect the signal. It is typically a sturdy metal rack that is designed to hold the bulk of cables that are coming from all over the building. The same frame might also hold networking equipment such as routers, switches, and backup drives.

25-pair

A *25-pair* cable consists of 25 individual pairs of wires all inside one common insulating jacket. It is generally not used for data cabling but is often used for telephone cabling, especially for backbone and cross-connect cables, which reduces the "cable clutter" significantly. This type of cable is often referred to as a *feeder cable*, because it supplies a signal to many connected pairs. Figure 2.28 shows a 25-pair cable.

FIGURE 2.28   A 25-pair cable

100-pair

For very large telephone company installations, you can use *100-pair* feeder cables. As should be obvious, they combine 100 pairs of wires into one large insulated cable. To keep the pairs unique, you must use colors other than the traditional networking colors. You don't need to know the colors, but just know that this is another way to make a more organized telephone wiring installation. Figure 2.29 shows a 100-pair cable.

110 block

A newer type of wiring distribution point, called a *110 block*, has replaced most telephone wire installations and is also being used for computer networking. On one side of it, wires are punched down, while the other side has RJ-11 (for phone) or RJ-45 (for network) connections. The 110 blocks come in sizes from 25 to more than 500 wire pairs. Some are capable of carrying 1Gpbs connections when used with CAT 6 cables. Figure 2.30 shows a 110 block.

FIGURE 2.30   A 110 block wire connector

Demarc

The point at which the operational control or ownership changes from your company to a service provider is referred to as a *demarcation point*, or *demarc*. This is often at the MDF in relation to telephone connections and the CSU/DSU in regard to WAN connections. (I will discuss the CSU/DSU in Chapter 3, "Network Devices.") When troubleshooting, network administrators will often test for connectivity on both sides of the demarc to determine whether the problem is internal or external.

Demarc Extension

If your offices are in a building with many other tenants, you then have another section of wiring with which to contend. Most office buildings have a central location where service provider terminates fiber and copper connections. From there, it's either up to the building owner or up to the individual tenants to get the communications cables to the office suites. The length of copper or fiber that is after the demarc but still not up to your office is referred to as a *demarc extension*. Many cabling companies specialize in installing and upgrading these extensions. If you are considering office space, you should verify that these connections are solid and offer you the connectivity and bandwidth you need.

Smart Jack

A special network interface is often used between the service provider's network and the internal network. The device provides for code and protocol conversion, making the signal from the service provider usable by the devices on the internal network, such as the CSU/DSU. This device, called a *network interface device* or *smart jack*, often also serves as the demarcation point between the inside wiring and the outside wiring. It often contains the connections and electronic testing equipment to perform local loopback tests and other types of troubleshooting. Figure 2.31 shows an example of a modern smart jack.

FIGURE 2.31   A modern smart jack

Verify Wiring Installation

It's amazing how many installers simply assume they have made no mistakes. They may test a few cables for good measure, but they leave most cables untested and keep sketchy records or no records at all. However, most truly professional installers will verify each cable's connectivity and keep detailed records of when it was tested and when it passed the connectivity test.

Many things can go wrong when pulling a network cable. Copper cables could be pulled a little too close to a magnetic source and could be affected by EMI. Cable jackets could be ripped off when pulling the cable through a tight space or around a corner. Cables could be cut wrong and extend beyond the maximum length for their type. Fiber-optic cables could be broken by mishandling or poor installation.

The best cable installer companies assume that some of these things will go wrong, and therefore they will test, test, and test again. If you are doing your own installation, then you should consider yourself as your own customer — you want to keep yourself happy, don't you? Seriously, the old carpenter's rule of "measure twice, cut once" applies to cable installations as well, both literally and figuratively. You should test frequently during installation and once more when all is complete, keeping detailed records for later use.

Verify Wiring Termination

The number of things that could go wrong when terminating copper wires completely dwarfs that of pulling cables! With a minimal amount of training and a little patience, almost anyone can pull a network cable without damaging it — at least most of the time. Proper termination of copper cables to a punch-down block is much trickier and requires practice to get it right. Therefore, you should always inspect the installation and verify that the wires are terminated properly and in the right order.

Fiber-optic termination requires extra special equipment and training. Unless your installers have spent hours cutting, stripping, polishing, and terminating the fiber-optic cable and then examining their mistakes with a magnifying glass or a microscope, they probably won't get it done right the first time. You should always test a new connection with the appropriate tool. I will discuss the tools used to test connections in Chapter 5, "Network Tools."

Exam Essentials

Know the components of wiring distribution.   You should know the purpose of horizontal cross connects, vertical cross connects, patch panels, MDFs, IDFs, and other network equipment. In addition, you should understand the use of special feeder cables such as 25-pair and 100-pair cables. Finally, you should know that a smart jack at the demarc is often used to isolate whether a network problem is internal or external.

Understand the importance of verifying wiring installation and termination.   You should realize that a network wiring job in a large building can be a complex undertaking. You should understand that many people may be involved and that their relative skill levels will vary greatly. Because of this, a competent network wiring installation will involve extensive testing and documentation.

Review Questions

1. Which of following cable types are designed to carry up to 1000Mbps signals? (Choose two.)

   A. CAT 3

   B. CAT 5

   C. CAT 5e

   D. CAT 6

2. If your main goal in a wiring installation is to provide the most resistance to EMI at any cost, which of the following should you use?

   A. CAT 6 cable

   B. Fiber-optic cable

   C. Coaxial cable

   D. STP cable

3. What is the maximum distance of all twisted-pair cable runs before they must be terminated at a switch or multiport repeater?

   A. 500 feet

   B. 328 feet

   C. 1,000 feet

   D. 100 feet

4. Which of the following is a type of fiber-optic connector that uses a push-pull mechanism similar to common audio and video plugs?

   A. ST

   B. LC

   C. RS-232

   D. SC

5. How many connections would a full mesh with seven members require?

   A. 42

   B. 14

   C. 121

   D. 21

6. Which pins are used in both the 568A and 568B standards of network wiring?

   A. 4, 5, 7, 8

   B. 1, 2, 3, 4

   C. 1, 2, 3, 6

   D. 2, 4, 6, 8

7. Which type of cable should you use to connect a router to a PC for the purpose of transmitting data?

   A. Crossover

   B. Straight

   C. Rollover

   D. Coaxial

8. What is the main advantage of using Frame Relay instead of a dedicated link like a T1?

   A. Frame Relay is much more reliable than a T1.

   B. Frame Relay connections are typically faster than dedicated links.

   C. Frame Relay generally costs less than multiple dedicated links.

   D. Frame Relay provides full-duplex connections, whereas dedicated links are always half-duplex.

9. How many B channels does ISDN PRI use?

   A. 2

   B. 24

   C. 1

   D. 23

10. What are the two main tunneling protocols used in VPNs? (Choose two.)

   A. PPTP

   B. LPTP

   C. P2TP

   D. L2TP

Answers to Review Questions

1. C, D. Category 5e (CAT 5e) and Category 6 (CAT 6) are designed to carry signals up to 1000Mbps (1Gbps). CAT 3 is capable only of 10Mbps, and CAT 5 is capable only of 100Mbps.

2. B. Fiber-optic cable will provide complete protection from electromagnetic interference (EMI), since it uses light instead of electricity for a signal.

3. B. All twisted-pair cable runs have a maximum distance of 100m (328 feet) before they must be terminated at a switch or other type of multiport repeater, such as a hub or a bridge. In today's networks, switches are used most of the time, and these cable runs are kept well shorter than 100m.

4. D. The standard connector (SD) is a type of fiber-optic cable connector that uses a push-pull mechanism similar to common audio and video plugs. These are most often used with multimode fiber-optic cable.

5. D. A full mesh requires [n(n–1)] / 2 connections, where n is the number of members. In this case, it's [7(7–1)] / 2 = 21.

6. C. Pins 1, 2, 3, and 6 are the only pins that are used in both the EIA/TIA 568A and 568B standards. The only question is which color goes on which pin. These standards can be intentionally combined on a cable to create a crossover cable.

7. A. You should use a crossover cable to connect devices that are similar, such as a router to a router. Since a PC is actually a type of "router," connecting a router to a PC requires a crossover cable or at least a crossed-over connection.

8. C. Frame Relay connections to multiple locations typically will cost much less than multiple T1 connections to the same locations. Often businesses don't need the dedicated links, if they can save money using Frame Relay instead.

9. D. ISDN PRI uses 23 B channels and 1 D channel. All channels are 64Kbps DS0s.

10. A, D. Tunneling is a process of encapsulating a network protocol with another protocol to send it through a public network and still keep the message private. The two main tunneling protocols used in today's networks are Point-to-Point Tunneling Protocol (PPTP) and Layer 2 Tunneling Protocol (L2TP).

Chapter

3

Domain 3 Network Devices

COMPTIA NETWORK+ EXAM OBJECTIVES COVERED IN THIS CHAPTER:

✓ **3.1 Install, configure, and differentiate between common network devices**

- Hub
- Repeater
- Modem
- NIC
- Media converters
- Basic switch
- Bridge
- Wireless access point
- Basic router
- Basic firewall
- Basic DHCP server

✓ **3.2 Identify the functions of specialized network devices**

- Multilayer switch
- Content switch
- IDS/IPS
- Load balancer
- Multifunction network devices
- DNS server
- Bandwidth shaper
- Proxy server
- CSU/DSU

3.1 Install, configure, and differentiate between common network devices

The components that are used in a network have a tremendous effect on the capabilities of the network and on your ability to control traffic within the network. Network components have evolved with time because of the need to create fast, efficient network designs for many computers. You should be able to identify the purpose, features, and functions of each of the main network components. In addition, you should be able to install and perform basic configuration on each of these devices. In the following sections, I will discuss each of the main network components in detail.

Hub

A *hub* is a device that has multiple ports into which connections can be made. All devices connected to a hub are also connected to each other. A hub does not filter any communication or provide any intelligence in regard to the data stream; it simply lets all the information flow through it and connects anything and everything that is connected to it. Hubs are generally used to connect network segments of computers that are physically close to each other, such as all the computers on one floor of a building or in a computer classroom. There are two major types of hubs: active and passive. An *active* hub is generally plugged into a power source so that it can amplify signals as well as connect them. A *passive* hub does not provide power but provides only connectivity. An example of a passive hub is a patch panel in a network closet. Figure 3.1 shows an active hub.

Installing a hub is quite simple. All you need to do is connect the hub to power and connect all the devices to the hub. Most devices, such as PCs and routers, will connect to the hub using a patch cable. If you decide to connect the hub to another hub or to a switch, then you should use a crossover cable. Once all the devices are connected and the power is supplied to the hub, you should see link lights on the hub that indicate the ports that are transmitting data traffic.

FIGURE 3.1   A four-port active hub

Repeater

A *repeater* could be referred to as an "electronic parrot." Whatever it hears, it repeats — louder than it heard it! You won't see repeaters used often in today's networks because they don't really serve much of a purpose anymore. In networks of the past, repeaters were used simply to amplify signal so a cable run could go a little farther without suffering from attenuation. Most were made for coaxial connections, but some were made for twisted pair as well. Repeaters did not have very many ports, because their purpose was usually to extend a specific cable segment just a little further. Now, switches in network closets serve as multiport repeaters.

There wasn't much to installing a repeater. You would simply attach the cables to it and install it in the middle of the segment at a place where you could also find power. Once you plugged in the repeater, there was usually a link light to indicate that traffic was flowing. Some of the original repeaters didn't even have the link light.

Modem

The term *modem* stands for "modulator/demodulator." *Modulation* is the process of converting digital data into analog data, usually in the form of sound. *Demodulation* is the reverse of this process whereby the transmitted sounds are converted back into digital data on the other side of the connection. Modems are typically used to communicate on normal telephone wires using computers. The most common types of modems used on standard telephone lines can communicate at a maximum speed of 56Kbps. It is also possible to use multiple telephone lines simultaneously to increase the speed of communication. Simple 56Kbps modems are built into many of the computers sold today, but they are becoming less and less common.

If a modem is not installed in a computer, it is simple to install one. Most of today's modems are either on a PCI-type card, which installs into a PCI bus on a computer, or on a USB connection, which simply plugs into a USB port. Some modems also may connect to the PCMCIA (PC slot) on the side of older laptops. After the modem and its drivers are installed, simply connect the modem to a regular (POTS) phone line. Figure 3.2 shows examples of internal modems.

FIGURE 3.2   Internal modems

NIC

Network interface cards (NICs) are used to connect a computer to the network. A network interface card is like a small computer in itself. Figure 3.3 shows a common NIC. Its job is to translate a stream of serial data (one bit at a time) into several streams of parallel data that will be used by the computer. The network interface card also examines every packet on the network cable to determine whether the packet has a destination MAC address that matches its MAC address. If it does not, then the NIC does nothing more with the packet. However, if the address does match, then the NIC will forward the packet to the appropriate port of the computer based on the information contained in the packet.

Installing a NIC is very much like installing a modem. Some NICs are made to be inserted into a PCI slot on a computer, while others may install as a USB or PCMCIA device. Once the NIC and its drivers are installed, it's simply a matter of connecting the patch cable to the network by plugging in the RJ-45 connectors at each end of the connection. Link lights on the device will indicate whether it has found an active network. Some NICs come with their own diagnostic software in case you have to do a little troubleshooting.

FIGURE 3.3 A NIC

Media Converters

As I discussed in Chapter 2, "Domain 2 Network Media and Topologies," today's networks may use many different types of media to transfer data. Often media type changes, such as fiber-optic cable to twisted pair, will mark the end of one network segment and the beginning of the next. Sometimes multiple media types are used within the same segment. To facilitate this process, you use devices that can connect multiple media types and convert the signal of one type to the signal of another. These devices are appropriately called *media converters*.

Installing a media converter involves attaching the appropriate media types to the appropriate interfaces on the converter and configuring the converter to perform the function that you need. It's very specific to the media converter you are using. Media converters will also generally require power, and they may also require additional software installed into the devices to which they are connected.

Basic Switch

A switch, also called a basic switch, resembles a hub from the outside, but that is where the resemblance stops. Switches are considerably more expensive than hubs because of their advantages. Whereas a hub simply lets traffic flow through it, a switch controls traffic through it to automatically optimize traffic flow on your network. A switch works at layer 2 (Data Link) and learns the physical address (MAC address) of all the devices that are connected to it and then uses the MAC address to control traffic flow. Rather than forwarding all data to all the connected ports, a switch can forward data only to the port where the computer with the destination address actually exists. This process automatically segments the network and dramatically decreases the traffic in the segments that are less used. Because of this, switches are often used to connect departments of a company so that communication between two or more departments does not affect other departments that are not involved in the communication. Also, large files can be transferred within the same department without affecting the traffic flow in any of the other departments. Switches can also be used to create virtual local area networks (VLANs) that improve the flexibility of a network design.

Installing a basic switch involves connecting the network cables and plugging the switch in. Most switches are programmed with a basic configuration at the factory, so they come out of the box with the ability to perform simple switching operations such as frame filtering and frame forwarding. You can add an IP address and a default gateway to the switch to facilitate remote management, but these are not necessary for the switch to function in the network as a basic switch. Figure 3.4 shows a basic switch.

FIGURE 3.4   A basic switch

Bridge

A *bridge* is similar to a basic switch in that it can provide some intelligence to segment a network. Bridges, like switches, can learn the MAC address of all the hosts connected to them and use the address to control traffic to each of their ports. Bridges, however, are slower than switches, so they have been largely replaced by switches as devices used to segment traffic. You should be aware of two main types of Ethernet bridges:

Transparent bridge   A *transparent bridge* can connect two dissimilar networks, but it is "invisible" to both networks, and it does not provide translation of any kind. For example, if your network contained two Ethernet segments with one Token Ring segment in between, a transparent bridge could connect communication from one of the Ethernet segments through the Token Ring segment to the other Ethernet segment. The Ethernet traffic would not be interpreted by the Token Ring segment.

Translational bridge   A *translational bridge*, as you might expect, actually performs a translation between two dissimilar networks. For example, if you wanted to translate data from an Ethernet segment to a Token Ring segment, you could use a translational bridge.

Installing a bridge involved understanding both of the networks and what was expected in regard to communication between and within them. Based on these factors, the bridge could be connected and configured to carry the traffic in the appropriate manner. Bridges did not have as many ports as today's switches, so a network administrator had to plan carefully as to where to install the bridge for maximum benefit. Bridges also required a power source to function properly on a network.

Wireless Access Point

A *wireless access point* (WAP) is a hub or switch that is used by wireless devices. Typically, a WAP looks just like any other hub except that it has an antenna. The WAP is connected to the wired network of an organization so that any devices that can make a wireless connection to it will also be connected to the wired network. Wireless devices typically connect to the WAP using the 2.4GHz radio frequency. Since wireless networks are continuing to grow in popularity, you're likely to see many more WAPs. I will discuss how to install a wireless access point later in this chapter. Figure 3.5 shows a WAP.

FIGURE 3.5 A WAP

Basic Router

Routers are the devices that connect the Internet and make the World Wide Web possible. They use a higher level of intelligence than that of bridges or switches. Routers work at layer 3 (Network) of the OSI model and forward traffic from one network (or subnet) to another. Routers first determine whether the traffic belongs on their network; then they deliver it to the appropriate network hosts while forwarding the traffic that does not belong on their network to another router. Routers determine where to forward traffic by consulting a routing table. An administrator can enter the routing table manually, or the router can learn it by using routing protocols.

Installing a router may involve connecting the physical media, configuring the interfaces with IP addresses, configuring the security of the router, and verifying its connectivity with other network components. Whereas a switch can perform basic switch operations when installed with no configuration, a router is a "big dumb expensive brick" until a network administrator enters basic configuration information so that the router knows what networks it is connected to and what protocols it is using to make connections. Installing a router properly takes a fair amount of technical expertise.

Basic Firewall

A basic *firewall* is a hardware or software system that is used to separate one computer or network from another. The most common type of firewall is used to protect a computer or an entire network from unauthorized access from the Internet. Firewalls can also be used to control the flow of data to and from multiple networks within the same organization. Firewalls can be programmed to filter data packets based on the information that is contained in the packets.

The main benefit of a firewall is that it allows you to control traffic into and out of computers and networks, thus increasing the security of the network and hiding the resources within it. An organization can use a corporate firewall to keep its network separated from other networks and from the Internet. A corporate firewall can provide a barrier that keeps attackers from accessing or changing a company's sensitive data.

Installing a firewall involves first knowing which side is "in" and which side is "out." The most proactive way to filter using a firewall is to stop all traffic from flowing through the firewall and then carefully build a list that includes all the necessary addresses and protocols. Of course, if you forget something, then some users are not going to be able to access resources that they could before, but that's better than the alternative. What exactly is the alternative? Well, you could let all traffic flow through the firewall except for what you specifically remember should be stopped by it, and then you could filter that data so it does not go through the firewall. In this case, there wouldn't be much complaint, but you might end up with a huge security risk of which you aren't even aware. Most secure organizations employ a system that is much more like the first scenario than the second.

Basic DHCP Server

Most clients should not be assigned a static IP address but rather should obtain the IP address automatically. This is because the automatic assignment of IP addresses to clients drastically improves the security and manageability of a network. This method also makes changing an IP configuration much easier.

Automatic configuration is usually accomplished using a Dynamic Host Configuration Protocol (DHCP) server. A DHCP server can automatically configure clients with an IP address, subnet mask, default gateway, DNS server address, and much more. The configuration of the DHCP server is generally the responsibility of the network administrator.

After a DHCP server is configured, clients should be configured to obtain their IP addresses automatically from the DHCP server. If the clients are configured properly, they will broadcast on the network when they are first started in order to obtain an address from a DHCP server. Figure 3.6 shows a Windows XP client connection that is set to obtain an IP address automatically.

FIGURE 3.6   A Windows XP client set to obtain an IP address automatically

Exam Essentials

Know the purpose of common network devices.   You should know the major components used in today's networks. You should be able to describe the purpose of each network component and its role in the network. For example, you should understand that switches and bridges work at layer 2 and use MAC address, whereas routers work at layer 3 and use IP addresses.

Know the functionality of each network component.   You should know how each of the major network components function. For example, you should know whether a component has any intelligence or makes any decisions about the traffic flow within a network. You should be able to differentiate between the types of network components and their capability to control network traffic, such as filters on a firewall. You should also understand the main factors in the installation and configuration of each of the most common network devices such as DHCP servers and WAPs.

3.2 Identify the functions of specialized network devices

So far, I have discussed the oldest and most common of all network devices such as hubs, basic switches, and basic routers. Many more network devices have "evolved" over time to meet the needs of growing and changing networks. These devices usually perform a specific function in a network that assists the network speed, security, and/or efficiency. Some of these actually combine multiple network support roles in a single device. In the following sections, I will discuss the function of the specialized network devices.

Multilayer Switch

Whereas a basic switch works solely at layer 2 (Data Link) of the OSI model, a multilayer switch can work at both layer 2 and layer 3. *Multilayer* switches (also called *layer 3 switches*) are essentially basic switches with a router module installed in them. They are especially useful in networks with VLANs because you can create the VLANs and decide how the VLANs will be routed — all within the same switch. Multilayer switches can be connected to other multilayer switches and to basic switches to extend VLANs through an organization. I will discuss VLANs in greater depth later in this chapter.

Content Switch

In today's networks, much of the user's data is stored off the user's computer in server farms. These may consist of many servers that have redundant drives and are clustered together to provide for load balancing and fault tolerance. The actual physical connections that provide these services can be very complex, but the logical connection to the user should be as transparent and simple as possible. A special switch called a *content switch* can help make this possible.

A content switch allows one virtual IP address to be known to the network for a specific resource or server, while the resource actually exists in multiple locations on several real IP addresses. This means users can access the resource just as if it were on their desktops, but the administrator can feed the resource from anywhere. Not only that, but the administrator can change the physical location of the data without having to make any changes to the user configuration. These changes will be completely transparent to users, who don't really care where the data is actually stored.

IDS/IPS

Today's networks often need more than just a firewall to protect them from intrusion. Hackers have developed sophisticated means of "tricking" protocols into giving them information that they can then use against the network and its resources. In addition, software is now available on the Web that requires very little actual network expertise to launch effective and potentially devastating attacks against a network. It's a war out there!

In response to this, many devices have been developed that do more than just filter packets. These devices actually understand the protocols that the networks use and can determine whether the correct protocol language is being "spoken" and whether the steps of the protocol are being performed in the right order. Two of these devices are the Intrusion Detection System (IDS) and the Intrusion Prevention System (IPS).

Actually, an IDS and an IPS are very similar, but there are some important differences. The main difference between the two is that the IDS is a "passive" device that allows an administrator to recognize an attack and respond accordingly, whereas the IPS is a "reactive" device that allows the administrator to program it to take specific actions when specific threats are discovered. This might include shutting ports or resetting connections.

Many devices can be changed from an IDS role to an IPS role simply by reconfiguring them. IDS/IPS systems can be network-based (NIDS) or host-based (HIDS), and they generally use multiple sensors, a console for monitoring, and a central engine that records the events and may take action if configured for IPS. They can be programmed with common attack signature to recognize, and they can learn the normal behavior of a network and look for anomalies.

Load Balancer

As I mentioned before, typically in today's networks the resources that are essential for a user are actually stored off the user's computer, sometimes in multiple locations for the same resource. When this is done, the user can gain access to the resources by going to a specific logical location, and the network devices can quickly decide how to obtain the user data and from which physical location to obtain it, completely unbeknownst to the user. The device that makes all this magic happen is a *load balancer.*

Actually, a load balancer is more of a network role than it is a network device. Many devices can be configured to provide a load balancing function. Servers can be configured with multiple NICs and clustered together, routers can be configured with multiple associated interfaces or subinterfaces, and switches (such as the content switch mentioned earlier) can be configured to direct traffic and to change the physical location on each request. This is sometimes referred to as *round robin* since the physical connection just keeps going round and round. These types of load balancing techniques can dramatically improve the speed of the network for the user.

Multifunction Network Devices

The network needs in a small office are often the same as those in a larger office but on a smaller scale. This is especially true if the small office is a branch office connected to a larger corporate data center. In this case, the branch office might still have a need for a router, a secure switch, a firewall, and an IPS, or at least the services provided by each device. Although it might not make sense to have a separate device (such as those in a corporate setting) to provide all these services, it might make perfect sense to use one device that provides them all.

Multifunction network devices combine many network roles such as routing, switching, a firewall, a DNS server, IDS/IPS, and more into one device that is easy to install and configure for a small or branch office. These devices, manufactured by Linksys, Netgear, D-Link, and other companies, usually come with software wizards for easy installation. They are becoming more common for use in small office home office (SOHO) environments as well.

DNS Server

As its name implies, the Domain Name System (DNS) provides domain name resolution on a network. Specifically, a *DNS server* provides hostname to IP address resolution, and vice versa. Queries that are used to resolve a hostname to an IP address are referred to as *forward lookup queries*. Queries that are used to resolve a known IP address to a hostname are referred to as *reverse lookup queries*. Clients are configured by the administrator or by the DHCP server with the address of the DNS server. The client can then use the server(s) for name resolution. Name resolution is extremely important in today's networks.

Often, a DNS server does not work alone but instead refers queries to other DNS servers, a process called *forwarding*. Also, many networks have multiple DNS servers that share the same databases used to resolve queries. These shared databases are referred to as *zone database files*. These can be shared by DNS servers through a process called *zone transfer* or by attaching the information to other transfers, such as Active Directory with Windows 2000 and Windows Server 2003 servers. DNS servers are an essential part of today's networks.

Bandwidth Shaper

As I mentioned earlier, the real job of a network administrator is to keep users happy and productive. This means that any device that can understand your bandwidth requirements for specific traffic and allocate resources accordingly will improve the user's speed on the network and make you a hero. In the past few years, network appliances (add-ons) called *bandwidth shapers* have been developed that can be quickly installed and can intelligently delegate bandwidth. You may want to consider using a bandwidth shaper if you have recurring user latency problems when a user is working with a bandwidth intensive application, such as video streaming.

Proxy Server

A *proxy* is a person or an agent that performs an action on behalf of someone else. In the legal world, the term is used when an attorney is permitted to sign on behalf of the client. In the information technology (IT) realm, it means relatively the same thing. A *proxy server* is, therefore, a device that makes a connection to another location, most often a website, on behalf of the user.

If an organization wants to centralize access to the Internet to control it and track its usage, it can configure the browsers on the user computers to use the address of the proxy server to get any information from the Internet.

When the user makes a request on a browser, the proxy server will actually make the request to the Internet on behalf of the user. This allows the organization to control access to the sites users can visit and determine who can visit them and when. Typically, the proxy server will also keep a detailed record of these Internet requests. If a person is being reprimanded or fired for improper Internet use, the HR team often has these reports in hand as Exhibit A!

Also, since the proxy keeps a record of the addresses that go through it, it can be used in other creative ways. For example, as a hostname is resolved to an IP address for one user to access a resource, this information can be stored in the proxy and used by other users. A proxy server that provides this type of service is referred to as a *caching proxy*. This type of server is often used to speed access to commonly used Internet and intranet sites.

CSU/DSU

The *channel service unit/data service unit* (CSU/DSU) is a digital interface device used to connect a router to a digital circuit, such as a T1 or T3 line. On one side of the device is the WAN, and on the other side is the entrance to the LAN. The CSU/DSU is actually two devices in one, each with a specific purpose. The CSU provides the termination of signal, connection integrity, and line monitoring. The DSU converts the T-carrier line frames into frames that the LAN can interpret. You can generally lease a CSU/DSU from your service provider, or you can buy one of your own. In either case, a CSU/DSU is an indispensable piece of equipment in a network with digital circuit connections.

Exam Essentials

Know the purpose of specialized network devices.   You should understand the purpose of these specialized network devices. You should know where one is likely to be needed and therefore used in a network. For example, you should understand that a multilayer switch works at layers 2 and 3 and not just layer 2. Also, you should be able to compare and contrast an IPS with an IDS.

Understand the functionality of specialized network equipment.   You should understand the basic functionality of specialized network devices such as a multilayer switch, content switch, bandwidth shaper, and CSU/DSU. You should know basically how each one operates and what it actually does for the administrator as well as the user.

3.3 Explain the advanced features of a switch

Switches and the technologies that they employ have changed tremendously over the past several years. New features, and enhancements to older features, make switches easier to deploy on a network and more effective in regard to controlling network traffic. In the following sections, I will discuss some of the advanced features used on switches in today's networks.

Power over Ethernet (PoE)

Sometimes the location of a remote router or wireless access point is a place that is not close to a power outlet. In these cases, it's possible to power some devices from the current provided on standard POTS lines. This feature is PoE. Many switches, IP telephones, embedded computers, and wireless access points can use this feature for convenient installation.

Spanning Tree

In today's networks, switches are often connected with redundant links to provide for fault tolerance and load balancing. Unfortunately, these redundant links can also create physical loops in the network. If these physical loops were allowed to be seen by data traffic as logical loops, the result could be broadcast storms, multiple copies of the same frame sent to hosts, and MAC database instability on devices. To prevent the logical loops from occurring while still maintaining physical redundancy, modern network switches use the Spanning Tree Protocol (STP).

The original STP is defined by the IEEE as 802.1D. Many other faster and more sophisticated spanning tree protocols have been developed over the past 10 years, including RSTP, MSTP, and PVSTP. Each of these protocols has the same goal in mind: to provide multiple viable paths for data fault tolerance and load balancing without creating loops and the problems they cause.

VLAN

A *virtual local area network* (VLAN) is a subnet created using a switch instead of a router. Because of this fact, VLANs have many advantages over subnets created by routers. One of the main advantages of VLANs is that the logical network design does not have to conform to the physical network topology. This gives administrators much more flexibility in network design and in the subsequent changes of that design.

Subnets created by a router are, by definition, local to the interface from which the subnet was created. In addition, all the hosts off each router interface are in the same subnet. This might be fine if all the hosts in a specific geographic area were always in the same department or security group of the organization, but often this is not the case. This means that an administrator cannot set up security policies for resource use by department and use the subnet address to control the policy, because many departments might be mixed into the same subnet.

VLANs solve this problem by creating the subnets using a switch or even groups of switches. Ports on the switches are assigned to a specific VLAN and therefore in a specific subnet. Now here is the important difference, so pay attention — all ports that are assigned to the same VLAN are logically in the same subnet regardless of where those ports are located in the organization. Because of this fact, the administrator can manage the network and its resources by departments represented by subnets, regardless of where each of the users actually resides. This offers a tremendous advantage to an administrator.

Trunking

Now, you may be wondering how all the switches know about all the VLANs. Well, the administrator will assign some ports on a switch to carry all the VLAN information to the other switches. These ports, which allow all VLANs to pass through them, are referred to as *trunks*. A VLAN switch that is connected to other VLAN switches will have at least one trunk port. Switches that are central to a topology may have multiple trunk ports.

Another advantage of VLANs is that the traffic that is communicated within the interfaces of the VLAN is only on the interfaces of that VLAN and on the trunks. This increases the security in an organization. Furthermore, connecting one VLAN's traffic to another VLAN requires a centrally located (logically) layer 3 device such as a router or a multilayer switch. The administrator can place access lists on this device that will control all traffic between the VLANs. This represents a tremendous improvement over placing separate access lists on all the routers in the organization. Because of these advantages, VLANs are commonly used in many of today's networks.

Port Mirroring

Some devices, such as the sensor on an IDS/IPS system, require the ability to monitor all network traffic. Since the VLANs separate the traffic for security reasons, monitoring all traffic sometimes requires getting a copy of network packets from one switch port sent to another switch port, strictly for the purpose of monitoring and logging them. This process, called *port mirroring*, is becoming a more common practice as organizations continue to install more IDS/IPS systems. It is referred to as Switched Port Analyzer (SPAN) on Cisco switches and as Roving Analysis Port (RAP) on 3Com switches.

Port Authentication

You can enhance your security by also requiring *port authentication* based on the MAC address of a source. When port authentication is configured, the switch will check the MAC address of a frame to determine whether it is allowed to forward that frame. Please note that I said "enhance" and that I did not say that this should be your only security, since MAC addresses are notoriously easy to spoof.

Port authentication is accomplished using different commands for different vendors, but the basic idea is the same; the ports on a switch are statically or sometimes automatically configured to accept only specified MAC addresses. In the case of static configuration, the network administrator manually configures the MAC addresses that the ports can accept. In the case of automatic configuration, some switches can be programmed to accept only the first address, or any set number of addresses on a port, after the configuration is enabled. This is referred to by Cisco as *sticky learning*.

So, you may be wondering what happens if another MAC address attempts to enter into the port of a switch that is configured not to accept it. Well, the switch can usually be configured to do one of the following:

Restrict   This means the switch will not allow the traffic that does not meet its security criteria to pass through it, but it will still remain up and pass the traffic that does meet its criteria.

Shut down   In this case, the switch will shut the port on the first attempt of a security violation. Generally, an administrator will need to reset the port manually to open it again. This is usually accomplished by shutting the interface and then reopening it.

You can use this type of security within an organization in many practical ways. For example, suppose you have a conference room that is used for presentations on company laptops. You want to be able to connect these laptops to the wall jacks to obtain a connection to the Internet. However, the same conference room is sometimes used as a waiting area for a visitor to your company. For security reasons, you do not want the visitor to be able to use the ports in the conference room. In this case, you could configure the switch ports connected to the wall jacks in the conference room to accept only the MAC addresses of the company laptops. If the visitor tried to plug in his laptop, he could be restricted or the port could be shut down altogether. Since the visitor would have no way of guessing the MAC addresses that you would accept, it is very unlikely that he could spoof the right address to defeat your security. This type of port authentication is often used in today's networks.

Note that port authentication on switches refers to the actual physical port (or interface) on the switch. This should not be confused with logical ports on layer 4 of the OSI model.

Exam Essentials

Know the purpose and use of advanced features on network switches.   You should understand the purpose of advanced features such as Power over Ethernet, STP, VLANs and trunking, and port mirroring and port authentication. In addition, you should be able to describe the appropriate use of each technology.

3.4 Implement a basic wireless network

The days of working from a desk in an office are long gone for many people. It's now possible to obtain the resources we need to do our jobs no matter where we happen to be at the time. As I write this, I'm in an airport club room on my laptop, which is connected to the airport's wireless network. In addition to "talking" to you about wireless networking, I'm currently using it to keep track of my email and research my facts when necessary. Yes, I use Google too!

Since wireless networks are becoming increasingly popular, you need to know how to implement a basic network. This includes installing the wireless clients as well as installing the WAP. In addition, you should know how to provide the best security available for your clients, based on client software and the type of WAP you use. Finally, you should know how to "tweak" the wireless settings to avoid interference caused by other devices. In the following sections, I will discuss the basic implementation of a wireless network.

Install Client

In the past, installing a wireless client was much more difficult than it is today. Wireless vendors now provide software that walks you through the installation of their card and their drivers. You can purchase many different types of wireless cards with PCI, USB, and PCMCIA interface types, depending on your needs. Most laptops have a wireless card installed and ready to use. The Microsoft Windows XP and Vista operating systems have a default client called the Windows Zero Configuration (WZC) client on Windows XP and the WLAN AutoConfig service on Vista. Need I say more?

More than 90 percent of the time, the wireless installation will be seamless when you follow the vendor's wizards. However, since you're the network administrator, you are supposed to know what to do when that other 10 percent kicks in and you have to troubleshoot an installation. For this reason, I will now walk through all the typical settings found in the configuration of a wireless client.

The Network Connections Dialog Box

If the software wizards included with your wireless device do not provide you with the connection you need, you can begin troubleshooting the problem by finding the connection and changing its properties. The first tool you should use to find the connection is the Network Connections dialog box. You can access this tool from the Control Panel on all Microsoft clients. It contains a list or group of icons for all the connections on a computer. Figure 3.7 shows the Network Connections dialog box on a Windows XP client. You should find your wireless connection in this tool.

FIGURE 3.7   Network Connections dialog box

The Wireless Network Connection Dialog Box

If you have wireless connections in your computer, they will be listed in Network Connections in the Control Panel. You should right-click on the wireless connection and then select Properties to access the Wireless Connection dialog box. The Wireless Network Connection dialog box has three tabs. You can manually configure your wireless network using the settings provided in this tool. The General tab, pictured in Figure 3.8, allows you to view and set the network properties, such as the network card, the wireless client, and the protocol (typically TCP/IP). The Wireless Networks tab, pictured in Figure 3.9, allows you to view the networks that are available to your computer. You can click the View Wireless Networks button on this tab to see a list of networks that are available, and then you can click Refresh to get the latest networks when there are changes. In addition, by selecting a specific network and clicking Properties, you can view and configure the authentication, encryption, and connection options, as shown in Figure 3.10. You should configure these options to match the settings of your wireless access point. Later in this chapter, I will discuss how to configure these options on the wireless access point. Finally, on the Advanced tab, you can configure the Windows Firewall and Internet Connection Sharing — just as you can with other network connections. Understanding all these tools should help you tweak any settings that the vendor client software does not set properly.

FIGURE 3.8   Wireless Network Connection dialog box, General tab

FIGURE 3.9   Wireless Network Connection dialog box, Wireless Networks tab

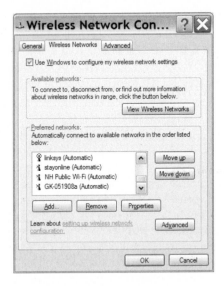

FIGURE 3.10　Viewing the wireless network properties

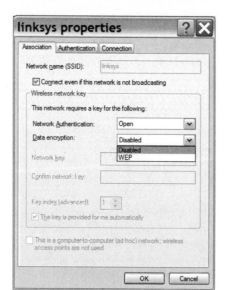

Access Point Placement

You can dramatically increase the effectiveness of your wireless network by placing the wireless access points in the best locations. Wireless communication on 802.11 networks relies on radio waves. In the same way that the AM signal in your car fades when you go under a bridge, the radio waves of your network can be affected by the infrastructure of the building where they are generated. Actually, because of the number of variables involved, this is more of an art than a science. However, there are some best practices to follow when placing access points.

Physical Location of WAPs

Generally speaking, the WAPs should be away from large metal objects and areas of electrical interference as much as possible. This is not always easy, but you should keep this in mind during installation. A friend of mine was responsible for installing WAPs in a gigantic freezer used to store ice cream for a large grocery chain. You can imagine the challenges in that installation. Often the WAPs were installed in a high ceiling, and he had to get on a cherry picker just to get to the areas where they were to be mounted. I hope your physical challenges won't be as great as his were, but you may have a few of your own that even he didn't experience.

You should think through the range that your devices can handle and install enough WAPs to cover the range, based on the radius of the rooms in which they will be used. To clarify, if you were to draw a large circle from wall to wall, the radius would be half of that circle. In this way, you can ensure that all clients have adequate access to the WAP's signal.

Wired or Wireless Connectivity

The next question is where you should connect the network cables and how many cables you should have. It's possible to connect a WAP to a WAP and to "daisy chain" a wireless solution that simply relays the signal until it finally gets to the wired LAN. The advantage of this is that the wired connections don't have to go to all the WAPs, which may save cable, installation time, and, therefore, money. The major disadvantages of this system are that a failure in one WAP could mean a failure in the whole system. Also, the fact that traffic will build as it works its way back to the LAN cable could cause a serious bottleneck on the way there. For these reasons, this type of configuration is generally not recommended.

Another option is to connect each of the WAPs to its own network cable and connect all of the cables to a common switch or series of connected switches. This takes more work and more wire in the beginning but could be a much more reliable system in the long run. A failure of one WAP would affect only the area in which that WAP resides. Also, the problem of traffic bottlenecks is greatly reduced. Whichever way you decide, or even if you choose a combination of methods, the placement of the WAPs is just the first of many decisions in regard to installing a wireless network.

Install Access Point

The central device in a wireless network is the WAP. It functions like a switch but allows the clients to make a connection to it through the air without using a network cable. This provides a tremendous convenience to the user, as long as you have the WAP configured properly so that it recognizes the client computer and allows it to make the connection. Otherwise, the wireless network can become a serious headache for users who are just trying to make the connection to get the resources they need to do their jobs. Because of this, it's important that you understand the proper installation of a WAP, including configuring encryption, configuring channels, and configuring the way WAP will identify itself to users, called the *ESSID beacon*, for connectivity as well as security. In the following sections, I will cover each of these important topics.

Configure Appropriate Encryption

The appropriate encryption for wireless clients will vary depending on the client operating systems that you are using to connect to the WAP. Additionally, encryption options will generally be "bundled" with authentication options. You should configure the access point for the highest security possible based on your client computers. Often the wizard included with the WAP will ask you about the clients and set the appropriate parameters based upon your answers, but you should know the basics about each of the encryption options you may be offered.

Disabled   This should be rather self-explanatory. A wireless network with the encryption disabled will pass all traffic in clear text. Anyone could easily "sniff" the data, including your username and password, right out of the air! You should never use this option to connect to your bank accounts or to conduct any financial transactions or important business, especially if you are in a public place such as an airport or coffee shop. With this option selected on WZC, you will not get the options for authentication.

Wired Equivalent Privacy (WEP)   Contrary to its name, this is the least secure of all wireless security types. You should use it only as a last resort when you have clients prior to Windows 2000 that do not support the more secure encryption types discussed next. It consists of a manually entered key comprised of alphanumeric or hexadecimal characters. The keys can be 40-bit, 64-bit, 128-bit, 153-bit, or 256-bit, depending on version of the software and the vendor, with 40-bit, 64-bit, and 128-bit being the most common. WEP "security" has been broken for many years now.

Wi-Fi Protected Access (WPA)   This encryption protocol is much more secure than WEP but is still not the most secure. It adds security using two additional components, TKIP and EAP. Temporal Key Integrity Protocol (TKIP) encrypts the keys used for authentication and encryption so they are more difficult to intercept and decipher. Extensible Authentication Protocol (EAP) can be used to ensure that the user is a valid network user. EAP can be used in many ways such as with Kerberos (Active Directory), smart cards, and biometric scanning devices such as retinal and fingerprint scanners. WPA can be used with an 802.1x authentication server, or it can be used in preshared key (PSK) mode, requiring each user computer and WAP to be configured with the same passphrase. In the case of PSK, the ultimate security of the network will be based on the complexity and security of the passphrase. The passphrase can be up to 63 characters long, although much shorter passphrases are often used.

Wi-Fi Protected Access version 2 (WPA2)   This encryption and authentication algorithm is one of the strongest. WPA2 offers Advanced Encryption Standard (AES) to provide as secure a wireless network connection as possible. It can also be used in an 802.1x mode with an authentication server or in PSK mode. This is the recommended mode for the latest Microsoft clients such as Windows XP and Windows Vista.

Configure Channels and Frequencies

Most of the wireless networks used today work in the 2.4GHz radio band. The key word here is *band*. They don't all work on one frequency but rather on a range or band of frequencies depending on how the administrator sets up the connection. The channels you choose may be affected by other devices that are in your organization. Typically, the most used channels by small and large business alike are 1, 6, and 11, because these channels will not interfere with each other.

Depending on whether you are receiving interference from other sources that also work in the 2.4GHz band, you may want to "tweak" the channel and/or frequency from time to time. Other devices that use the 2.4GHz band include wireless phones and Bluetooth devices such as wireless keyboards and mice. These can potentially interfere with communication on your wireless network. Changing the channel and/or frequency on the other device is sometimes an option, but when this is not possible, you should know how to make the change on the wireless access point. Where you change these settings will vary depending on your devices, but you should start with the advanced options on a specific network.

Set ESSID and Beacon

WAPs can send out a signal to let people know they exist and the names of the network to which they are connected. In fact, this is usually the default behavior of a WAP unless you change it. The name of the wireless network is referred to as its *extended service set identification* (ESSID). It is typically sent out by a WAP with a special signal called a *beacon*. The beacon and the ESSID allow one wireless network to be distinguished easily from another wireless network.

For security reasons, it's also possible to turn off or disable the beacon. This does not mean that the network will no longer exist or cannot be found. It means only that it won't be as easy to find. If you need to connect to a network that is not emitting a beacon, the wireless administrator can give you the ESSID to enter manually. You can enter it in your wireless software along with any credentials needed for encryption and/or authentication, thereby creating the new network in your software and allowing it to connect to the WAP.

Verify Installation

In general, the best way to implement and verify a wireless network installation is in "baby steps." Whenever possible, you should take very small steps so that troubleshooting will be much easier. The following list is an example that you might follow when creating a wireless network for multiple clients:

1. Configure the WAP with no security.

2. Configure the first computer without a wireless client.

3. Connect the client to the wired network, and verify connectivity.

4. Add the wireless client software to the computer without encryption or authentication, disconnect the cable, and verify connectivity to the WAP.

5. Add the appropriate encryption and authentication protocols at the WAP and the client, and verify connectivity again.

6. Install the other clients with same configuration as the first.

Exam Essentials

Know the basics of installing wireless client software. You should understand that most of today's wireless software contains wizards that will complete the majority of the installation. In addition, you should realize that you may have to adjust some of the settings. Finally, you should know the basic tools provided by Windows XP and Vista to allow you to change these settings.

Know how to install and verify a wireless network. You should know the fundamentals of placing access points in areas that are free from physical and electrical interference. In addition, you should understand the differences between the encryption and authentication protocols offered with wireless products, such as WEP, WPA, and WPA2. Finally, you should realize that the best way to implement and verify a wireless network installation is to start off "wired" and then take baby steps with the first computer and WAP. After a successful combination is found, it can then be duplicated with other computers and even other WAPs.

Review Questions

1. Which of following is true about bridges and switches? (Choose two.)
   A. Bridges are faster than switches.
   B. Switches are faster than bridges.
   C. Bridges have more ports than switches.
   D. Switches have more ports than bridges.

2. Which of the following is a special hub or switch that can be used by clients without cables?
   A. WLAN
   B. WPA
   C. WEP
   D. WAP

3. Which of the following are true about a firewall? (Choose two.)
   A. Firewalls are always a software solution.
   B. Firewalls only filter traffic that is coming into a network.
   C. Firewalls can be programmed to filter data packets based on information they contain.
   D. Firewalls are often used in business environments.

4. Which of the following are not true in regard to DHCP? (Choose two.)
   A. DHCP servers can automatically configure clients with the address of a DNS server.
   B. Client computers are generally configured to broadcast for a DHCP server.
   C. DHCP servers can resolve hostnames to IP addresses.
   D. You should use a DHCP server only when a static client configuration is not possible.

5. Which of the following is a network device that can detect an intruder and respond to the attack automatically?
   A. Firewall
   B. IDS
   C. IPS
   D. UPS

6. Which of the following is a device used to connect a router to a digital circuit such as a T1 or T3 line?
   A. CSMA/CD
   B. WAP
   C. CSU/DSU
   D. Modem

7. Which of the following protocols is used on today's switches to prevent problems caused by loops but still maintain physically redundant links?

   A. VLANs

   B. STP

   C. VTP

   D. UDP

8. Which of the following are options for port authentication responses on layer 2 switches? (Choose two.)

   A. Restrict

   B. Filter by IP

   C. Filter by protocol

   D. Shut down

9. Which of the following is a wireless client built in to the Windows XP operating system?

   A. WAP

   B. WEP

   C. WZC

   D. W-2

10. Which of the following would be considered the strongest form of wireless security?

   A. WEP

   B. WAP

   C. WPA

   D. WPA2

Answers to Review Questions

1. **B, D.** Switches have largely replaced bridges in today's networks because they have many more ports than bridges and they are much faster in regard to segmenting network traffic.

2. **D.** A wireless access point (WAP) is a special hub or switch that can be used by client computers without the need for cables, as long as the client computers are configured with the appropriate hardware and software.

3. **C, D.** Firewalls can provide hardware, software, or a combined solution to filtering data traffic. They are typically programmed to filter traffic coming into and going out of a network, based on what is contained in the data packets. Firewalls are used by most businesses to prevent unwanted traffic and network intrusion.

4. **C, D.** Dynamic Host Configuration Protocol (DHCP) servers can automatically configure clients with an IP address, subnet mask, default gateway, DNS server address, and much more. You should use a DHCP server whenever possible and use static configuration only when a DHCP server is not available. Client computers are configured to send short broadcast communication to obtain their addresses from a DHCP server. DHCP servers do not provide name resolution; DNS servers do.

5. **C.** An administrator can configure an Intrusion Prevention System (IPS) to detect common attacks and respond to the attacks by shutting ports or resetting connections.

6. **C.** A CSU/DSU is used to connect a router to a digital circuit such as a T1 or T3. The WAN is on one side of the device, and the entrance to the LAN is on the other side.

7. **B.** Spanning Tree Protocol (STP) is used in today's networks to provide fault tolerance by maintaining physically redundant links while still preventing the problems caused by network loops.

8. **A, D.** Port authentication on layer 2 switches works by MAC addresses, not by IP addresses or ports, which are at layers 3 and 4, respectively. The main two options are to restrict network traffic to only those frames identified by specifically configured or learned MAC addresses and allow all other traffic or to shut down the port immediately when an address that is not configured or learned is presented to the switch.

9. **C.** Windows Zero Configuration (WZC) is built in to the Windows XP operating system. It can generally detect any wireless access point or computer that is beaconing and can be used to connect to the device.

10. **D.** Wi-Fi Protected Access version 2 (WPA2) with Advanced Encryption Standard (AES) is considered the strongest form of wireless security for today's wireless networks.

Chapter 4

Domain 4 Network Management

COMPTIA NETWORK+ EXAM OBJECTIVES COVERED IN THIS CHAPTER:

✓ **4.1 Explain the function of each layer of the OSI model**

- ▪ Layer 1: physical
- ▪ Layer 2: data link
- ▪ Layer 3: network
- ▪ Layer 4: transport
- ▪ Layer 5: session
- ▪ Layer 6: presentation
- ▪ Layer 7: application

✓ **4.2 Identify types of configuration management documentation**

- ▪ Wiring schematics
- ▪ Physical and logical network diagrams
- ▪ Baselines
- ▪ Policies, procedures, and configurations
- ▪ Regulations

✓ **4.3 Given a scenario, evaluate the network based on configuration management documentation**

- ▪ Compare wiring schematics, physical and logical network diagrams, baselines, policies and procedures, and configurations to network devices and infrastructure
- ▪ Update wiring schematics, physical and logical network diagrams, configurations, and job logs as needed

✓ **4.4 Conduct network monitoring to identify performance and connectivity issues using the following:**

- Network monitoring utilities (e.g., packet sniffers, connectivity software, load testing, and throughput testers)

- System logs, history logs, and event logs

✓ **4.5 Explain different methods and rationales for network performance optimization**

- Methods:

  - QoS

  - Traffic shaping

  - Load balancing

  - High availability

  - Caching engines

  - Fault tolerance

- Reasons:

  - Latency sensitivity

  - High bandwidth applications

  - VoIP

  - Video Applications

  - Uptime

✓ **4.6 Given a scenario, implement the following trouble-shooting methodology:**

- Information gathering: identify symptoms and problems

- Identify the affected areas of the network

- Determine if anything has changed

- Establish the most probable cause

- Determine if escalation is necessary

- Create an action plan and solution identifying potential effects

- Implement and test the solution

- Identify the results and effects of the solution

- Document the solution and the entire process

✓ 4.7 Given a scenario, troubleshoot common connectivity issues and select an appropriate solution

- Physical issues:
  - Cross talk
  - Nearing cross talk
  - Attenuation
  - Collisions
  - Shorts
  - Open impedance mismatch (echo)_
  - Interference
- Logical issues:
  - Port speed
  - Port duplex mismatch
  - Incorrect VLAN
  - Incorrect IP address
  - Wrong gateway
  - Wrong DNS
  - Wrong subnet mask
- Issues that should be identified and escalated:
  - Switching loop
  - Routing loop
  - Route problems
  - Proxy ARP
  - Broadcast storms
- Wireless issues:
  - Interference (bleed, environmental factors)
  - Incorrect encryption
  - Incorrect channel
  - Incorrect frequency
  - ESSID mismatch
  - Standard mismatch (802.11 a/b/g/n)
  - Distance
  - Bounce
  - Incorrect antenna placement

4.1 Explain the function of each layer of the OSI model

To understand anything and then develop it, you need a way to relate to it, and computer communication is no exception. As computer communication became a reality, we needed a common language that we could use to communicate regarding computer communication. In the early 1980s, representatives from more than 60 countries, collectively known as the International Standards Organization (ISO), developed a model of communication upon which hardware and software could be developed and connected. They named the model the Open System Interconnection (OSI) model, and then they began to use it to create new hardware and software.

Initially, the OSI model was supposed to include an OSI protocol as well, but the OSI protocol was never fully developed. Every protocol that has been developed, however, can be loosely mapped to the OSI model. Since the OSI model is the basis for all computer communication and for all protocols, you should understand the structure, purpose, and function of the model. In the following sections, I will discuss how each layer of the OSI model functions.

The concepts of this chapter are covered in greater depth in *CompTIA Network+ Study Guide* (Sybex, 2009) and *CompTIA Network+ Deluxe Study Guide* (Sybex, 2009).

The Seven Layers of the OSI Model

The OSI model is composed of seven layers (see Figure 4.1). Each of the layers has a defined purpose. The layers are numbered from the bottom up. In the sections that follow, I will discuss the name, number, and function of each layer of the model, beginning with the top layer. Figure 4.1 shows the OSI model and some of the protocols that work at each of the layers.

FIGURE 4.1   The OSI model

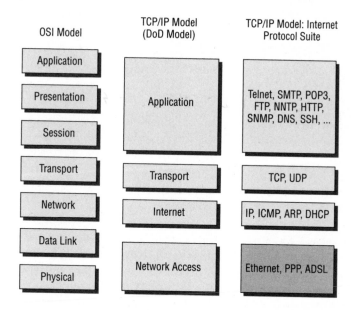

 A good way to remember the layers of the OSI model from the top down is to remember the mnemonic: All People Seem To Need Data Processing.

Application Layer

The Application layer (layer 7) is the highest layer in the OSI model. It contains applications that facilitate network communication. These are not applications like Microsoft Word and Excel but rather application protocols such as Hypertext Transfer Protocol (HTTP) for browsing the World Wide Web and File Transfer Protocol (FTP) for transferring files on networks and over the Web. At the Application layer, the data still resembles something that people can read and interpret.

Presentation Layer

At the Presentation layer (layer 6), data is first converted into a form that can be sent over a network. At this layer, data is compressed and decompressed and encrypted or decrypted, depending on which direction it's traveling. You can think of the Presentation layer as the translation layer.

Session Layer   *[handwritten: Socket]*

The Session layer (layer 5) is responsible for establishing, synchronizing, maintaining, and then terminating communication sessions between computers. It also handles error detection and notification. You can think of the Session layer as the traffic cop that directs the network traffic and lets the appropriate traffic flow at the appropriate time.

Transport Layer   *[handwritten: voice of IP   UDP]*

The Transport layer (layer 4) handles the actual processing of data between devices. This layer is responsible for error correction and virtual circuits in the form of ports. It resends any *dropped packets*, which are packets that do not receive an acknowledgment from the destination address. It's also responsible for any problems that are associated with the fragmentation of packets.   *[handwritten: Connsion / orientionless   TCP   UDP]*

Network Layer

The Network layer (layer 3) is responsible for providing the mechanism by which data can be moved from computer to computer or from network to network. The Network layer does not actually move the data; instead, it provides the addressing information and the protocols that are used to provide logical paths through the network that are necessary to move the data to the appropriate location. The Network layer contains many protocols that facilitate these services, including Internet Protocol (IP), Internet Control Message Protocol (ICMP), Internet Group Multicast Protocol (IGMP), and Address Resolution Protocol (ARP).   *[handwritten: Routing]*

Data Link Layer

The Data Link layer (layer 2) is responsible for sending data to the Physical layer so that it can be put onto the "wire" or network media. The Data Link layer is subdivided into two other layers: the Logical Link Control (LLC) and Media Access Control (MAC) layers. The LLC connects the Data Link layer to the higher-level protocols such as IP at the Network layer. The MAC layer connects the Data Link layer to the physical connection and provides the MAC address. The Data Link layer also defines the technology that is used for the network. This layer can also perform checksums, which are calculations that the system uses to make sure packets are not damaged in transit.

Physical Layer

The Physical layer (layer 1) defines the physical characteristics of the network, such as the type of cable that must be used as well as the voltage that will be used to transmit data through the network. Since the Physical layer defines these characteristics, it also establishes the topology of the network. Many standards are defined at this layer, such as the IEEE 802.3 standard for Ethernet as well as the IEEE 802.5 standard for Token Ring networks.

[handwritten: TCP /]

Exam Essentials

Be able to list the names and the order of each layer of the OSI model.   The OSI model has seven layers as follows:

7. Application

6. Presentation

5. Session

4. Transport   *P D y*

3. Network   *P o c ᴌ e T*

2. Data Link   *Ar o m p*

1. Physical   *B i T*

Understand the function of each layer of the OSI model.   You should understand the main purpose and function of each layer of the OSI model. In addition, you should be familiar with the types of protocols found at each layer. For example, Application: user protocols such as HTTP, FTP, and so on; Presentation: translation; Session: establishes, maintains, and terminates connection; Transport: error correction, virtual circuits through ports, TCP, and UDP; Network: logical addressing and routing; Data Link: LLC and MAC, physical addressing, putting data on the wire; Physical: electrical, mechanical, and procedural standards.

4.2 Identify types of configuration management documentation

It's with good reason that the person who manages a network is called the *network administrator*. A fair amount of documentation is involved in managing today's complex networks. Some of the documentation that a network administrator uses on a day-to-day basis includes wiring schematics, physical and logical network diagrams, baselines, polices, and regulations. In the following sections, I'll discuss each of these important documents.

Wiring Schematics

One day maybe most networking will be wireless, but for now this is not the case. In fact, most networks have thousands of feet of wiring that works its way around a building. I'm using the word *wiring* here in a loose sense, because the backbone of a network often consists of fiber-optic cable. Still, the network administrator must understand where all the wiring is connected and therefore what the options are in regard to fault-tolerant connections and changes to the network design.

To facilitate this knowledge, most companies keep detailed wiring schematics that show how cables are wired throughout an organization, what is connected to each one, and where there are cables that can be used for growth. The network administrator must keep these wiring schematics up-to-date when changes are made to the network.

Physical and Logical Network Diagrams

As we discussed in Chapter 2, "Domain 2 Network Media and Topologies," there is a big difference between the physical shape of a network and the logical shape of a network. The *physical shape* is what the network looks like to the "naked eye;" but the *logical shape* defines the path that a packet takes to get from one part of a network to another. Since these concepts are so different, the diagrams that represent them will also be very different.

A physical network diagram might describe where you have routers, switches, servers, client workstations, and other network equipment and what cables are being used to connect devices. It might look very much like a wiring schematic, except that the emphasis will be on the devices at the ends of the wires rather than the multitude of wires connecting them. Detailed information about the devices currently being used and their limitations could also be listed. This type of diagram could be used for planning the network or eventually replacing outdated equipment that is hampering network performance.

A logical network diagram, which describes the path the traffic takes to get from one router or switch to another, might be used for troubleshooting. Often network designers use multiple paths through various network devices to load balance a network and provide fault-tolerant routes when needed. This type of diagram will usually list the IP addresses of the devices and will take into account the configuration of devices such as VLANs on switches or access lists on routers. If traffic is suddenly not able to get from one part of a network to another, then a diagram showing the exact path that the traffic is supposed to take would be of great value to a person troubleshooting the problem.

Baselines

If you go to a doctor and your temperature is 104 degrees Fahrenheit, what does that indicate? You have a fever, right? How do know that you have a fever? When I said 104 degrees, you compared that to 98.6 degrees, which is the normal temperature for a healthy human being. Well, there are also normal readings for a network, but they aren't as simple as 98.6 degrees Fahrenheit. In fact, they may be customized to a type of network or even to your specific network.

There are four lifeblood resources to any network or any devices on the network: processor, memory, disk subsystem, and network subsystem. A serious weakness in any of the network resources can easily spread and affect the other resources. When a lack of a resource causes this type of problem, this is generally referred to as a *bottleneck*. How do you prevent bottlenecks? You must understand what your network looks like in regard to these resources when it is healthy so that you can determine what to change when it is not. A record of measurements taken by network diagnostics and system-monitoring equipment when the network is healthy is referred to as a *baseline* of the network. You should have a baseline of your network because although your network may be similar to other networks, no two networks are exactly alike. Typically, baselines are stored in log files that are accessible to the network administrator when needed for comparison.

Policies, Procedures, and Configurations

Each organization will determine its own policies for designing, configuring, and managing their own network. These policies and procedures should be created by the network teams who know the system best and should be "signed off" on by a high-level management person, such as an executive of the company. They should reflect the overall goals of the company in regard to network connectivity, disaster recovery, fault tolerance, security, and so on. Each company will need to decide what is important to them. Only after the policies and procedures are in place can the correct configurations be initiated and administered by the networking teams.

Regulations

While deciding on their policies and procedures and therefore their configurations, organizations should also take care to comply with the governmental regulations in their geographic area. For example, wiring that goes through the plenum of a building will have to consist of the right type of cable with an insulation that will not burn or wick. If the wrong type of cable is used in a plenum, the building might not pass an inspection, or it might not be covered by the company's insurance policy if a fire were to occur. It is to the advantage of the organization to be aware of and to abide by the regulations in its geographic area.

Exam Essentials

Understand the purpose and function of a wiring schematic.   You should understand that a wiring schematic shows the cabling of a network. You should know that it is essential for troubleshooting the physical layer of a large network. Finally, you should understand that the wiring schematic must updated whenever there is a change in the network.

Understand the difference between a physical network diagram and a logical network diagram.   You should understand that a physical network diagram shows the devices in a network and contains information about their location and their platform. In contrast, a logical network diagram traces the path that a packet takes as it traverses the network. It also takes into account the configurations of the devices, such as VLANs on switches or access lists on routers.

Understand the purpose of a baseline.   You should understand that the purpose of a baseline is to have a record of what a network looks like when it's "healthy" so you can determine what is different when it doesn't seem healthy anymore. You should know that there are four main resources in network systems: processor, memory, disk subsystem, and network subsystem. Finally, you should understand that a weakness in any of these areas can create a bottleneck, which can affect all of the resources.

You should understand the policies, procedures, and regulations of your network. Although there are general guidelines for policies and procedures, each organization will decide how to define and enforce the policies. These should then be signed off by upper management to give them the authority of the organization. You should be familiar with policies and procedures regarding networking and security in your organization.

4.3 Given a scenario, evaluate the network based on configuration management documentation

The objective here pretty much says it all. You have to do more than just memorize each of these concepts — you must be able to apply them to a scenario-based question and decide which tool should be used based on the information provided and the intended goal. You must also understand that it's important to document any changes made to the network, whether they are logical or physical. In short, you must understand the material presented in the previous section and then be able to think through the question to decide which answer is best. In the following sections, I'll discuss some strategies related to scenario-based questions. At the end of this chapter, we provide some scenario-based questions with which you can practice.

Compare Wiring Schematics, Physical and Logical Network Diagrams, Baselines, Policies and Procedures, and Configurations to Network Devices and Infrastructure

The main question here is "Does this scenario relate to the physical, logical, performance, or procedural aspects of my network?" That question may seem rather straightforward, but the scenario might be such that more than one aspect is affected, and therefore more than one tool should be considered. For example, if I were to upgrade a switch in my network so that I could use more VLANs to manage traffic and security better, which of these aspects of my network could be affected? Certainly, the physical network diagram of the network will change with the upgrade of the switch, but you should also understand that the logical network diagram would also change because of the additional VLANs. In addition, since security can now be managed better, the policies and procedures documentation might also be affected. Finally, if the upgrade of the switch improves network performance, then I might need a new baseline as well. In sum, you should recognize that one change can have a domino effect on many documents.

Update Wiring Schematics, Physical and Logical Network Diagrams, Configurations, and Job Logs As Needed

You should always keep documentation as up-to-date as possible. This may not be as easy as it sounds. Any replacement or upgrade of network equipment could well require an update to a physical network diagram. Any change in configuration on a router or a switch, such as a new router interface or a new VLAN, will require a change in the logical network diagram. To track these changes and their documentation, many companies use job logs that list the change that was made, when it was made, and when it was documented. Microsoft, as well as other companies, offer software to facilitate this process.

Exam Essentials

Understand how to apply a scenario to various network documents.   You should understand how to apply a scenario to the use of a wiring schematic, physical diagram, logical diagram, baseline, and list of policies and procedures.

Understand the need to update network documentation.   You should understand the frequent and consistent need to update network documents such as wiring schematics, logical and physical diagrams, and baselines. You should know that job logs are often used to track changes to the network and when the change was recorded in each of the documents.

4.4 Conduct network monitoring to identify performance and connectivity issues

You can use many different tools to identify performance and connectivity issues on a network. These tools have become more sophisticated over time and can give you a tremendous amount of information about the network and the data traffic that is flowing through it. Tools such as network-monitoring software can be used the gather information. Other tools such a system logs, history logs, and event logs can record information for future use and troubleshooting. In the following sections, I'll discuss the use of these tools to improve the performance of network.

Network-Monitoring Utilities

Network-monitoring utilities, commonly referred to as *sniffers*, are like electron microscopes that you can use to examine what is going on inside a network cable. With these tools, a network administrator can look inside each packet at the detailed information it contains. To identify and troubleshoot performance and connectivity-related issues on a network, you should concentrate on the header of the packet, rather than the data it carries. The header information at the beginning of the packet will tell you what protocol is being used, the IP address, the MAC address, and the port that is being used for the source and destination of a connection. By comparing the information gained from the sniffer to the normal ports and expected IP addresses (based on your logical diagram), you can then determine where the communication is breaking down.

Many third parties have developed sophisticated equipment to perform other network tests such as connectivity, load, and throughput tests. These products use both hardware and software to analyze the network performance and make recommendations for improvement. Companies such as Fluke Networks (www.fluke.com) specialize in equipment and software to test and evaluate networks.

System Logs, History Logs, and Event Logs

One thing that computers and network devices are very good at doing is keeping track of exactly what they are doing and what they've already done. With the proper configuration, most devices can give you a wealth of information about how they have been used, what changes have been made to their configuration, when these changes were made, and who made them. You can generally create system logs, history logs, and event logs on servers, PCs, and network equipment such as routers and switches.

System logs are generally used with servers to determine what services are available to the users and what system resources are being used to provide the services. Figure 4.2 shows a System log on Windows Server 2003. History logs, as you might imagine, keep track of events that have already happened and changes that have already been made to a system. They are sometimes very useful in isolating the source of a problem that was introduced by a change or another network event. Event logs can be used to track changes to configurations; security auditing; and the starting, refusing to start, and stopping of services. Windows servers combine many of these logs in a tool called Event Viewer, which allows you to view and manage the System, Application, and Security logs.

FIGURE 4.2   System log on Windows Server 2003

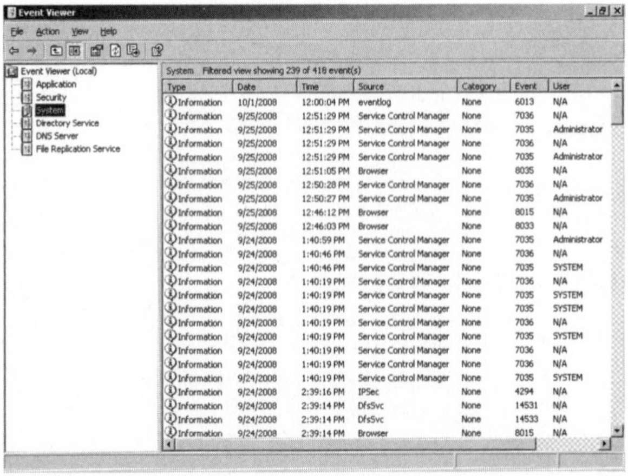

Exam Essentials

Understand the purpose of network-monitoring utilities.   You should understand that network-monitoring utilities can be used to get packet-level information to determine the behavior of a network component and then troubleshoot it. You should realize that these types of tools can create a tremendous amount of information but that they generally also have a component that logs the information into a file that can be used for future troubleshooting.

Understand the purpose of system logs, history logs, and event logs.   You should understand that system logs are typically used to track what services are available for users and what is currently in use. History logs generally track what has occurred on a system and can be used to troubleshoot where any failure may have occurred. Event logs generally track changes to configurations; security auditing; and the starting, refusing to start, and stopping of services.

4.5 Explain different methods and rationales for network performance optimization

The main role of a network is to make its resources available to the end user. End users generally don't know how the network functions, and they don't want to know. All they need is to get their documents and emails so that they can do their job. On the other hand, you must be aware of the latest networking technologies so that you can continue to make the resources transparently available to end users. To facilitate this, you can employ many methods to make the network more efficient. In the following sections, I'll discuss the most common of these methods and the specific reasons for their use.

Methods

One of the main jobs of network administrator is to create and preserve available bandwidth. This is the bandwidth available to the users after the network administrator factors out the overhead of running the network. In other words, a 1Gbps connection does not really give the users 1Gbps but instead gives them a share of the bandwidth that remains after the overhead of the network is considered. Administrators use many technologies to keep overhead to a minimum and assure that each type of user traffic gets the share of available bandwidth it requires. In the following sections, I'll discuss the most common of these technologies.

QoS

Quality of service (QoS) is an overall term that refers to the ability to provide different types of traffic flow with different types of service through the network. In other words, some types of traffic can receive priority and custom queuing through the network. This type of service is especially useful for video and voice applications that must maintain a consistent data flow in order to function properly. With good QoS, even a congested network can handle these types of applications.

Traffic Shaping

Traffic shaping is controlling computer network traffic to optimize performance and/or reduce latency. This technology works to slow down some traffic flows that do not need all the bandwidth in the path they are using. In this way, it increases the available bandwidth for other traffic flows that need it. Traffic shaping uses bandwidth throttling, which is typically applied to specific connections on the network edges. Traffic shaping can also be applied to specific devices at the network interface card.

Load Balancing

Today's networks often have multiple connections from a source to a destination. One of the reasons for this type of configuration is *load balancing*. When more than one path exists from a source to a destination, you can use each of the multiple paths to, in essence, "spread out" the traffic flows, thereby maximizing your available bandwidth on each connection. This is generally accomplished using routers or multilayer switches. Some of the most common types of traffic that are load balanced in today's networks include websites, FTP, DNS, and Internet Relay Chat.

High Availability

High availability is a system design protocol that sets a limit on unplanned downtime during a given period of time. Organizations that manage significant amounts of money or even human lives will generally strive for very high availability for their computer systems and network connections. In some organizations, for example, one of the goals is to provide 99999 uptime, which means that the system must be available 99.999 percent of the time. In other words, there can be no more than 0.001 percent of unplanned downtime. Since there are exactly 525,600 minutes in a year, this equates to 5.26 minutes per year ($525,600 \times .00001$)!

Unplanned downtime is due to a network failure. Another type of downtime, referred to as planned downtime, includes maintaining and upgrading the network during periods of low traffic.

Caching Engines

Computers and people tend to do the same things over and over. The principle of a *cache* is to store the resources that a device or a user needs to perform a task in a much closer location than the first time the task was performed. For example, if many users are accessing a popular website, a caching engine can be used to keep the links and data for the website at a location closer to the users to keep them from using the network bandwidth over and over again. Caching engines can also be used for files and resources internal to an organization so that the users can get to them while still conserving available bandwidth. This service typically requires no user configuration and is transparent to the user.

Fault Tolerance

Earlier, we mentioned that one of the reasons for redundant connections is load balancing. Another reason for redundant connections is fault tolerance. *Fault tolerance*, in regard to network connections, is the ability to lose one connection without losing the connectivity that a user requires. It is generally accomplished using routers or multilayer switches, which provide multiple connections from a source to a destination. In this case, if one connection fails, the other connection(s) are still available to user traffic. This in turn increases the high availability of the network resources.

Reasons

In an uncongested network, none of the strategies previously discussed would be necessary. In today's networks, however, powerful PCs are often used to download pictures, videos, and other large files. Because of this load, the biggest and best networks can still suffer from congestion. This can be because of latency sensitivity, high-bandwidth applications, and large uptime requirements. In the following sections, I'll discuss each of these reasons.

Latency Sensitivity

Latency is defined as the time delay between the moment when a process is initiated and the moment when one of its effects becomes detectable. In regard to networking, *latency sensitivity* refers to the susceptibility of an application or service to the speed or consistency of a network connection. In other words, some applications that people use on a network are not as sensitive as others to latency because they do not require a real-time or even an interactive connection to the user. Other applications and services require a high degree of consistent user interaction and are therefore considered to have high latency sensitivity.

High-Bandwidth Applications

Many applications that people use today require a tremendous amount of bandwidth relative to the applications used in the past. The types of applications that we use have evolved. Very early programs used batch processing that simply requested a list or set of information from a server and then waited for a response. Then we progressed to interactive applications that had to be able to give the user quick answers so that they could make the next decision. Nowadays, many of the applications that we use are considered real-time, which is to say that the user is watching, listening to, and interacting with the application itself. These include, but are not limited to, VoIP and video-streaming applications. I will discuss each of these emerging technologies in this section.

Voice over Internet Protocol (VoIP)

If you think about it, it's all come full circle. We started with the telephone in the late 1800s, which used only voice. This technology remained in place for quite a while. Then we began to add computers to the telephone lines in the late 1970s. After this, many new communication lines were developed (such as T1, Frame Relay, ATM, SONET, and so on) to enhance the communication between computers. These new types of communication lines have become very sophisticated and powerful. Now, we have decided that we can achieve great speed and quality advantages for telephones by putting those voice connections onto the sophisticated lines that were first developed for computers. VoIP provides a merging of voice, data, and video technology that allows easy collaboration of information between people for business and personal use. Obviously, it requires a network that supports its bandwidth requirements.

Video Applications

I can remember sitting down with my mom and dad at 6 p.m. every night to find out what was going in the world by watching the news on one of our three channels! We didn't have a clue what had happened that day until the news told us at that time. We also got only one chance to take it all in, because we certainly had no way to record it. Today, we can all watch the videos of anything we choose whenever we want to over the Internet. We can find out about what's going on in the world in a matter of minutes and sometimes even watch as it happens on our own computers. Video applications come in many forms, and the vendors' names are not important. The most important thing for you to understand is that these applications are real time in regard to the way they are watched by the user and therefore require a tremendous amount of bandwidth to operate effectively.

Uptime

As I mentioned earlier, *uptime* for a network is a measure of the amount of time that a network system is "up" and therefore available to the user. It is often used as a measure of network stability and reliability. The greater the uptime, the better the network is for the users. Many businesses strive for 99.999 percent uptime of the network and its essential components.

Uptime can also be defined the amount of time that a specific component has been up and has not been restarted. This is a very different definition than that for a network, because with network uptime, higher is always better. On the other hand, an extremely high uptime for a specific server might indicate negligence, since updates and patches often require a reboot that will reset uptime for that device.

Exam Essentials

Understand methods of network performance optimization   You should be aware that QoS is an overall term that refers to the ability to provide different types of traffic flow and different types of service within the network. In addition, you should understand that Traffic Shaping can be used to control bandwidth and therefore increase available bandwidth for those traffic flows that need it. High availability is a system design protocol that sets a limit on unplanned downtime during a given period of time. Caching engines can be used to keep files and resources close to users after they are used for the first time. Finally fault tolerance, in regard to networking, is the ability to lose one connection without losing the connectivity that a user requires.

Understand reasons for network performance optimization   You should know that latency sensitivity is the susceptibility of an application or service to the speed or consistency of a network connection. In addition, you should understand that many of the applications that we use today, such as VoIP and video applications, are interactive and therefore are considered high-bandwidth applications. Uptime is generally considered as the amount of time that a network or resource is available to the user; however the same term can also be used to designate the amount of time since a resource was restarted.

4.6 Given a scenario implement network troubleshooting methodology

Generally speaking, troubleshooting is a process of isolation. The best troubleshooters will try to determine what still works and how far it continues to work and then determine exactly where it breaks down. The more you know about the interworkings of a network, the better you will be able to determine the weakness or the problem based on its symptoms. There are many different troubleshooting methodologies, but all share the same basic steps. In the following sections, I'll discuss the steps involved in troubleshooting a network.

To facilitate this discussion, I will also present a scenario upon which you will apply your troubleshooting methodology. For this scenario, I will use technical information and terminology that I have previously discussed. Specifically, say you have a user who is complaining that she cannot access any intranet or Internet resources. Now, let's apply a troubleshooting methodology to this scenario.

Information Gathering: Identify Symptoms and Problems

The user is complaining that she cannot access intranet or Internet resources on the network. You are in the area, so you go to the user's computer. By typing **ipconfig /all,** you determine that the computer is set to obtain an address from a DHCP server, but the address it has assigned itself is 169.254.2.1; that looks like an APIPA address, doesn't it? I wonder how far this problem goes?

Identify the Affected Areas of the Network

Next you decide to ask around and see whether others are having the same problem. Some users report that they have a connection that seems to be working fine, while others have now lost their connection as well. You go to one of the other computers that recently lost its connection and type **ipconfig,** only to see that it also has an APIPA address of 169.254.5.67. You wonder what's causing this to happen; what has been done to the network servers?

Determine Whether Anything Has Changed

You ask another network administrator, who informs you that the only servers that were due for maintenance last night were the DHCP servers, but they were supposed to be put back online by this morning. He says he will check into it and get right back to you. Could that be the problem?

Establish the Most Probable Cause

You reason that if the DHCP servers were not available at the time when the users' computers were trying to renew their leases, then the computers would end up with an APIPA address. You are now convinced that the DHCP servers are to blame and that it will be determined that they were not put back online. You run a quick check from one of the affected computers by typing **ipconfig /renew,** but it is not able to renew its address, further confirming your suspicion.

Determine Whether Escalation Is Necessary

You haven't heard from the other administrator, yet your users are still down. You decide that someone may have "dropped the ball." You need to get those DHCP servers up and running, or you need to assign static addresses to those clients for now. In either case, this will require that you escalate the issue and get some results. You call the senior network administrator and tell her your situation. She checks into it and finds that the DHCP servers are not online as they should be. The team was falling behind and did not fully understand the urgency of the situation. How could they not have understood the importance of a DHCP server?

Create an Action Plan and Solution Identifying Potential Effects

The senior network administrator asks you to send her an email relating the entire situation and how it all transpired since this morning once the problem is resolved. Based on what you say about the situation, the senior network administrator will recommend training for the server administrators regarding the principles of DHCP, the frequency of lease renewals in your organization, and the effects of not having a DHCP server available to the client computers when needed. In the meantime, she will make a few calls and put some fire under those DHCP server technicians!

Implement and Test the Solution

The DHCP server technicians humbly apologize for their mistake and get the DHCP servers back online. You ask the affected users to restart their machines and thereby pick up a new address from the DHCP server. (It's the easiest way to tell them how to do it.) You then ask each of the users to send you a quick email as soon as each is online and functional; then you watch for the emails to flow in. As each of the users sends you an email, you quickly respond and tell them you are sorry about the problem and that plans are in place to keep this from happening again.

Identify the Results and Effects of the Solution

You verify that there are no other computers affected and that the DHCP servers are now back online. As a final test, you renew your own address using the `ipconfig /renew` tool, which functions normally and renews your lease. This proves that the DHCP servers will also work for the client computers when needed.

Document the Solution and the Entire Process

You sit down and write that email to the senior network administrator. You focus it not on who was at fault (everyone makes mistakes) but on documenting the actions and/or inactions in regard to the DHCP server and how quickly it lead to problems for users in your organization. You also document how it was eventually resolved and the final test that you performed to ensure that all was well again. Now you are ready to move on to your next challenge!

Exam Essentials

Know the steps involved in the troubleshooting methodology.   You should know the basic steps involved in this troubleshooting methodology. You should also understand the need for and how to document what was done in each step in the troubleshooting methodology.

Know how to relate the steps to a troubleshooting scenario.   You should be able to relate each of the troubleshooting methodology steps to a scenario and answer questions regarding the importance of each step.

4.7 Given a scenario, troubleshoot common connectivity issues and select an appropriate solution

Today's networks can be much more complex than networks of the past, but the rationale behind them is still the same: to provide connectivity so that users can share information and resources. When connectivity is affected, the users are brought to a standstill, and productivity quickly declines. Because of this, you need to understand the major issues that can affect network connectivity. You can divide these into three main categories: physical issues, logical issues, and wireless issues. In addition, there are other issues that should be identified but will often need to be escalated to a higher level of network authority in a large enterprise network. In the paragraphs that follow, I'll discuss each of these network connectivity issues.

Physical Issues

Because most of today's networks still consist of large amounts of copper cable, most networks can still suffer from the physical issues that have plagued all networks since the very beginning of networking. Newer technologies and protocols have lessened these issues but have not resolved them completely. The physical issues that still affect networks include crosstalk, attenuation, collisions, shorts, open impedance mismatch, and interference. I'll discuss each of these issues.

Crosstalk

As I mentioned in Chapter 2, *crosstalk* is the occurrence of signal bleed between two wires that are carrying a current and are adjacent to each other. Network cable designers minimize crosstalk inside network cables by twisting the wire pairs together, in effect putting them at a 90-degree angle to each other. The tighter the wires are twisted, the less the crosstalk will affect them. Newer cables, such as CAT 6 cable, minimize the effect of crosstalk with a tighter twist, but it still exists and can affect network communications when network speeds are very high.

Near-End Crosstalk

A specific type of crosstalk measurement, referred to as *near-end crosstalk*, is the measure of the electromagnetic interference that a wire bleeds to adjoining wires at the point where the current is first induced into the wire. This is considered to be the strongest potential point for crosstalk, since the crosstalk signal itself can "suffer" from attenuation as it moves down the wire. In other words, if you are going to have a crosstalk issue, it's likely to show up in the first part of wire where it's connected to a switch or a NIC.

Attenuation

As a signal moves through any medium, the medium itself will degrade the signal. This phenomenon is referred to as *attenuation* and is common among all networks. As you might imagine, signals on fiber-optic cable don't attenuate as fast as signals on copper cable, but they still eventually attenuate as well. As I discussed in Chapter 2, you should know that all copper twisted-pair cables have a maximum segment distance of 100 meters before they will need to be amplified, or "repeated," by a hub or a switch. On the other hand, single-mode fiber-optic cables can sometimes carry signals for miles before they suffer from attenuation. The bottom line is that if attenuation is a concern, consider fiber-optic cable.

Collisions

A network *collision* happens when two devices attempt to communicate on the same physical segment at the same time. In early Ethernet networks, collisions were a constant concern, and carrier sense multiple access with collision detection (CSMA/CD) was used to detect and respond to collisions on the network. In today's more modern networks, switches are used to separate the network into multiple collision domains. When only switches are used and all hubs are removed from the network, the switches will learn the MAC addresses of the devices attached to them and thereby create a type of permanent virtual circuit from every device to every other device on the network, thereby eliminating collisions.

Shorts

A *short circuit*, which is sometimes called a *short*, is a situation that allows current to flow on a different path than was originally intended in the circuit. In networks, shorts are typically caused by a physical fault in the cable. They can be detected using circuit-testing equipment. Often, the best and fastest remedy will be to use a different cable until the cable that has the short can be repaired or replaced.

Open Impedance Mismatch

Open impedance is an indication on cable testing equipment that the cable or wires are not completing the circuit that you are testing. If this occurs on only one wire, it's probably because of an improper or damaged connection. If it occurs at the same place on all wires in the same cable, then it's probably an indication that the cable has been accidentally cut at that point. Some testing equipment will also give you the location of the cut, even if it is inside a wall. The most common solution will be to repair the connection or use a different cable.

Logical Issues

In addition to physical issues, there are also many logical issues that plague today's networks. Many of these logical issues are the result of the improper configuration of a device or service. The logical aspects of a network that can affect its performance include port speed, port duplex mismatch, incorrect VLAN, incorrect IP address, wrong gateway, wrong DNS, wrong subnet mask, routing and switching loops, and broadcast storms. In the following sections, I'll discuss each of these logical issues affecting networks.

Port Speed

Since networks have evolved for many years, there are various levels of speed and sophistication mixed into networks, often within the same network. Most of the newest NICs can be used at 10Mbps, 100Mbps, and 1000Mbps. Most switches can support at least 10Mbps and 100Mbps, and an increasing number of switches can also support 1,000Mbps. Most switches can also autosense the speed of the NIC that is connected and use different speeds on various ports. As long as the switches are allowed to autosense the port speed, few problems will generally develop that result in a complete lack of communication. If you decide to set the port speed manually, then you should take care to set the same speed on both sides of a link.

Port Duplex Mismatch

Each port of a network switch generally has three duplex settings: full, half, and auto. For two devices to have an effective connection, the duplex setting must match on both sides of the connection. If one side of a connection is set to full and the other is set to half, the result will be a mismatch. Likewise, if both sides are set to auto but the devices are different and therefore one side defaults to full and the other to half, the result will be a mismatch as well.

Duplex mismatches can cause network errors and even the lack of a network connection. This is partially because setting the interfaces to full duplex disables the CSMA/CD protocol. This is not a problem in a network that has no hubs and therefore no shared segments in which there could be collisions, but it could be a problem in a network where hubs are still being used. Therefore, your settings will be determined based on the equipment in your network. If you have all switches and no hubs, then you can generally set all interfaces to full duplex. On the other hand, if you have hubs, then you have shared networks and will need to keep the settings to half duplex.

Incorrect VLAN

A VLAN is a subnet that is created using ports on a switch. Switches can have multiple VLANs and can be connected to other switches using trunks. Often VLANs are used to represent departments or functions of users. This makes the configurations of security policies and network access lists much easier to manage and control. On the other hand, if a port is accidentally assigned to the wrong VLAN in a switch, it's as if that client were magically transported to another place in the network. The security policies that should apply to it will not, while other policies will apply that should never have applied to that client computer. As you can imagine, the correct VLAN port assignment of a client is essential.

Incorrect IP Address

The most common addressing protocol in use today is IPv4. This protocol provides a unique IP address for each host on a network. Often, client computers obtain their addresses from DHCP servers. In contrast, the network administrator typically statically assigns servers and router interfaces. An incorrect address on a client will keep that client from being able to communicate on the wire and possibly cause a conflict with another client on the network. On the other hand, an incorrect IP address on a server or router interface can potentially affect many users. For this reason, you should set up DHCP servers very carefully and also configure the static addresses assigned to servers and router interfaces very carefully.

Wrong Gateway

A *gateway*, sometimes called a *default gateway* or an *IP default gateway*, is an address of a router interface that is configured into a device to serve as a pointer to forward traffic that has a destination IP address that is not in the same subnet as the device. In other words, if a device compares where a packet wants to go with the network that it is currently on and finds it needs to go to another network, then the device will send that packet to the gateway to be sent out of that network and to the other network. Every device needs a valid gateway to obtain communication outside its own network. Therefore, you should be careful when considering the gateway configuration of devices in a network.

Wrong DNS

Networks and the clients within them commonly use DNS servers to resolve hostnames of computers to IP addresses. They can also facilitate communication on today's modern networks by allowing clients to find the appropriate server to give it the resources it requires, such as a domain controller during the login and authentication process. Often, the DHCP server configures DNS addresses automatically on the client. If a DHCP server is not used, then the DNS server settings must be configured statically along with the IP addressing information. A wrong DNS configuration can result in a computer's network applications failing, since many applications rely on hostname resolution.

Wrong Subnet Mask

Every IP address configuration is actually "viewed" by a network device as a combination of the IP address and the subnet mask. The device uses the subnet mask to determine which portion of the address represents the network address and which portion represents the host address. For this reason, a wrong subnet mask configuration will have the same effect as a wrong IP address configuration. The subnet mask of network clients is generally configured by the DHCP server. If addresses are entered manually, then the subnet mask must also be entered carefully to avoid the misconfiguration of the entire addresses.

Wireless Issues

Wireless networks can be convenient for the user, but they can also require much more configuration for the network administrator. When you decide to use wireless connections on your wired network, you don't substitute one set of challenges for another; instead, you simply add a whole new set of wireless challenges to the wired challenges you already face. Some of these wireless challenges include interference, incorrect encryption, incorrect channel, incorrect frequency, ESSID mismatch, wireless standard mismatch, distance, bounce, and incorrect antenna placement. In the following sections, I'll discuss each of these wireless issues.

Interference

Since wireless networks rely upon radio waves to transmit signals, they are subject to interference from many factors. Other wireless devices (such as Bluetooth keyboards, mice, or cell phones) that are close to their frequency can cause a signal bleed and inhibit or even prevent wireless communication. Even microwave ovens have been known to affect some wireless networks. Other environmental factors, such as the distance between the client and the wireless access point (WAP) as well as the type of construction that is between them, can also affect the power of the intended signal and therefore make any interference from other signals more pronounced. You should take care as to where you place a WAP and be sure that there are no other devices in the area that can cause interference. If the interference is on the client side, you may be able to move the client away from the source of the interference.

Incorrect Encryption

As I discussed in Chapter 2, wireless networks can use encryption to secure the communication between two devices. Many forms of encryption are available for wireless networks, from WEP to WPA2 with AES. To ensure the greatest degree of security, you should configure your wireless networks with the highest encryption protocol that both the WAP and the clients can support. The main point here is that the WAP and the clients must be configured with the same type of encryption. If the WAP requires higher security than the clients are able to provide (or vice versa), then the clients will not be able to communicate with the WAP.

Incorrect Channel

Wireless networks use many different frequencies within a band of frequencies (typically the 2.4GHz or 5GHz band). These frequencies are sometimes combined to provide greater bandwidth for the user. A combination of these frequencies that can be used by the end user is referred to as a *channel*. For the WAP and the clients to communicate, they must be on the same channel. Most often, wireless networks use channels 1, 6, or 11.

Incorrect Frequency

As I stated earlier, setting the channel, in effect, sets the frequency or frequencies that wireless devices will use. It is also possible on some devices to "tweak" those settings and choose a specific frequency. Of course, if you do this on one device, then you must configure the same setting on all the devices that you want to communicate with each other.

ESSID Mismatch

When a wireless device comes up, it will scan for service set identifiers (SSIDs) in its immediate area. These can be basic service set identifiers (BSSIDs), which identify an individual client, or extended service set identifiers (ESSIDs), which identify a WAP. In your own wireless LAN, you will likely want the devices to find the ESSID that you are broadcasting. This is typically not a problem, since your broadcast should be stronger than any neighbors because it is closer. The exception to this rule might be an office building that has many WAPs that are assigned many different ESSIDs because they belong to the various tenants in the building. It is then possible that your neighbor's ESSID broadcast could be stronger than yours, depending on where the clients are in the building. If a user reports that they are connected to a WAP but are still not able to see the resources they need or not able to authenticate to the network, you should verify that they are connected to your ESSID and not your neighbor's. You can generally just look at the information "tool tip" on the wireless software icon to determine this information.

Standard Mismatch

As I discussed in detail in Chapter 2, wireless networks have many standards that have evolved over time, such as 802.11a, 802.11b, 802.11g, and 802.11n. Standards continue to develop that make wireless networks even faster and more powerful. The catch is that some of these standards are backward compatible, while others are not. For example, most devices purchased today can be set to 802.11b/g/n, which means that they can be used to communicate with other devices of all three standards. On the other hand, most devices cannot be configured to be backward compatible to 802.11a, since it used OFDM rather than DSSS. You should take care in setting the type of networks that a device can use and make sure that the standards on the WAP match the standards on the client or at least are backward compatible.

Distance

Two potential problems are associated with the distance of wireless networks: not far enough and too far from the WAP. If the WAPs used do not have the power to provide a connectivity point for the intended clients, you can increase the distance that the WAP can transmit by changing the type of antenna it uses. You might also use multiple WAPs connected to the same switch or set of switches. On the other hand, if the signal is too strong, then it can go out into the parking area or even further out to other buildings and businesses. To prevent this occurrence, you should place the WAPs as close as possible to the center of the area in which they are used. You can also "trim" the signal using special antennas. In addition, you should verify that you have the latest security features to keep imposters from authenticating to and using your network.

Bounce

In a wireless network that spans a large geographical distance, it's possible to install repeaters and reflectors to *bounce* a signal and thereby carry it up to over a kilometer. If this is the intention of the administrator, then it's a good thing. On the other hand, if signal bounce is not tightly controlled, the network could spread well past the original intended boundaries of its creators. You can determine the effects of signal bounce by conducting a thorough wireless site survey.

Incorrect Antenna Placement

As I mentioned earlier, the best place to put a WAP and/or its antenna is close to the center of the planned wireless network. Some antennas can be placed away from the WAP but connected to it with a cable. This would be done if you need the antenna to be in a location that would not be convenient for the WAP.

If you use multiple WAPs, then more sophisticated means may be used to determine where to best place the WAPs. You can use third-party tools, such as AirMagnet, on a laptop or a tablet PC to survey the site and determine how far your WAPs are transmitting. You can also hire a consultant to conduct a survey for you. Many companies specialize in assisting organizations with their wireless networks and with the correct placement of antennas and WAPs. It's important to place the antennas in the correct place, because an incorrect placement can lead to interference and poor performance.

Issues That Should Be Identified and Escalated

Some issues in a network go far beyond the objectives of Network+ certification. These issues are best handled by escalating them to a senior network engineer who has the additional experience and knowledge required to resolve these problems. Some of the issues that should be escalated include switching and routing loops, routing problems, proxy ARP, and broadcast storms. In the following sections, I'll discuss each of these issues.

Switching Loops

Today's networks often connect switches with redundant links to provide for fault tolerance and load balancing. Protocols such as the Spanning Tree Protocol (STP) prevent switching loops while at the same time maintaining the fault tolerance. If the STP should fail, it takes some expertise to reconfigure and repair the network. For this reason, this type of issue should be identified and then escalated.

Routing Loops

Routing protocols are often used on networks to control traffic efficiently while preventing routing loops. In a case where a routing protocol is configured improperly or a change has not been taken into consideration, a routing loop could occur. This could potentially affect the traffic flow for normal users. Also, if network administrators have configured conflicting static routes, the same result can occur. Because of the complexity of these fixes, these issues should be identified first and then escalated to network administrators.

Routing Problems

Routing packets through the many subnets of a large enterprise while still maintaining security can be a tremendous challenge. A router's configuration might include access lists, NAT, PAT, and even authentication protocols. An errant configuration change can potentially trigger a "domino effect" that could cause traffic to take the wrong path or to not be able to traverse the network at all. Because these configurations can be complex and specific to a device, they should be identified and then escalated to the network administrative team leaders.

Proxy ARP

As I discussed earlier, the ARP is a service that resolves IP addresses to MAC addresses. Proxy ARP is a technique by which a host answers ARP queries for network addresses that it does not have configured for itself. This, in effect, fools the network so that it directs all the traffic that would have gone to those hosts to the proxying host instead, effectively "capturing" the traffic. The captured traffic is then typically routed to the destination host via another interface or a tunnel. In this way, an existing network can be extended without the knowledge of the upstream router. As you can see, proxy ARP is a complex topic that is generally used in advanced networks. Therefore, a problem relating to proxy ARP should be escalated to the senior network administrator.

Broadcast Storms

When a switch receives a broadcast, the normal behavior of the switch is to flood the broadcast, sending it to all the ports except for the one on which it came in. If the STP protocol fails between switches, it's possible that the traffic could continue to be flooded repeatedly through the switch topology. If this happens, the network can get so busy that normal traffic will not be able to traverse the network properly. This situation is referred to as a *broadcast storm*. As you can imagine, this is certainly a time to identify the issue and then escalate it!

Exam Essentials

Know when to escalate an issue to a senior network administrator. You should know that there are specific issues that are more encompassing than one device or even one segment of the network. Issues such as switching loops, routing loops, proxy ARP, and broadcast storms must be escalated to the senior network administrators who are responsible for the entire network and can see the bigger picture.

Review Questions

1. Which connectionless protocol works at the Transport layer of the OSI model?
   - **A.** IP
   - **B.** UDP
   - **C.** TCP
   - **D.** ICMP

2. Which layers of the OSI model define 802 standards, such as 802.3? (Choose two.)
   - **A.** Application
   - **B.** Data Link
   - **C.** Physical
   - **D.** Network

3. Which of the following are true regarding a physical network diagram and/or a logical network diagram? (Choose two.)
   - **A.** A physical network diagram is a representation of all the equipment and connections without regard to the traffic flow of the network.
   - **B.** A physical network diagram traces the path that a packet takes within the network.
   - **C.** A logical network diagram includes only cables and connectors, not devices.
   - **D.** A logical network diagram traces the path that a packet takes within a network.

4. Which type of log is typically used with servers to determine what services are available to the users and what resources are being used to provide the services?
   - **A.** History
   - **B.** Event
   - **C.** Resource
   - **D.** System

5. Which of the following refers to the ability to provide different types of traffic flow with different services, based on the type of traffic?
   - **A.** QoS
   - **B.** Load balancing
   - **C.** High availability
   - **D.** Caching engine

6. Which of following terms describes the occurrence of signal bleed between two wires in the same cable?

    A. EMI

    B. Bounce

    C. Attenuation

    D. Crosstalk

7. If you have the right IP address configured but the wrong subnet mask, which of the following is true?

    A. The combination of IP address and subnet mask is wrong because it's not in the right network.

    B. The IP address will function but only within its own subnet and not to other subnets.

    C. The hostname can be used instead of the IP address.

    D. The IP address will function properly because a correct subnet mask is never needed.

8. Which of the following is a broadcast that identifies a WAP?

    A. BSSID

    B. Ad hoc

    C. Bounce

    D. ESSID

9. Which of the following wireless standards are backward compatible with 802.11b? (Choose two.)

    A. 802.11a

    B. 802.11g

    C. 802.11n

    D. 802.11c

10. Which of the following is a type of problem that should be escalated to senior network administrators? (Choose two.)

    A. Incorrect IP address assignment

    B. Routing loop

    C. Incorrect wireless channel

    D. Proxy ARP

Answers to Review Questions

1. B. User Datagram Protocol (UDP) is a connectionless protocol that works at the Transport layer of the OSI model. IP is connectionless, but it works at the Network layer. TCP works at the Transport layer, but it is connection oriented. ICMP works at the Network layer and not the Transport layer.

2. B, C. Standards such as 802.3 and 802.11 are defined at the Physical layer of the OSI model.

3. A, D. A physical network diagram shows the devices, cables, and connections in a network without regard to the path that the packet takes when traversing a network. A logical network diagram traces the path that a packet takes through a network.

4. D. System logs are used to determine what services are available to users and what resources are being used to provide them. History logs keep a record of events that the administrator can review later. Resource logs focus on the four main resources: processor, memory, disk, and network. System logs keep a record of network services such as DNS and DHCP.

5. A. Quality of service (QoS) provides specific types of traffic with specific types of service and bandwidth through a network, based on the type of traffic and its needs. For example, voice and video applications can be configured for a QoS and thus be allowed to traverse the network when other traffic may not. This frees up the bandwidth for the applications that need it most. Load balancing is making more efficient use of multiple devices or services by dividing the work or traffic between them. High availability is the concept that the network must be available to the users for a predefined percentage of time. A caching engine is a service that keeps the resources that were required to perform a task close to the user so that the same task can be performed more quickly the next time and subsequent times.

6. D. The occurrence of signal bleed between two wires in the same cable is crosstalk. This is prevented by twisting the wires pairs together inside the cable. EMI is electromagnetic interference from an external source, such as an electric motor or a fluorescent light ballast. Bounce is a property of electricity that will cause it to turn around and come back down a wire it has traversed, if it is not absorbed in some manner. Attenuation is the degradation of signal because of the medium itself.

7. A. A network address is viewed by a network device as a combination of the IP address and the subnet mask. For this reason, a wrong subnet mask will have the same effect as a wrong IP address because the network address will be wrong.

8. D. A wireless access point (WAP) broadcasts an ESSID, which identifies that access point. It's important that your clients access your ESSID. A BSSID is a basic set ID that generally identifies another wireless computer. Ad hoc is a mode of wireless communication between two wireless devices without using a WAP. Bounce is a property of a wireless signal that causes it to be reflected off physical objects.

9. B, C. Both 802.11g and 802.11n are backward compatible with 802.11b. Conversely, 802.11a is not compatible with 802.11b. 802.11c is part of a bridging standard for wireless communication and is not an active network standard.

10. B, D. Some issues affect the entire network and should therefore be escalated to senior network administrators. Two of these include routing loops and proxy ARP. Others include switching loops and broadcast storms.

Chapter

5

Domain 5
Network Tools

COMPTIA NETWORK+ EXAM OBJECTIVES COVERED IN THIS CHAPTER:

✓ **5.1 Given a scenario, select the appropriate command line interface tool and interpret the output to verify functionality**

- Traceroute
- Ipconfig
- Ifconfig
- Ping
- Arp Ping
- Arp
- Nslookup
- Hostname
- Dig
- Mtr
- Route
- Nbtstat
- Netstat

✓ **5.2 Explain the purpose of network scanners**

- Packet sniffers
- Intrusion detection software
- Intrusion prevention software
- Port scanners

✓ 5.3 Given a scenario, utilize the appropriate hardware tools

- Cable testers
- Protocol analyzer
- Certifiers
- TDR
- OTDR
- Multimeter
- Toner probe
- Butt set
- Punch down tool
- Cable stripper
- Snips
- Voltage event recorder
- Temperature monitor

5.1 Given a scenario, select the appropriate command line interface tool and interpret the output to verify functionality

Many troubleshooting utilities are built into the most popular operating systems. Most of these utilities are based on the command line and are not obvious to the end user. As a network administrator, your knowledge of the existence and proper use of these tools will set you apart from your peers. In the following sections, I will discuss and illustrate the proper use of the most common troubleshooting utilities.

Traceroute

Suppose that you use the ping tool (which I will discuss in detail later in this chapter) and find that you have a problem with connectivity in your network. Now let's suppose that your network is a complex configuration of switches and that routers carry information to all the hosts within it. Furthermore, suppose that the computer you are pinging is located on the other side of your network and that you have to transmit through multiple routers to get to the subnet of the destination computer. If you do not get a reply, then how could you possibly know where the communication is breaking down? The answer is that you cannot — at least not with the ping tool.

The *traceroute* tool (also called the *tracert* tool) is a network utility that uses ICMP to create a list of routers through which a packet is transmitted. Using the traceroute tool, you can determine not only that the connection cannot be made to a computer but also which router could not forward the packet to the next subnet. In other words, you can isolate a network failure to a specific location in your network.

The terms traceroute and tracert are sometimes used interchangeably, but they are not actually the same; traceroute is the generic term for this type of tool, which can be used by Novell, Cisco, and other types of TCP/IP hosts, while tracert is specific to Microsoft clients and servers in a TCP/IP network.

You initiate the tracert tool on a Microsoft client by typing **tracert** at the command prompt followed by a space and then the IP address or hostname of the computer to which you want to test connectivity. You can find a complete list of tracert commands by typing **tracert /?**, as shown in Figure 5.1.

FIGURE 5.1   The tracert tool

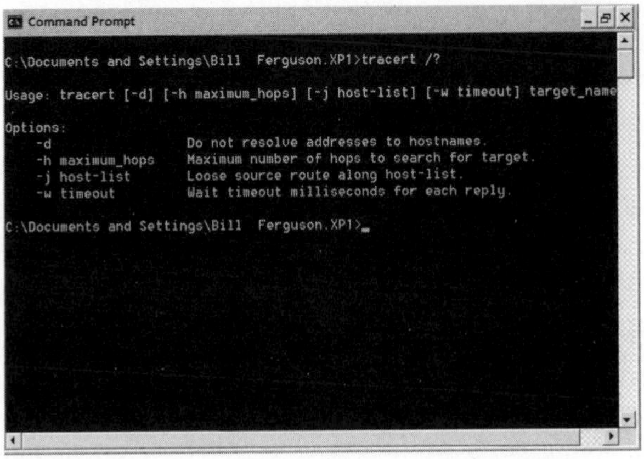

For example, if you wanted to perform a tracert to mct.billfergusonv.net, you could type the following at the command prompt:

tracert mct.billfergusonv.net

The tracert tool sends echo request packets much like the ping tool, but it makes an important change in each of the packets. This change affects the *time to live* (TTL) of the packet, which is the number of hops it can take through a network before it is discarded by a network device.

In a normal ping request from a Microsoft client, each echo request packet has a TTL of 128. This means it can bounce around a network until it has gone through 128 router interfaces (sometimes through the same interfaces many times) before it is discarded. The reason that packets have a TTL is so that they can be discarded by the network in the event they cannot be delivered.

Each router decrements the TTL as it forwards the packet. If the result of decrementing the TTL is that the TTL is reduced to a value of 0, then the router is responsible for discarding the packet and sending a message back to the network identifying itself by its IP address and noting that it has discarded the packet. The tracert tool uses this fact to gather information about the route the packets are taking through the network, as shown in Figure 5.2.

FIGURE 5.2   A tracert example

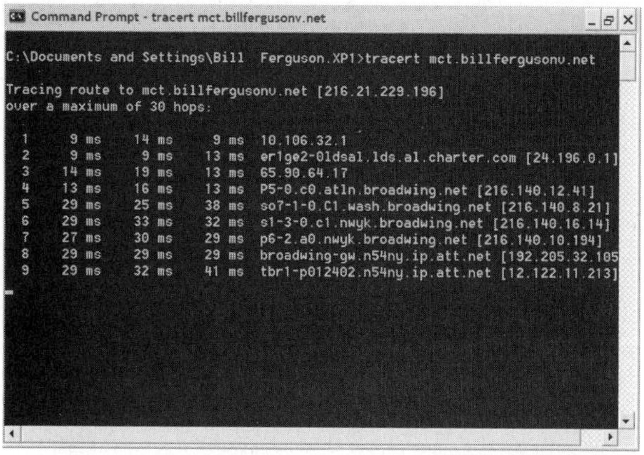

```
Command Prompt - tracert mct.billfergusonv.net                          _ 🗗 ×

C:\Documents and Settings\Bill  Ferguson.XP1>tracert mct.billfergusonv.net

Tracing route to mct.billfergusonv.net [216.21.229.196]
over a maximum of 30 hops:

  1      9 ms     14 ms      9 ms   10.106.32.1
  2      9 ms      9 ms     13 ms   er1ge2-0ldsa1.lds.a1.charter.com [24.196.0.1]
  3     14 ms     19 ms     13 ms   65.90.64.17
  4     13 ms     16 ms     13 ms   P5-0.c0.atln.broadwing.net [216.140.12.41]
  5     29 ms     25 ms     38 ms   so7-1-0.C1.wash.broadwing.net [216.140.8.21]
  6     29 ms     33 ms     32 ms   s1-3-0.c1.nwyk.broadwing.net [216.140.16.14]
  7     27 ms     30 ms     29 ms   p6-2.a0.nwyk.broadwing.net [216.140.10.194]
  8     29 ms     29 ms     29 ms   broadwing-gw.n54ny.ip.att.net [192.205.32.105
  9     29 ms     32 ms     41 ms   tbr1-p012402.n54ny.ip.att.net [12.122.11.213]
```

When you initiate the tracert request, an echo request packet is first sent out with a TTL value of 1. This means that the first router it encounters will discard it and send a message back through the network indicating that it has done so. The message that the router sends back is recorded as the first hop that the packet has to take through the network. The time (in milliseconds) that elapses between sending the packets and the message returning is also recorded. After this is done, the tracert tool automatically sends out a new packet with the TTL value of 2. The first router simply processes the packet normally, decrementing the TTL to 1 and forwarding it to the next router. The second router, however, discards the packet and sends a message back through the network identifying itself by its IP address. This becomes the second hop on the tracert report. This process continues until all the hops between the local computer and the destination host are listed or one of the routers fails to reply. If a router fails to reply, then you have isolated the source of your problem.

As you may have guessed, the best scenario in which to use the traceroute utility is when you are troubleshooting a connectivity problem that must be followed through multiple routers. You would likely use the ping tool first to establish connectivity (or in this case the lack thereof) and then use the traceroute tool to isolate the problem. In addition, since the traceroute tool records statistics about the time that routers take to forward packets, it can also assist you in discovering network weaknesses before they become a major problem. In other words, if the times seem unusually high, then you might want to take a closer look at the routers or the interfaces with longer times. Routes that have the longer time are said to have a higher *latency*. One of the jobs of a network administrator is to control traffic to create low latency.

Ipconfig/Ifconfig

The *ipconfig* tool displays network configuration values and refreshes addresses configured by DHCP servers on Microsoft computers. You can also use it for a wide range of other troubleshooting scenarios. The *ifconfig* tool is the same sort of command that is used by Unix and Linux systems. You should know the purpose and main functionality of both of these commands, which I'll cover in the following two sections.

Ipconfig

When you type **ipconfig** at the command line without any switches, or *options*, it displays the IP address, subnet mask, and default gateway of all the network adapters on a computer. You can use it as a very quick method of verifying a basic IP configuration. By adding switches, you can get much more information about the configuration, and you can control other network parameters such as the DNS resolver cache on a computer. In addition, you can release and renew IP addresses that are assigned by a DHCP server provided that the computer is configured to obtain an IP address automatically. Table 5.1 shows the additional options available when you type **ipconfig** and what each one enables you to do.

TABLE 5.1   Common Ipconfig Commands

Ipconfig Option	Purpose
ipconfig /all	Displays the full TCP/IP configuration for all adapters. (Adapters include physical interfaces as well as dial-up connections.)
ipconfig /renew	Releases and renews the IP address on an adapter. (The computer must be configured to obtain an IP address automatically.)
ipconfig /release	Releases an IP address that was obtained automatically but does not renew an address. This is a useful tool when moving a computer from one subnet to another.
ipconfig /flushdns	Flushes the DNS client resolver cache. This can be a useful tool when you're troubleshooting name resolution problems.
ipconfig /displaydns	Displays the contents of the DNS client resolver cache. It includes entries that are preloaded from the Hosts file as well as recently obtained resource records.
ipconfig / registerdns	Initiates manual dynamic registration for the DNS names and IP addresses that are configured on a computer. It's especially useful when troubleshooting DNS name resolution problems.
ipconfig /showclassid	Shows special DHCP server configuration options on the client when it is configured. This tells the DHCP server to give the client a different set of options based on its class.

TABLE 5.1 Common Ipconfig Commands *(continued)*

Ipconfig Option	Purpose
ipconfig /setclassid	Used to configure the class of a client so as to match the configured classes in a DHCP server. This ensures that the client will receive the appropriate options from the DHCP server based on its class.
ipconfig /?	Displays help and syntax for the command.

Ifconfig

The ifconfig tool is used in Unix and Linux operating systems to configure interfaces and view information about configured interfaces. The syntax of the ifconfig tool is very different from ipconfig, as shown in Figure 5.3. You will be glad to know that you will not have to memorize the syntax of the ifconfig tool, but you should know the general uses of the command. You can find information about the entire syntax and use of the ifconfig tool on the Web at www.linux.com.

FIGURE 5.3 The ipconfig tool

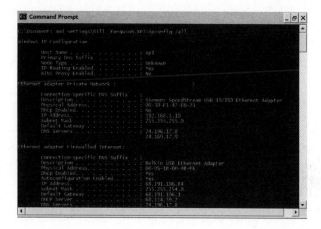

Ping

The *ping* tool, which stands for Packet Internet Name Groper, is one of the most common utilities used by network administrators. It is primarily used to establish general network connectivity, but it can also be used to test name resolution in a network. The ping tool includes switches that allow you to customize your test. You should know how the ping tool operates and its most common uses in network troubleshooting.

You initiate a ping request simply by typing the word **ping** at a command prompt followed by a space and then the IP address or hostname of the host to which you would like to test connectivity. You can also use many options in ping to make a request more specific, as shown in Figure 5.4.

FIGURE 5.4   The ping tool

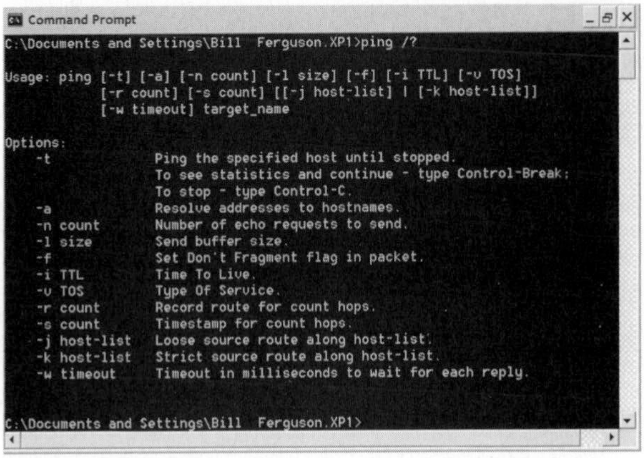

For example, to ping a host with the IP address of 192.168.1.105, type the following at the command prompt:

ping 192.168.1.105

Similarly, to ping a host with the hostname of xpclient, type the following at the command prompt:

ping xpclient

When you ping a host from a system using a Microsoft client, four packets are transmitted onto the wire with the destination address that you specified. These are referred to as *echo request packets*. When the host identified by the destination address receives the packets, it will reply with special packets called *echo reply packets*. When the computer from which you are initiating the ping request receives the echo reply packets, this establishes that there is general network connectivity between the two computers. An error message such as "destination host unreachable" or "request timed out" indicates that there is no connectivity between your computer and the other computer.

If you want to establish only general network connectivity, then you should ping the IP address of the host on the network. To take the ping tool a step further, you can also ping the hostname of the client instead of just the IP address. For a ping request with a hostname to be interpreted by the network, the hostname must be resolved to an IP address by a name resolution mechanism such as DNS or WINS. After the hostname is resolved to an IP address, then the packets can be delivered to the computer with that IP address. In this way, pinging the hostname of a computer on the network will test both your name resolution systems as well as the general connectivity of the computer to the network.

Now let's put this into practice. Suppose you have a troubleshooting scenario whereby a client cannot connect to a server using a specific application, for instance, an email application such as Microsoft Outlook. Since the essence of all troubleshooting is isolation, you might first want to make sure the client has general connectivity to the server. By successfully pinging the IP address of the server from the client that is having the problem, you can eliminate the possibility that the problem is of a physical nature, such as wiring, cable connections, and so on. You will also eliminate the possibility that the IP address of the client is not configured properly. On the other hand, if you do not get a reply, then you will know that the problem is either of a physical nature or due to an improper configuration, and therefore it probably has little to do with Outlook.

To take the test a little further, you could also ping the hostname of the server from the client that is having the problem. If you received a reply when you pinged the IP address but you do not receive a reply when you ping the hostname, then the problem is likely related to name resolution. This test does not completely solve your problem, but it's a first step that does make sure you are setting off in the right direction to solve it. To customize your ping request, you can use the switches provided with the tool. The switches give you the option to send a set number of packets, a continuous ping, and so on. To see a list of the all the switches, type the following at the command prompt:

`ping /?`

Arp Ping

Address resolution protocol ping (arp ping) is another tool that you can use to test connectivity to a host. You can use it on an IPv4 network to ping hosts by using the ARP protocol (discussed next) rather than the ICMP protocol used by a conventional ping. IPv4 devices must respond to ARP packets and may be reachable even when personal firewalls are in place to prevent ICMP packets from reaching a host. However, since ARP is a broadcast protocol, it can be used to test connectivity only to computers that are on the same subnet as the computer on which the tool is being used.

Arp

Arp is a service that works in the background and resolves IP addresses to MAC addresses so that packets can be delivered to their destination. As you may recall, each computer keeps an *arp cache* of entries that have been recently resolved (within the past 10 minutes). First the computer checks the arp cache; then, if the entry is not in the cache, arp will be used to broadcast into the local network and request that the computer with a specific IP address respond with its MAC address so that the packet can be addressed and delivered.

Since the packets cannot be delivered until the MAC address is discovered, arp is a crucial component in the system. Because of this, you should know how to identify problems that might be caused by an errant arp cache. In addition, you should know how to troubleshoot the arp cache when necessary.

You can access the arp tool and the syntax for its use by typing the following at a command prompt:

arp /?

The two general types of entries found in an arp cache are dynamic and static, as shown in Figure 5.5. Your knowledge of both types of entries is essential to understanding how arp operates and therefore how to troubleshoot it. You should be able to distinguish between dynamic and static entries in an arp cache. Static entries are indicated with an s, whereas dynamic entries are indicated with a d.

FIGURE 5.5   The arp tool

Dynamic entries are automatically added to the cache when arp is used to resolve an IP address to a MAC address. The lifetime of these entries varies between operating systems but is generally no more than about 10 minutes, unless they are used within the 10 minutes, in which case the clock starts again. Dynamic entries typically do not cause problems. They are clearly marked as dynamic.

Static entries, on the other hand, are very different from dynamic entries. Static entries must be added by an administrator and, once added, become a permanent entry in the cache unless they are deleted. For example, if you wanted to add a static entry to an arp cache for a computer with an IP address of 192.168.1.10 and a MAC address of 00-aa-00-62-c6-09, you would type the following at the command prompt:

arp -s 192.168.1.10   00-aa-00-62-c6-09   *Added*

Now, before you start adding static entries to all your computers, I'll discuss the advantages and disadvantages of static entries. There is only one reason to add a static entry to an arp cache: faster IP to MAC address resolution between two computers on the same network. Adding a static entry might increase performance, but this is very doubtful on today's modern networks. In addition, adding a static entry to resolve an IP address to a MAC address does not affect the name resolution time to resolve the hostname to an IP address, which usually must occur first.

Although the advantages of adding a static entry are ambiguous, the disadvantages are very real. Adding a static entry to an arp cache ties a specific MAC address to a specific IP address. This might be fine as long as you don't change the NIC on the computer identifying the entry. If the NIC should fail and be replaced by another NIC, the static entry for the IP address will override the dynamic entry that would otherwise be created in the cache. In other words, since the IP address of the computer will already be listed in the static entry, another IP address and MAC address (the dynamic entry) will not be added. Of course, the new NIC would have a different MAC address, so the arp cache would be incorrect. Consequently, computers with the static entry would not be able to communicate with the computer containing the new NIC.

To troubleshoot the problem, you should remove the static entry from the arp cache. You can remove the static entry for the previous example by typing the following at a command prompt:

`arp -d 192.168.1.10     00-aa-00-62-c6-09`

You can also use a wildcard (*) in place of the IP address and MAC address to delete all hosts from the arp cache.

Nslookup

DNS is an essential component in most networks. This is especially true if you are using Windows 2000 Server or Windows Server 2003 with Active Directory. The *nslookup* utility allows you to troubleshoot problems related to DNS. You can use nslookup to research information about a DNS server or to set a DNS configuration on the server. You can use nslookup in either noninteractive or interactive mode. You should know the difference between these two methods of use.

To use nslookup in noninteractive mode, simply type the command that you want to initiate. At the command prompt, you can enter interactive mode to determine what to type. To do this, type **nslookup,** press Enter, and then type **?** to see a list of all the commands you can execute. Determine the command you want to use, and then type **exit** to get out of interactive mode. You can use many commands with nslookup. It's not necessary that you know all of them (thank goodness!), but you should know that they all relate to hostname resolution in one way or another and that the tool is generally used on large domain-based networks.

To use nslookup in interactive mode, type **nslookup,** and then press Enter. You can then execute multiple nslookup queries and commands from within the nslookup utility. To exit the utility, simply type **exit.** The commands in interactive mode are the same as those in noninteractive mode, except that you don't have to type **nslookup** before each command. Figure 5.6 shows the nslookup tool in interactive mode.

FIGURE 5.6   The nslookup tool in interactive mode

Hostname

If you are troubleshooting connectivity between two hosts, then you had best know two things: the name of the host to which you are attempting to connect and the name of the host on which you are making the attempt. If you are already at a command prompt, the fastest way to determine the name of the host to which you are connected is to type **hostname** at the prompt. This action will then "promptly" return the hostname of the computer to which you are connected. Figure 5.7 shows the hostname prompt.

FIGURE 5.7   The hostname tool

Dig

Domain Information Groper (Dig) is a flexible tool for interrogating DNS servers. Some administrators choose Dig over nslookup because of its ease of use and clarity of output. It can be used with all forms of DNS servers including Microsoft, Linux, and even legacy Berkeley Internet Name Daemon (BIND) servers. You can begin to use dig by typing **dig** on the command line. To get more information about dig, type **dig /?**.

Mtr

My tracert (mtr) is a command-line tool that combines the functionality of traceroute and ping into one tool. Some network administrators prefer mtr over tracert for troubleshooting networks. Like tracert, the mtr tool manipulates the TTL of the packets and then records the information provided by the routers. The output of mtr can provide the administrator with information such as the routers that were traversed along the path, the average round-trip time for the packets, and the packet loss on each router in the path. In this way, it can assist the administrator in finding the links that are causing network utilization problems. You can begin using the mtr command by simply typing **mtr** on the command line. To get additional information about mtr, type **mtr /?**.

Route

You can use the *route* tool on Windows and clients to set up static routes on the client itself. By building a table in the client device, it will, in effect, be a router for some traffic that it receives. This might be useful if the device is also being used to provide access to a cable modem or DSL router that has a connection to the Internet. You can view what is in the table by typing `route print` on the command line, as shown in Figure 5.8. You can also add or delete routes from the table using the switches provided. Table 5.2 shows the most common switches used with the route tool.

TABLE 5.2   Common Route Options

Route Option	Display
route print	Displays the current routes known by the client including the local loopback and broadcast
route add	Can be used to add a route to the existing table if needed
route change	Can be used to change an existing route when needed
route delete	Can be used to permanently delete a route from the table when no longer needed
route /?	Displays route help to see more detailed information and syntax

FIGURE 5.8 The route tool

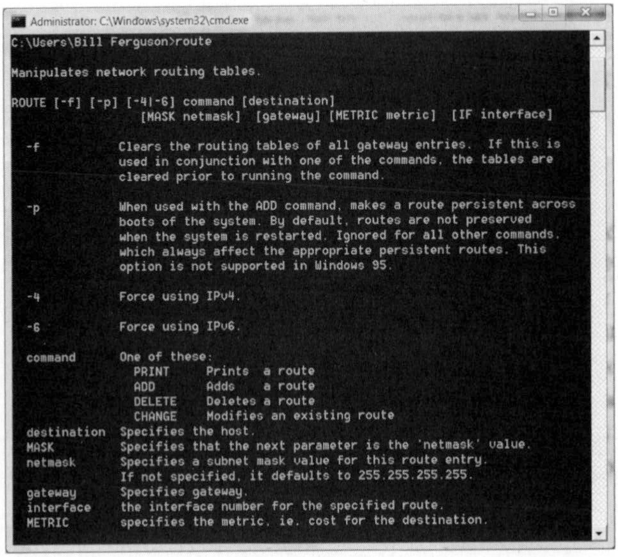

Nbtstat

NetBIOS over TCP/IP (NetBT) resolves NetBIOS names to IP addresses. TCP/IP provides many options for NetBIOS name resolution, including cache lookup, WINS server query, broadcast, DNS server query, and Lmhosts and Hosts file lookup. Since name resolution can become very complex, you need a tool that can assist you in sorting out what is working and what is not working. The *nbtstat* utility lets you troubleshoot name resolution problems. In addition, you can use this tool to remove or correct a preloaded entry in the NetBIOS name cache.

The nbtstat utility has a fairly complex syntax that allows you to customize a query. You can also keep it simple and just use the beginning of the syntax to obtain a broader range of output. You can view the syntax of nbtstat and the options available by simply typing **nbtstat** at a command prompt and pressing Enter. Table 5.3 lists the most common options used with nbtstat.

TABLE 5.3 Common Nbtstat Options

Nbtstat Option	Display
nbtstat -n	Displays names registered locally by the system
nbtstat -c	Displays NetBIOS name cache entries
nbtstat -R	Purges the NetBIOS name cache and reloads it from the Lmhosts file

TABLE 5.3 Common Nbstat Options *(continued)*

Nbtstat Option	Display
nbtstat –RR	Releases NetBIOS names registered with the WINS server and then renews their registration
nbtstat – a *name*	Performs a NetBIOS adapter status command against the computer specified by *name* and displays the local NetBIOS name table for the computer and the MAC address of the computer
nbtstat –S	Lists the current NetBIOS sessions and their status, including statistics

Netstat

Suppose that you are troubleshooting an application for a user and you know the application uses a specific protocol and therefore a specific port or ports, for example, FTP and ports 20 and 21. If the user's computer is having a problem running the application, you might want to make sure that computer is active and listening on the appropriate ports. This is the type of scenario that might require your use of the *netstat* tool.

You can use the netstat tool to display protocol statistics and current TCP/IP connections, as shown in Figure 5.9. The netstat tool has many options that you can use to customize the output for your situation. Table 5.4 lists the options available in netstat and the general function of each option. You can list the syntax and all the options by typing the following at the command prompt:

netstat /?

When you use it with no options, netstat simply displays active TCP/IP connections.

FIGURE 5.9 The netstat tool

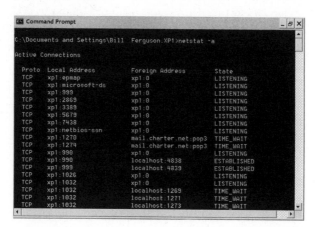

TABLE 5.4   Common Netstat Options

Netstat Option	Display
netstat -a	Displays all connections
netstat -r	Creates a routing table of the computer and all active connections
netstat -o	Processes IDs so you can view the owner of the port for each connection
netstat -e	Displays Ethernet statistics, such as packet discards and errors
netstat - s	Displays per-protocol statistics, such as detailed TCP and UDP statistics
netstat -n	Does not convert addresses and port numbers to names but instead shows them as IP addresses

Exam Essentials

Know when to use the ping tool.   The ping tool is one of the most commonly used of all network tools. It is typically used to verify physical network connectivity between computers but can also be used to test name resolution by pinging the hostname of a computer instead of the IP address.

Know when to use the tracert (traceroute) tool.   Tracert (also referred to as traceroute) is typically used to determine more information about a network problem after a ping was unsuccessful. This utility manipulates the TTL of the packets that it sends onto the network so as to force each of the routers to send its identity when it discards the packet. You can use the tracert tool to isolate a network failure to a specific interface on a router.

Know when to use the arp tool.   The arp tool is primarily used to modify the arp cache, which is used to resolve IP addresses to MAC addresses. There are two types of arp entries: dynamic and static. Dynamic entries are much less likely to cause a problem than static entries. Changing a NIC on a computer for which other computers have a static arp entry can cause the computer to be unavailable on the network.

Know when to use the netstat tool.   The netstat tool displays protocol statistics for active and listening ports. It can be used to determine whether an application is failing because the ports that it requires are not functional. The netstat utility has many options (switches) that enable you to customize a query.

Know when to use the nbtstat tool.   The nbtstat tool displays information about the NetBIOS name cache, which is a factor in NetBIOS name resolution. You can use the nbtstat tool to troubleshoot name resolution problems by displaying information as well as by clearing invalid information from the cache. You should be able to list the most common options for the nbtstat command.

Know when to use ipconfig/ifconfig.   Ipconfig and ifconfig enable you to view information about interfaces and to configure interfaces. The ipconfig tool is used on Microsoft systems, whereas the ifconfig tool is used on Unix and Linux systems. Be familiar with the most common options used with these commands.

Know when to use the nslookup tool.   You can use nslookup to troubleshoot hostname resolution. You can use this utility in either noninteractive or interactive mode. The nslookup tool would most likely be used to troubleshoot name resolution in a large domain-based network.

5.2 Explain the purpose of network scanners

A network scanner in the hands of a competent administrator is a powerful tool that can be used to analyze network traffic at the packet level. In other words, it can be used to look inside the packet and observe the detailed information that it contains. This could include information in the header of the packet, such as the source IP address, destination IP address, protocol, and port, or it could include even more detailed information such as the data that the packet contains. A network administrator can use many different types of network scanners to monitor and control network traffic. Some of these types include packet sniffers, intrusion detection software, intrusion prevention software, and port scanners. I will discuss each of these types of network scanners in the following sections.

Packet Sniffers

As I discussed in Chapter 4, "Domain 4 Network Management," a *packet sniffer* is like a powerful electron microscope for network traffic. It allows the network administrator to examine the information within the packets carefully and thereby make more informed decisions about the network. For example, an administrator may use a packet sniffer to find a failing network interface card that is putting out a constant stream of data onto the network, sometimes referred to as a *chatty NIC*. The administrator would be able to find the specific

NIC based on the source MAC address, which could be found in the packet sniffer's output for each packet. This is only a small example of how you might use a packet sniffer. Other uses include scanning the network for protocols, getting the IP source and destination addresses, and even examining the data itself, provided that it is not encrypted.

Windows clients and servers include Network Monitor, which is a very basic packet sniffer. In addition, many third parties have developed sophisticated packet sniffers that also can perform other network tests such as connectivity tests, load tests, and throughput tests. These products use both hardware and software to analyze the network performance and make recommendations for improvement. Companies such as Fluke Networks (www.fluke.com) specialize in equipment and software to test and evaluate networks.

Intrusion Detection Software

As I mentioned in Chapter 3, "Domain 3 Network Devices," *intrusion detection software* (IDS) enables you to monitor network traffic and look for anomalies in the traffic. The IDS knows what to look for in the network in two main ways. Either the software is updated by the vendor with the latest attack signatures (much like with antivirus software) or the software "listens" to your network, learns the normal patterns, and looks for anything out of the ordinary. Most software allows you to set a combination of the two methods so you can begin using it with signatures and then let it become even more effective as it learns your specific network. In either case, IDS will not take any action on its own except to notify the administrator by text, by email, or even by phone.

Intrusion Prevention Software

Sometimes IDS also functions as *intrusion prevention software* (IPS). The main difference is that IPS will take some action such as resetting connections or even closing ports if necessary. IPS will rarely be set to launch a counterattack of any kind but will do only what is necessary to defend the network and the hosts within it. Often, the only difference between setting up IDS and IPS is the different configuration options.

 IDS/IPS systems can be network-based (NIDS) or host-based (HIDS) and generally use multiple sensors, a console for monitoring, and a central engine the records the events and may take action if configured for IPS.

Port Scanners

Port scanners are software programs that are specially designed to search for and analyze traffic on open ports of a network host. You can use one to verify the security of your network. Attackers, on the other hand, can use it to compromise your system. You can scan one device to determine what ports are listening on it and what protocols and IP addresses are being used, known as a *portscan*, or you can use multiple devices at the same time for a specific listening port or group of listening ports, addresses, or protocols, referred to as a *portsweep.* Many third-party port scanners are available on the Web, including NMAP, SuperScan, and PacketTrap, just to name a few. Figure 5.10 shows some common output from the SuperScan software.

FIGURE 5.10   The SuperScan software

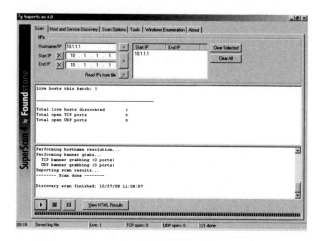

Exam Essentials

Know the purpose and use of a packet sniffer.   You should understand that packet sniffers are used to see inside packets flowing through the network or into a device. This assists the administrator in making more informed decisions about the network. Windows servers and clients have a very basic packet sniffer called Network Monitor. You can also purchase or download many other third-party packet sniffers.

Know the purpose of IDS/IPS and the difference between them.   You should know that IDS/IPS can monitor the traffic on the network and look for anything unusual that might be an attack or cause problems on the network. The latest attack signatures should be installed to ensure network protection continuously remains up-to-date. The software can also learn the normal patterns of your network and then alert the administrator or even take action to prevent damage during an attack. The main difference between IDS and IPS is that IDS will only monitor the traffic and report it to the administrator; whereas IPS can actually reset connections or even close ports when necessary. Most software actually functions as both IDS and IPS, and the main differences between the two are generally the different configuration options.

Know the purpose of a port scanner.   You should understand that a port scanner is a software program that is designed to search for and analyze active ports on a network host. It can be set to detect protocols, IP address ranges, and other network-related information and create a report for the administrator. You can you use port scanner software to test the security of a single system or to sweep an entire network to determine security vulnerabilities.

5.3 Given a scenario, utilize the appropriate hardware tools

Some aspects of network maintenance and troubleshooting require that you get out there with some hardware and do a little manual labor. The term *manual* is actually a stretch here because most of the hardware tools that you will use for your network are actually very sophisticated in themselves and don't require much muscle to use. In fact, many of these tools include both software and hardware components. In the following sections, I will discuss the most common of these hardware tools.

Cable Testers

If you buy a patch cable that is made by an official vendor, there is a very good chance it will be pinned correctly and that the connectors will be securely crimped. On the other hand, if you inherit a patch cable that was made in the field by some other technician, you may not be so lucky. If you cannot make a connection from one device to another and you suspect the cable, the best thing to do for the immediate fix is to try another cable. If the new cable works, then the other cable was probably faulty, but maybe it just wasn't created properly in the first place. Before you throw it way or begin to repair it, you may want to use a cable tester to find out whether there is anything wrong with it and, if there is, on which wire or wires the problem is located. A *cable tester* is a tool with which you connect both ends of the cable to test its connectivity on each of its wires. There are many different types of cable testers and they vary greatly in design, but most use lights or LCD screens to indicate the connectivity through the cable. They can be very useful when you need to decide whether to continue to use, replace, fix, or discard a cable.

Protocol Analyzer

When you first look at the term *protocol analyzer,* you probably think about software and not hardware. In fact, some vendors refer to their packet sniffers as protocol analyzers. However, in its hardware interpretation, a protocol analyzer is a specialized piece of hardware that is made to be carried around to various areas of the network and get information about the traffic in that area. Since the protocol analyzer can be physically moved to the network it will analyze, it can get the most accurate and reliable information possible.

At first glance, a protocol analyzer might look very much like a laptop, but if you look closer, you might see a difference in the keyboard as well as the types of connecting ports on it. You might also notice a more rugged design. Companies such as Network Instruments and MetricTest specialize in this type of product.

Certifiers

With today's modern networks, it's often not good enough just to say that something works and therefore it's set up properly. As I discussed in Chapter 2, "Domain 2 Network Media and Topologies," there are specifications associated with every type of network media. For example, if you install CAT 6 cable, then you expect that it will provide 1000Mbps bandwidth for your data. But the only way that it will do this is if all the wall jacks, patch panels, connectors, and so forth, are installed properly. You could just let the users be the guinea pigs and test it all for you, but the right way is to make sure it's working properly by using a device that can test the network segment to which it's attached and compare the result with what it should be for that type of segment. This device is called a *certifier*. Many different types of certifiers exist, and they are available for copper, fiber, and even wireless networks. Some devices even combine certain aspects of all three types of networks.

TDR

A *time domain reflectometer* (TDR), as its name implies, is a pretty sophisticated piece of network-troubleshooting equipment. It sends a low-level electromagnetic pulse and listens for any reflection of that pulse (similar to radar). In fact, it's like radar for finding breaks or even weaknesses (bad splices or connections) in copper network cables. If you are troubleshooting a problem with a copper cable, a TDR can tell you exactly how far the problem is from where you are testing. That way, if the wire is buried or is in a wall, you will know that you should probably just try to use a different cable (if one is available). On the other hand, if the problem is accessible, then you may be able to fix it. Either way, knowing exactly where the problem exists is half the battle.

OTDR

If a TDR can be called sophisticated, then an *optical time domain reflectometer* (OTDR) is positively out of the space age! An OTDR performs the same function as a TDR but does it with light on fiber-optic cables. Whereas most of the cables that you test with a TDR will be shorter than 100 meters long, you can test cables that are several kilometers long with an OTDR. An OTDR can also detect the fiber cable length and therefore tell you exactly where a break is in the fiber. It can also make you aware of bad splices or connections along the entire route of the fiber cable. For these reasons, OTDRs are an indispensable tool for working with today's long and sophisticated fiber-optic cable runs.

Multimeter

Now that I have discussed the expensive and sophisticated tools, let's return to the basics while using a little ingenuity as well. You can test the continuity of the wires in a cable and determine whether there is current on the wire with a plain old multimeter. Actually, there was a day when a multimeter was as fancy a tool as there was, because we used a different tool to check continuity than we did voltage. Now a multimeter is a staple tool for anyone who is involved in networking or electronics of any kind.

Most of today's mulitmeters can provide you with a digital readout of a myriad of tests, including continuity, resistance, voltage, current, and so on. You simply set the multimeter for what you need. Some troubleshooting might require taking two measurements, one of known good connectivity and the other of what you are troubleshooting and then comparing the two. It might not be as automatic as some of the other more sophisticated tools, but a multimeter can give you many answers if you just know how to ask the right questions.

Toner Probe

Another tool that you can use to test the connectivity of wires that run through walls and other obstructions is a toner probe. This is a less sophisticated tool that produces a signal (or tone) on one end and then determines whether that signal can still be heard on the other end. The device that produces the signal is called the *tone generator.* There is also another device that is mentioned less often, called the *tone locator.* You can use the tone locator to find the signal in the wire on the other end from the tone generator and therefore prove the connectivity of the wire through the obstruction.

The tone generator and the tone locator are sometimes referred to as the *fox and hound.* It is not usually necessary to strip any insulation from the wires in order to locate the tone. The tone locator can usually find the tone through the insulation just by placing it close to the wire. The only real disadvantage of a tone generator is that it generally takes two people to use one effectively to test several wires in a cable.

Butt Set

Your computer network is closely tied to your telephone network, especially if you are still using modems. For this reason, you may also want to have one of the "old standby" tools in your arsenal that has been used by telephone company line repair technicians for many years. A *butt set* looks a phone with a cord and no base, but it's really much more than that. Butt sets have evolved over the years so that they can test all the latest connections. A butt set can connect to and test any pair of phone wires on any modular jack, punch down block, demark block, and so forth. It can also test for dial tone, open line, shorted line, and many other problems.

Punch Down Tool

As I discussed in Chapter 2, in order to increase the flexibility and fault tolerance of a network, most organizations do not use a continuous cable from end to end for each computer connection. Instead, each cable is connected through a series of patch panels. These patch panels provide a method for quickly changing a cable that is part of a computer's connection to the network. Typically, the front side of a patch panel has many RJ-45 connector ports. The back of the panel, however, does not have ports and instead is hardwired with the wires from the cables "punched down" into special connectors that hold them securely in place. This is where the *punch down tool* comes into play.

The process of punching down a wire properly takes a considerable amount of force. You could try to do it without the special tool, but you would probably break the wire or not be able to make the proper connection at all. The punch down tool, shown in Figure 5.11, assists you in applying the right amount of pressure in the right direction. As you push in with the tool, you load up a spring that then releases the proper amount of force to press the wire firmly into the connector while stripping the insulation off the side of the wire to assure a firm connection with the metal connector. With a little practice, you will be able to "punch down" wires with ease.

FIGURE 5.11   A punch down tool

Cable Stripper

To attach an RJ-45 jack to the end of a cable, you must strip about an inch and a half of the outer cable insulation without cutting any of the insulation on the eight wires that are inside the cable. It's possible to do this with a pocketknife, but it takes a little practice. An easier method is to use a tool that is designed to cut just the outer insulation and leave the other wires untouched. A *cable stripper* does just that. There have been many cable stripper designs over the years. Some tools double as a crimping tool and a cable stripper. Figure 5.12 shows a crimping tool with a cable stripper integrated into it.

FIGURE 5.12   A crimping tool with cable stripper

Snips

Of course, before you can strip the insulation, you have to cut the appropriate amount of cable off the cable spool. As you might imagine, *snips* are just pliers with a sharp blade that can easily cut through the entire cable and leave you with a nice even clean end with which to work. Snips should be in your toolbox if you are planning on creating custom-length cables for your network instead of buying patch cables.

Voltage Event Recorder

One of the most important resources upon which all networking equipment depends is good clean power. If the power source of a computer or network device has *sags* (downward fluctuations in current) or *spikes* (upward fluctuations in current), these could cause the systems to malfunction and might even damage sensitive hardware. Most organizations "smooth out" power using an uninterruptible power supply (UPS) on critical but not all equipment, so it's important to know whether the power company is providing reliable current. You can use a *voltage event recorder* to monitor the current from an electrical socket for a predefined period of time and create a report indicating line voltage and sags or spikes of current. This can be useful for network maintenance and planning.

Temperature Monitor

One of the nicer things about being involved in IT in a large organization is that you generally get the coolest room in the building, at least in regard to temperature. It's extremely important to keep servers, routers, switches, and other network equipment cooled down while they are running. The recommended temperature range for a data center is between 68 and 75 degrees Fahrenheit. Staying in this range will improve the reliability and longevity of the components; in other words, it saves the company money too!

Since this is very important, most companies don't trust the environment of a data center to the thermostat on the wall. Instead, more sophisticated and sensitive *temperature monitors* are used throughout the data center to ensure that the correct temperatures are being achieved. These monitors may inform the administrator of a problem or may also be tied into the cooling systems in their respective areas.

Exam Essentials

Know how to utilize the most common hardware tools.   You should know how to utilize hardware testing tools such as a cable tester, protocol analyzer, certifier, TDR, OTDR, and multimeter. In addition, you should know how to use network installation tools such as a butt set, punch down tool, cable stripper, and snips. Finally, you should understand how to utilize hardware-monitoring tools such as voltage event recorders and temperature monitors.

Review Questions

1. Which of the following protocols does traceroute use?

    A. TCP

    B. TTL

    C. ICMP

    D. DNS

2. Which of the following are displayed with ipconfig and no additional options? (Choose two.)

    A. Default gateway

    B. IP address of DHCP server

    C. Subnet mask

    D. Hostname

3. Which of the following is resolved by ARP?

    A. MAC addresses to IP addresses

    B. Hostnames to IP addresses

    C. NetBIOS names to IP addresses

    D. IP addresses to MAC addresses

4. Which of the following Windows command-line tools displays the NetBIOS name registered locally by a system?

    A. netstat -a

    B. nbtstat -c

    C. nbtstat -n

    D. netstat -e

5. Which of the following can analyze network traffic to find threats to security and then take action, such as resetting a connection?

    A. IDS

    B. Proxy server

    C. Firewall

    D. IPS

6. Which hardware-troubleshooting tool should you use to determine the exact point of a short or a break in a CAT 5 cable running inside a wall?

    A. OTDR

    B. Cable tester

    C. Multimeter

    D. TDR

7. Which hardware tool is typically used to attach network wires to the back of patch panels?

   A. Screwdriver

   B. Hammer

   C. Punch down tool

   D. Cable stripper

8. What is the recommended temperature range for a data center?

   A. 68 to 75 degrees Celsius

   B. 60 to 70 degrees Fahrenheit

   C. 80 to 90 degrees Celsius

   D. 68 to 75 degrees Fahrenheit

9. Which of following devices looks similar to a laptop but is actually a sophisticated hardware tool that can be used to gather information locally in a network?

   A. Protocol analyzer

   B. Certifier

   C. OTDR

   D. Cable tester

10. Which network device can help you analyze the quality of power in a data center?

   A. UPS

   B. OTDR

   C. Voltage event recorder

   D. Protocol analyzer

Answers to Review Questions

1. C. The protocol used by traceroute is ICMP. Traceroute manipulates the TTL, but the TTL is not a protocol. TCP and DNS are not involved in traceroute.

2. A, C. The ipconfig tool used without any options displays the IP address, subnet mask, and default gateway. Neither the IP address of the DHCP server nor the hostname is shown. To see the additional information, you should use the /all option.

3. D. The Address Resolution Protocol (ARP) resolves IP addresses to MAC addresses. ARP is an essential protocol in the TCP/IP protocol suite. ARP does not resolve hostnames to IP addresses but instead resolves IP addresses to MAC addresses.

4. C. To display the NetBIOS names registered locally by a Windows system, you should type **nbtstat -n** on the command line. netstat -a displays active connections to a computer. nbtstat -c displays the local NetBIOS name cache. netstat -e displays Ethernet statistics associated with the device.

5. D. Intrusion prevention software (IPS) can analyze network traffic to find threats based on traffic signatures or based on normal network traffic. IPS can then take actions such as resetting the connection. IDS detects attacks but does not take action. A proxy server makes a connection to a resource on behalf of the user. A firewall filters packets based on IP addresses, protocols, or even the data they contain.

6. D. Since CAT 5 cable is a copper twisted-pair cable, you should use a time domain reflectometer (TDR) to find the exact point of the break in the cable that is running through the wall. An optical time domain reflectometer should be used for fiber cables. Neither a cable tester nor a multimeter can give you the detailed information you need.

7. C. A punch down tool is a specialized tool that assists you in applying the right amount of force in the proper place to insert a wire into the punch down block on the back of a patch panel while simultaneously removing its insulation so the metal can make a proper connection.

8. D. The recommended range of temperatures for a data center is between 68 to 75 degrees Fahrenheit. Actually, the devices could perform well at even cooler temperatures, but this range is low enough for the devices while still keeping things relatively comfortable for people and saving the company money at the same time.

9. A. A protocol analyzer (in its hardware definition) looks similar to a laptop but typically has physical ports and functionality that a laptop does not have. Since it is portable, it can be used to gather information locally on a network. A certifier is a device that automatically compares a test result with a standard. An OTDR is a device used to test fiber links for breaks or weaknesses. A cable tester is used to verify that a cable is properly constructed to carry data.

10. C. You can use a voltage event recorder to monitor the current from an electrical socket for a predefined period of time and create a report indicating line voltage and sags or spikes in current. A UPS is used to supply power in the event of a power outage from the power company. An OTDR is a device used to test fiber links for breaks or weaknesses. A protocol analyzer is a portable hardware device used to gather information locally in a network.

Chapter

6

Network Security

COMPTIA NETWORK+ EXAM OBJECTIVES COVERED IN THIS CHAPTER:

✓ **6.1 Explain the function of hardware and software security devices**

- Network-based firewall

- Host-based firewall

- IDS

- IPS

- VPN concentrator

✓ **6.2 Explain common features of a firewall**

- Application layer vs. network layer

- Stateful vs. stateless

- Scanning services

- Content filtering

- Signature identification

- Zones

✓ **6.3 Explain the methods of network access security**

- Filtering
  - Access control lists
  - MAC filtering
  - IP filtering
- Tunneling and encryption
  - SSL VPN
  - VPN
  - L2TP
  - PPTP
  - IPSEC
- Remote access
  - RAS
  - RDP
  - PPPoE
  - PPP
  - VNC
  - ICA

✓ **6.4 Explain methods of user authentication**

- PKI
- Kerberos
- AAA
  - RADIUS
  - TACACS+
- Network access control
  - 802.1x
- CHAP
- MS-CHAP
- EAP

✓ **6.5 Explain issues that affect device security**

- Physical security

- Restricting local and remote access

- Secure methods vs. unsecure methods

    - SSH, HTTPS, SNMPv3, SFTP, SCP

    - TELNET, HTTP, FTP, RSH, RCP, SNMPv1/2

✓ **6.6 Identify common security threats and mitigation techniques**

- Security threats

    - DoS

    - Viruses

    - Worms

    - Attackers

    - Man in the middle

    - SMURF

    - Rogue access points

    - Social engineering (phishing)

- Mitigation techniques

    - Policies and procedures

    - User training

    - Patches and updates

6.1 Explain the function of hardware and software security devices

One thing that you should never believe is that we network computers to improve security. In truth, we network computers to share resources, and then we have to address a myriad of security issues and threats. We address these network security issues and threats using both hardware and software. Also, many protocols have evolved over the past 20 years or so that are specifically designed to mitigate network security threats. In the following sections, I'll discuss specialized hardware devices, software, and protocols that are used to address network security threats.

Network-Based Firewall

A *firewall* is a hardware or software system that is used to separate one computer or network from another one. The most common type of firewall is used to protect a computer or an entire network from unauthorized access from the Internet. Firewalls can also be used to control the flow of data to and from multiple networks within the same organization. Firewalls can be programmed to filter data packets based on the information that is contained in the packets. A *network-based firewall* is generally located on the edge of a network where that network comes in contact with another network such as the Internet. Some network firewalls are used between two corporate networks to control the flow of information between the two divisions, such as between departments in the same company. In either case, the advantage of a network-based firewall is that it provides general protection for all the hosts behind it. However, the disadvantage is that the settings on the firewall will affect all the hosts behind it and therefore tend to be general settings and not specific settings for specific network hosts.

Host-Based Firewall

A *host-based firewall* addresses the issue of specific settings by applying its settings to only one host. Host-based firewalls are generally built into the operating system or installed as an application on a computer. Microsoft Windows XP and Vista have a host-based firewall called the Windows Firewall. The Windows Firewall can be configured on Windows XP to filter incoming traffic only, but on Vista the firewall can be configured with more specific filters that control network traffic to and from the host computer. Generally traffic is identified and filtered based on the header information that contains the source address, destination address, and protocol of the traffic. In other words, most host-based firewalls filter traffic based on where it came from, where it wants to go, and what it wants to do when it gets there. Figure 6.1 shows a simple host-based firewall on a Windows Vista client.

FIGURE 6.1   A host-based firewall on Windows Vista

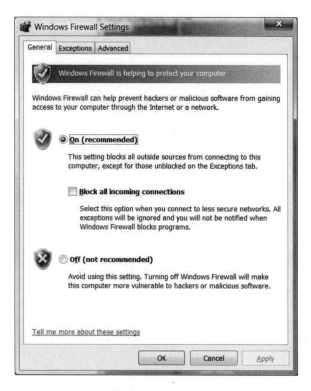

IDS

An *intrusion detection system* (IDS), as I discussed in Chapter 3, "Domain 3 Network Devices," is much more than a firewall. In effect, an IDS is an intelligent monitor of network traffic that "understands" what normal traffic is supposed to look like and what it is supposed to do and can therefore identify abnormal traffic as a threat. "How does it know?" you may ask. Well, either it's configured with the latest attack signatures from its vendor (much like antivirus software) or it simply "watches" your network for a while to learn what normal traffic looks like. Of course, the best system is a combination of the two. In addition, an IDS can be configured to alert the network administrator when it detects a threat. In fact, the only action that a true IDS takes in response to a threat is to alert the administrator with an email message or network message if configured properly. Often an IPS just logs the threat so the network administrator can address it later.

IPS

An *intrusion prevention system* (IPS) is very similar to an IDS but can take more action in response to a threat than an IDS. An IPS can address an identified threat by resetting a connection or even closing a port. Of course, the IPS can also be configured to alert the administrator of the threat and the action that was taken. In fact, in practice, the main difference between an IPS and an IDS is one of software configuration.

VPN Concentrator

A *virtual private network* (VPN) is a network connection that is made secure even though it is flowing through an unsecure network, typically the Internet. This is done by using an encapsulation protocol. The encapsulation protocol creates a tunnel between two devices. A device that is sometimes used to create this tunnel is referred to as a *VPN concentrator.* Most VPN concentrators use either the Point-to-Point Tunneling Protocol (PPTP) or Layer 2 Tunneling Protocol (L2TP) to create the tunnel. I will discuss each of these protocols and their use later in this chapter.

Exam Essentials

Understand network-based and host-based firewalls.   You should be aware that a network-based firewall is generally located on the edge of network to control access to the entire network and thereby protect all hosts on it. A host-based firewall, on the other hand, is located on a specific host, or computer. You should also understand that each of these firewalls serves a purpose even if both are used, since more security layers are generally considered better security.

Understand IDS vs. IPS.   You should know that both IDS and IPS are designed to identify abnormal traffic on a network. You should understand that the difference between IDS and IPS is that IDS detects only the abnormal traffic and warns the administrator, whereas IPS can also take proactive action to shut ports or reset connections. Finally, you should realize that many devices actually support both types of firewalls and that often the only difference between the two is the configuration settings.

Understand VPN concentrators.   You should know that a VPN is a network that is made private even though the data flows through an unsecure network. This is done by using a VPN tunnel, which encapsulates one protocol into another one. In addition, you should know that VPN concentrators are devices that are sometimes used to create the tunnel. Finally, you should understand that most VPN concentrators use either L2TP or PPTP as the tunneling protocol.

6.2 Explain common features of a firewall

Not all firewalls are the same. In fact, firewalls have changed tremendously over the past 10 years as technologies have evolved. Firewalls that first could filter packets only by their addresses and their protocols can now filter them by the data that they contain. As technologies used to examine packets and make filtering decisions improve, the sophistication of the firewalls and their ability to provide granular decision making also improves. In the following sections, I'll discuss the most common features of today's firewalls.

Application Layer vs. Network Layer

The biggest difference between an application-layer firewall and a network-layer firewall is the type of information that they identify and filter. Network-layer firewalls are also referred to as *layer 3 firewalls*, referring to layer 3 (Network) of the OSI model. These firewalls can filter traffic based on the source IP address, destination IP address, and protocol in the header information of the packet. By contrast, application-layer firewalls can work at layer 7 (Application) of the OSI model. This type of firewall can actually examine the data in the packet and not just the header information of the packet. Because of this, it can then detect malicious data traffic such as worms and other threats that would be missed by a network-layer firewall. Application-layer firewalls can also be configured to take action, much like an IPS, when they detect a threat and can filter the threat and alert an administrator while still allowing normal traffic flow. Application-layer firewalls are typically more expensive than network-layer firewalls, but many large organizations have purchased them because of the advantages they offer.

Stateful vs. Stateless

The difference between a stateful firewall and a stateless firewall is one of the intelligence with which the firewall examines the packets. A stateless firewall is configured only to recognize static attributes in each individual packet, such as the source IP address, destination IP address, and protocol. It does not take into account a stream of data that would be normal for a protocol and therefore what packet it should be seeing next in the normal flow for that protocol. In contrast, a stateful firewall is able to hold in memory the significant attributes of each connection. The attributes, which are known as the *connection state*, might include IP addresses, ports involved in the connection, and sequence numbers that are being used for the connection. The most CPU time is spent at the beginning of the connection, because after that the stateful firewall can identify packets that are just part of an already established and "prescreened" sessions. This makes the filtering more efficient and more accurate for most communication session. Stateful firewalls were the first step in the technical evolution toward IDSs and IPSs.

Scanning Services

All firewalls perform a type of scanning service on the packets that pass through them. In other words, they examine the header and sometimes the data in the packet. Some firewalls can also take scanning to new levels combining virus protection or email protection software that blocks traffic containing viruses or any type of malware or spyware. You can even configure firewalls to block email messages that contain attachments that make these emails larger than a predetermined size. These types of scanning services can enhance security and network performance.

Content Filtering

The best thing about a firewall is that it can be configured to allow some types of traffic to flow through it while stopping the flow of other types of traffic. This type of *content filtering* is essential to organizations so that security and productivity can be maintained simultaneously. The biggest difference between the different types of firewalls is the level of content they filter. For example, a layer 7 stateful firewall can be configured to be much more selective than a layer 3 stateless firewall. For example, some firewalls can be configured to disallow access to websites that contain data or graphics that are not deemed acceptable by management standards. If a user tries to access a site that contains the unacceptable graphics or data, the site will be disallowed not because of an IP address or hostname, or even port address, but because the nature of the material on the site. This gives an administrator much more granular control over users.

Signature Identification

As I've mentioned, it's a war out there in terms of protecting your network. In response to this state of affairs, many firewall vendors have developed a system that allows network administrators to determine exactly what is filtered and therefore what else needs to be configured. These *signature IDs* are classified individually by the vendor with numbers and can generally be grouped together as well. These are broken into separate protocol segments such as IP, TCP, UDP, DNS, and HTTP signatures. For example, Cisco's signature "1202" triggers when the system detects a possible denial of service (DoS) attack. Many of these signatures were first discovered the hard way — when someone else's network was attacked.

Zones

Today's organizations must be very careful not to allow sensitive information to be available to attackers from the outside the organization. As I have discussed, a firewall provides a barrier between two networks, in effect creating two different security areas referred to as *zones*. Two or more firewalls can also be used to create even more zones.

In general, three zones are associated with firewalls: internal, external, and demilitarized (DMZ). The *internal zone* is the zone inside of all firewalls, and it is considered to be the protected area where most of your critical servers, such as domain controllers and sensitive information, are located. The *external zone* is the area outside the firewall that represents the network against which you are protecting yourself. This is generally, but not always, the Internet. The *demilitarized zone* comes into play only when you have more than one firewall. It is a zone that is between two firewalls. It is created using a device that has at least three network connections, sometimes referred to as a *three-pronged firewall*. Organizations generally place servers that are used from the internal network and from the external network in the DMZ. Servers that might be placed in the DMZ include web, VPN, and FTP servers. Higher-security servers, such as domain controllers and DHCP servers, should be placed in the internal zone behind both firewalls. A DNS server that connects to the Internet might be placed in the external zone. Placing the proper resources in the proper zones is essential to the security of your network.

Exam Essentials

Understand application-layer firewalls vs. network-layer firewalls.   You should know that the main difference between application-layer firewalls and network-layer firewalls is the type of information that they identify and filter. Network-layer firewalls are also referred to as layer 3 firewalls because they focus on layer 3 (the Network layer) information, such as the source and destination IP address and port designation of the traffic. Application-layer firewalls work much higher in the OSI model at layer 7 (the Application layer) and actually examine packet data. They are superior to network-layer firewalls because they detect malicious traffic such as computer worms that would be missed by a network-layer firewall.

Understand stateful vs. stateless firewalls.   You should know that stateful firewalls are more efficient than stateless firewalls because they can store in memory the connection state and therefore can allow packets from the connection state to continue without having to screen each packet. Stateless firewalls simply examine packets flowing through a network and compare them to the configuration that the network administrator has entered into the firewall. Since they have to examine all packets individually, they are less efficient.

Be familiar with common firewall services.   You should be familiar with common firewall services such as scanning, content filtering, and signature identification. All firewalls have scanning services that identify the type of traffic passing through them. Scanning refers to examining the headers of packets to get the information they need, such as source IP address, destination IP address, and port information and making the decision as to whether to allow the packet or deny it based on the administrator's configuration. Scanning services can also include more sophisticated techniques such as virus protection and granular email control. Content filtering goes deeper into the packet and actually examines the data and graphics that it contains. This can also allow for more granular control.

Signature identification is a process by which a firewall can detect harmful traffic because the signature (or behavior) of that traffic has been identified by the vendor and programmed into the firewall so that the firewall can identify that behavior characteristic. This means that you can often protect your network from what was learned when someone else's network was attacked.

Understand zones.   You should understand zones are security areas and that there are three zones that are associated with firewalls: internal, external, and DMZ. The DMZ applies only when you have more than one firewall. It exists between the two firewalls and generally contains resources that do not need the tightest security but do need to access a resource from within an organization and from outside the same organization. Servers such as web servers, VPN servers, and FTP servers might be placed in the DMZ. High-security servers, such as domain controllers, should be placed in the internal zone behind both firewalls. A DNS server that connects to the Internet might be placed in the external zone.

6.3 Explain the methods of network access security

In the following sections, I'll discuss the methods of network access security.

Filtering

As I mentioned, *filtering*, in regard to networking, is simply letting some traffic flow through the network while blocking other traffic. What you decide to filter and how you decide to apply a filter will depend on the network on which you are filtering traffic. For example, you might use a very different means of filtering for traffic that is local to your network than you would for traffic that comes from another network or from the Internet. In the following sections, I will discuss the most common technologies and protocols used to filter network traffic.

Access Control Lists

Generally speaking, an *access control list* (ACL) is a method of identifying traffic and then making decisions based on the attributes of that traffic. The attributes considered might be the source IP address, destination IP address, source MAC address, destination MAC address, protocol, or even specific port information in the header of the packet. What is identified and filtered will largely depend upon the type of device on which the list is configured. For example, ACLs on switches are very different from ACLs on routers. In the following sections, I'll discuss each of these types of ACLs and the filtering they provide.

MAC Filtering

As I discussed in Chapter 1, every host on a network has a 48-bit hexadecimal media access control (MAC) address. Also, every Ethernet packet contains a source MAC address and a destination MAC address, although sometimes the destination MAC address is a broadcast address such as FF-FF-FF-FF-FF-FF. MAC filtering, usually applied on switches working at layer 2 (Data Link) of the OSI model, focuses on these addresses in the packet and can be configured only to let specific MAC addresses through an interface on the switch. In addition, more sophisticated filters can let only specific addresses into one interface and out of another interface. In other words, the traffic can come in an interface only if it has a destination address for a specific host or group of hosts. MAC filtering is usually applied at the *access layer* of a computer network, where the host computers are connected to the switches. It is generally not used as the only means of security, because MAC addresses can easily be spoofed with the right software.

IP Filtering

The source IP address and destination IP address of the packet is contained in the IP header of a packet, sometimes referred to as *layer 3* (Network) addresses. *IP filtering*, usually associated with routers, is a process of configuring the devices to pass through only the IP traffic desired but block everything else. This is the most effective way to filter, since anything that is forgotten will not be passed through. Another method of filtering is to let all traffic pass through except what is specifically configured to be blocked. The problem with this method is that any traffic that is forgotten will be passed through; therefore, this method is much less secure.

As mentioned, IP filtering is most often associated with routers, but most devices have configuration options and settings for IP filtering. It can be applied in layer 3 switches, which are switches that have a router module within them, or in a number of firewall devices, such as a Cisco PIX firewall. In fact, even Windows XP clients have the option to filter IP addresses in their advanced network settings, although this is recommended only for a specific client with a specific reason. Otherwise, filtering at the router or firewall should be used. Figure 6.2 shows the IP filtering option in the advanced TCP/IP properties of a Windows Vista client.

FIGURE 6.2   IP filtering on Windows Vista

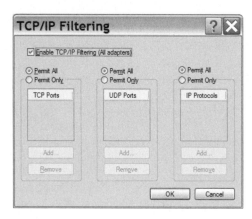

Tunneling and Encryption

For most companies with multiple locations, the prospect of installing dedicated leased lines, such as T1s or T3s, to each of their locations is cost prohibitive and unnecessary. It's unnecessary with today's networks because it's possible to use the Internet as a secure connection between the locations. As I discussed earlier in this chapter, *tunneling* is a process of encapsulating one protocol over another so as to provide a secure communication through an unsecure medium, typically the Internet. The processes and protocols used to create tunnels have changed over the past 10 years, and some tunnels are therefore more secure than others. Some tunneling protocols also encrypt the data contained in the packets, while others do not. In the following sections, I'll discuss the protocols used for tunneling and the security they provide.

SSL VPN

The *Secure Sockets Layer* (SSL) protocol uses cryptography to provide secure authentication and communication privacy over the Internet. It is typically used for e-commerce. When used in conjunction with a VPN on a site that is allowing e-commerce, the advantage SSL offers is that many of the filters are already configured. In other words, if a site wants to allow e-commerce using SSL, then the ports for SSL already must be allowed through any firewalls or other network filters. This means that an SSL-based VPN might be much easier to configure than one that requires that a new protocol and its ports be allowed through the firewalls of the network.

VPN

As mentioned, a *virtual private network* (VPN) is a network that is not really private, since it runs through an unsecure network. However, a VPN is made "virtually" private using an *encapsulation protocol*, also called a *tunneling protocol*. You can accomplish this using SSL and cryptography. There are also other protocols that are specifically designed to provide a tunnel that encapsulates a well-known protocol, for example, IP, with a secure protocol only known by the sender and receiver.

L2TP

Layer 2 Tunneling Protocol (L2TP) is one of the most common tunneling protocols in use today. The only Microsoft clients that support L2TP are Windows 2000 Professional and newer. Windows 2000 Server and newer servers also support L2TP.

L2TP authenticates the client in a two-phase process. First it authenticates the computer, and then it authenticates the user. Authenticating the computer helps to prevent a *man-in-the-middle attack*, where the data is first intercepted by another computer and then forwarded to the intended receiver. LT2P can also authenticate the end of the tunnel with an IP address so that it doesn't send data to an unintended receiver. L2TP works by using digital certificates, which means the computers that use L2TP must support digital certificates.

PPTP

Point-to-Point Tunneling Protocol (PPTP) is a protocol used to create a secure tunnel between two points on a network over which other protocols such as PPP can be used. This tunneling functionality provides the basis for many VPNs. Although PPTP is a widely used tunneling protocol, other tunneling protocols, such as L2TP, provide even greater security. PPTP cannot authenticate the end of the tunnel and thereby prevent a man-in-the-middle attack.

IPSec

Internet Protocol Security (IPSec) is a framework of protocols designed to authenticate connections and encrypt data during communication between two computers. It operates at the Network layer of the OSI model and provides security for protocols that operate at the higher layers of the OSI model. Because of this, you can use IPSec to secure practically all TCP/IP-related communications, including tunnels.

The function of IPSec is to ensure that data on network is safe from being viewed, accessed, or modified by anyone except the intended receiver. IPSec can be used to provide security within networks as well as between networks. To be more specific, IPSec has three main security services:

Data verification   This ensures that the data that is received is actually from the source from which it appears to have originated.

Protection from data tampering   This ensures that the data has not been changed in any way during the transmission between the sending computer and the receiving computer.

Privacy of transactions   This ensures that the data that is sent is readable only by the intended receiver.

There are two main modes of IPSec: *transport mode* and *tunnel mode*. Transport mode is used to send and receive encrypted data within the same network. Tunnel mode is used to send encrypted data between networks. It includes an encryption mechanism as well as an authentication mechanism. The only Microsoft clients that can use IPSec are Windows 2000 Professional and newer. Windows 2000 Server and newer servers can also use IPSec.

Remote Access

Generally speaking, *remote access* means that your user is not on a device that is connected within the LAN of your organization but is connected outside your LAN instead. The user may be connecting from home or from a hotel, but, in either case, the place from which they are connecting is not part of your organization. With remote access your goals are twofold. Your first goal is to provide the user with a user experience as close as possible to what they would have if they were connected within the LAN. Your second goal, though not second in importance, is to maintain the security of your system. This means that you need a method by which the user can authenticate to the network, and then you need a method by which the user can securely transmit sensitive data. In the following sections, I'll discuss the tools and protocols that can assist you in meeting these goals.

RAS

Remote Access Service (RAS) is a remote access solution that is included with Microsoft Windows server products. Its main function is to give users the same access to the network from a remote location as if they were actually sitting at their desks, although sometimes the access is much slower. RAS is implemented in Windows NT Server as RAS and in Windows 2000 Server and Windows Server 2003 as *Routing and Remote Access Server* (RRAS), but both product implementations offer the same basic functionality — remote access connectivity to a LAN environment. RAS servers can provide dial-up connections using modems as well as VPN connections using WAN miniports. Figure 6.3 shows an RRAS server on Windows Server 2003.

FIGURE 6.3   An RRAS server on Windows Server 2003

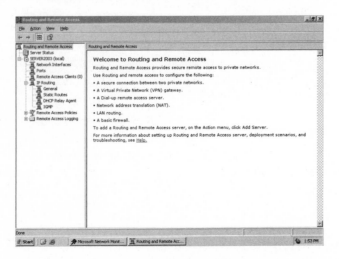

RAS is also capable of providing security using the tunneling protocols of which I've spoken, such as PPTP and L2TP, although L2TP is available only on Windows 2000 and newer servers. RAS and RRAS servers support remote connectivity to all the major client operating systems in use today.

RDP

Remote Desktop Protocol (RDP) is a protocol used by Microsoft to establish remote display and remote control capabilities between servers and clients on a Microsoft network. It is the protocol on which Windows Terminal Services operates. Originally, Terminal Services offered two options during installation: Remote Administration and Application Server. In later versions of Terminal Services (Windows Server 2003), only Application Server is offered. This is because Remote Desktop Connection, which also uses the RDP protocol, is now included with the Windows XP Professional and Vista client software and Windows Server 2003 and Windows Server 2008 server software. Figure 6.4 illustrates a Remote Desktop Connection tool in Windows Server 2008.

FIGURE 6.4   The Remote Desktop Connection tool

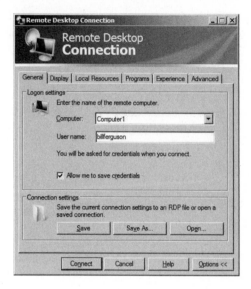

PPPoE

Point-to-Point Protocol over Ethernet (PPPoE) is a protocol that has become popular because of the growing number of people who use cable modems and DSL connections to access the Internet. PPPoE is a specification for connecting users on an LAN to the Internet through a common broadband medium such as a cable modem or DSL line. All the users on the LAN can share one common connection to the Internet. PPPoE can also be implemented with wireless devices that connect multiple users in a wireless LAN to the Internet.

PPP

Point-to-Point Protocol (PPP) is the standard remote access protocol used today. It provides for authentication mechanisms, error checking, and multiple protocol support. You can choose from among several authentication options, including Password Authentication Protocol (PAP), Challenge Handshake Authentication Protocol (CHAP), and Extensible Authentication Protocol (EAP).

 I will discuss each of these protocols in greater detail later in this chapter.

The PPP protocol establishes a session with this three-step process:

1. Framing rules are established between the client and the server. These include the size of the frames allowed as well as the data rates that can be used.

2. The client is authenticated by the server using the configured authentication protocol.

3. *Network control protocols* (NCPs) configure the remote client for the correct LAN protocols, TCP/IP, and so on.

After these three steps are successfully completed, the server and client can begin to exchange data.

VNC

Virtual Network Computing (VNC) was first developed in 2002 by Olivetti and Oracle Research Lab (ORL), which has since been acquired by AT&T. It is a graphical desktop sharing system that uses the *Remote Frame Buffer* (RFB) protocol to control another computer remotely. The RFB protocol transmits keyboard and mouse commands from one computer to another. VNC is platform independent, which means it can be used on many different operating systems and on servers as well as clients.

In fact, the computers using VNC take on the role of server and client. A server is a computer that has the resource that will be shared. A client is a computer on which the server will be monitored and controlled. By default, the connection between the client and the server is not secure and therefore should be tunneled using Secure Shell (SSH), much like the way Telnet is secured.

ICA

Independent Computing Architecture (ICA) is a proprietary protocol designed by Citrix for application server systems. It defines a specification for passing data between servers and clients but is not bound to any platform. ICA is commonly used on Citrix WinFrame and Citrix Presentation Server. It can be used on Windows, Mac, Linux, and even Unix clients as terminals, which are referred to as *thin clients*. These systems work best when only data is needed and do not function well in environments that require large graphics, movies, or live content such as streaming video or audio. Their communication can be secured using an application independent tunneling protocol such as L2TP.

Exam Essentials

Understand MAC filtering vs. IP filtering.   You should know that MAC filtering works on switches at layer 2 (Data Link) of the OSI model and uses the destination MAC addresses of frames to make filtering decisions. IP filtering works on routers, works on layer 3 switches, and can even be configured on individual clients and servers. It can use the layer 3 (Network) source and destination addresses (generally IP addresses) to make filtering decisions on packets.

Understand the various forms of tunneling.   You should understand that tunneling is a process of encapsulating one protocol over another and is typically used for secure data transfer through an unsecure network. You should know that there are various forms of tunneling including SSL VPN, VPN, L2TP, and PPTP. Each has its own advantages and disadvantages. For example, a VPN using SSL might be advantageous if SSL is already being used, since the correct filters would already be in place. In addition, L2TP is much more secure than PPTP but requires the latest clients and servers.

Understand IPSec.   You should know that IPSec is a framework of protocols that is designed to provide secure authentication and secure data transfer between two computers. It works at the Network layer of the OSI model and can be used to secure practically all TCP/IP-related communications including tunnels. It has three main security services: data verification, protection from tampering, and privacy of transactions. The only Microsoft clients that can use IPSec are Windows 2000 Professional and newer. Windows 2000 Server and newer servers can also use IPSec.

Understand Remote Access.   You should be familiar with remote access services such as RAS and RRAS. In addition, you should understand remote access protocols such as RDP, PPoE, PPP, VNC, and ICA. You should understand the appropriate use of each protocol and the difference between remote control protocols such as RDP and VNC and between solely remote access protocols such as PPP and PPPoE.

6.4 Explain methods of user authentication

Authentication is a process by which people prove their identities. For example, you have to use a driver's license or some other form of picture ID to prove that you are who you say you are when you check in for a flight. In person, this is not typically difficult, but over a network it can become much more complicated.

User authentication is process by which users prove their identity over the network. This is generally accomplished in one of three methods, or a combination of them, also called *factors*. The three factors by which users prove their identity are as follows:

- Something they know
- Something they have
- Something they are

Something a user knows could be a password or the personal identification number (PIN) that corresponds to their smart card. Something a user has could be a smart card or a cryptographic key. Something a user is would relate to biometric authentication, such as a fingerprint, voiceprint, cornea or iris scan, or a hand geometry print. You can also combine these factors to create even greater security called *multifactor authentication*.

Each of these factors of authentication uses different protocols. It's important that you understand your options in regard to each type of user authentication. In the following sections, I'll discuss the most common methods of user authentication.

PKI

Public Key Infrastructure (PKI) is a method of user authentication that falls into the "something I have" category. If the user possesses the right key (a series of mathematical computations), then the user can prove their identity and gain access to a resource. If the user does not have the right key, then they cannot gain access to the resource. The keys are stored in an electronic document called a *certificate*. An important part of PKI is the process of tracking the certificates themselves and to whom they are issued. The servers and services that verify a user's identity and track the certificate are called *certificate servers*.

You can use your own certificate server to track the certificates that you issue within your own organization. If you need to prove your identity to others, you can also use a third-party company, such as VeriSign, that specializes in verifying identities and issuing the appropriate certificates and keys. Most organizations use a certificate hierarchy whereby they trust someone because someone else trusts them.

PKI works by using a pair of keys called the *public key* and the *private key*. The public key identifies the user and can be used to encrypt data that will be sent to the user so that only the user can decrypt it. The public key does not decrypt data. Since it does not decrypt data, it can be freely distributed without a concern as to whether it will be stolen or intercepted. It's kind of like a key that only locks your house but will not unlock it. You wouldn't be worried if more people had a key that would only lock your house, would you?

The private key is the other key in the key pair and is very different from the public key. The private key is held only by the user and is not shared with anyone. It is stored by the user's operating system and automatically used by the operating system and by PKI-enabled applications. The private key simply decrypts anything that the public key has encrypted. In fact, it is the only key that can decrypt what the public key in its key pair has encrypted.

To put this into practice, let's say you wanted to send me an encrypted email. First, you would need for me to send you my public key. Using my email software, I would send you an email that contains my public key and gives you an opportunity to store it for use. You would then create your email and use my public key to encrypt the email. You would then send me the encrypted email, which I would then decrypt and open with my private key. The email software will actually handle the use of the keys for us; all we have to do is get the process started by selecting to use encrypted email between us. This is just one example, and there are many other uses of PKI for user authentication, encryption, and identity verification of the sender of a message.

Kerberos

Kerberos is an authentication protocol that was developed by MIT and named for the mythical three-headed dog that guards the gates of Hades over the River Styx. It is commonly used in LANs, and it is the default authentication protocol for Windows Active Directory and for Novell NDS systems. Kerberos was specifically designed to prevent *replay attacks* whereby a user records the process of authentication of a device to a resource and then "plays back" the appropriate pieces, thereby gaining access.

To prevent replay attacks, Kerberos uses a system of keys that expire as soon as they are used or after a definable period of time (usually five minutes). When users first log on, they receive a special token called a *ticket-granting ticket* (TGT). When they need access to a resource, their system will present the TGT to a server called a *key distribution center* (KDC), which is usually also a domain controller. The KDC will then give the user's computer either a key to access the resource or another TGT to access the next KDC that is in the path toward the resource. In a large network with multiple domains, this process may be repeated several times just to get access to the resource. In all cases, the TGTs and the keys obtained from them expire as soon as they are used and cannot be used again. Now you can see why they named it after the three-headed dog that guards the gates of Hades!

Kerberos works well when all the users are part of a network and are therefore authenticated by the domain controller. If the user is not from within the network, then special provisions can be made to make the user recognized by the network and therefore able to use Kerberos for authentication. These provisions will vary depending on the operating system, but it's often simpler to just use PKI for accounts that are not part of the network.

AAA

Authentication, authorization, and accounting (AAA, pronounced "triple A") is an overall term that defines the goals of an organization in regard to its data and resources. As I mentioned earlier, *authentication* is a process of users proving their identity. It essence, you are asking "Who are you?" *Authorization* is the process of determining what resources a user has access to once authenticated. Here you are asking "What are you allowed to do?" Finally, *accounting* is a process of tracking the resources the user has connected to and the resources they've used. It can be understood to ask "What did you do?" Many services and protocols have been developed that conform to AAA concepts. Two of the most common services that are used with remote access are RADIUS and TACACS+. I will discuss each of these services in the next sections.

RADIUS

Remote Authentication Dial-In User Service (RADIUS) is a service that provides a centralized system for authentication, authorization, and accounting. Remote access servers become clients of another server referred to as a RADIUS server. The authentication of the users is then actually performed by the RADIUS server based on certificates, Kerberos, or some other type of authentication. RADIUS uses UDP to broadcast the communication between the remote access servers (RASs) and the RADIUS server. The RAS becomes a go-between that opens the door, or doesn't, for the client computer to come in and use the resource. Also, because all requests are centralized through the RADIUS server, accounting for those requests is also centralized. RADIUS is supported on all the latest Microsoft Server systems such as Windows 2000 Server, Windows Server 2003, and Windows Server 2008.

TACACS+

Terminal Access Controller Access Control Systems+ (TACACS+) is a service that is similar to RADIUS but uses TCP to communicate between the RAS and the RADIUS server. It was developed by Cisco Systems to address the need for a more scalable AAA solution. The fact that it uses TCP (a connection-oriented protocol) instead of UDP (a connectionless protocol) offers several advantages, namely, that the RAS server receives an acknowledgment from the TACACS server that the authentication request has been received and is being processed. Also, because the two can communicate with a connection-oriented protocol, more sophisticated security mechanisms can be employed. For example, while RADIUS encrypts only the password in the packet that is passed from the RAS to the RADIUS server, TACACS encrypts the entire body of the packet including the information regarding the username and the service that the user is requesting. This makes TACACS a much more secure service than RADIUS. Of course, TACACS also keeps an accounting of all requests from a RAS, and that accounting can also be secured.

Network Access Control

Let's say that I have a device in a network that you can access and thereby gain access further into the network. That device may be a RAS or could be a wireless access point. It may not have the intelligence or the information to authenticate you, but it has a connection to a server that does. In this case, the device relays your credentials to the authentication server that does have the intelligence and the database to make the right decision. This is an example of *network access control*. The most common type of network access control is 802.1x, covered in the next section.

802.1x

802.1x is a standard developed by the Institute of Electrical and Electronics Engineers (IEEE). It defines a method for access control whereby the client computer (referred to as a *supplicant*) requests access to a network through a device such as a network appliance or a WAP (referred to as an *authenticator*), and the authenticator passes the request to the authentication server to be authenticated. The authentication server either accepts or rejects the request, based on its database, and then gives instructions to the authenticator to accept the request or reject it. 802.1x is commonly used for wireless network security in today's networks. The tricky part here is that the authenticator does not really authenticate the request at all — the authentication server does. The authenticator just acts as a gatekeeper.

CHAP

Challenge Handshake Authentication Protocol (CHAP) is a remote access authentication protocol that uses a password that is a shared secret between the server and client; however, the password is never sent in clear text. Instead, a three-way handshake is used in which the server sends the client a challenge to prove that it knows the password by inserting it into a challenge string sent by the server using a hashing algorithm. The client uses the hashing algorithm on the password to create a hash of the password, called a *message digest*, which it sends back to the server. When the server receives the message digest from the client, it compares it with the message digest of the true password using the same hashing algorithm. If the two message digests are the same, then the client knows the password, and the communication can continue. If they are not the same, then the communication will be terminated. In this way, CHAP establishes authentication without having to send a password in clear text. CHAP is the strongest authentication method that can be used when deploying a mixture of Microsoft clients and other types of clients, such as Novell, Unix, or Apple.

MS-CHAP

Microsoft Challenge Handshake Protocol (MS-CHAP) is Microsoft's variation on the CHAP protocol, which provides even greater security for authenticating Microsoft clients. Because MS-CHAP is specifically written for Microsoft, all clients must be running a Microsoft operating system. Although it's possible for any Microsoft client to use MS-CHAP, it is more likely that it will be used by Windows 95, Windows 98, and Windows NT Workstation clients. This is because the newer clients can use an even more secure protocol referred to as MS-CHAP v2.

   Microsoft Challenge Handshake Protocol version 2 (MS-CHAP v2) is a much stronger form of remote access authentication that can be used only by Windows 2000 Professional and newer clients or by Windows 98 clients using a VPN. Many new features in MS-CHAP v2 strengthen the security of the authentication mechanisms. The most important of these is that MS-CHAP v2 offers a two-way authentication method. This means a client can verify that a server is legitimate and not a rogue RAS server before it reveals its credentials to the server for authentication. This prevents an attacker from inserting a server into a network environment for the purpose of collecting user credentials for later use. MS-CHAP v2 is a good solution for networks with Microsoft Windows 2000 Server or Windows Server 2003 and clients that are Windows 2000 Professional and newer.

EAP

As the name suggests, *Extensible Authentication Protocol* (EAP) is an open set of standards that allows the addition of new methods of authentication. EAP can also use certificates from other trusted parties as a form of authentication. It is currently used primarily for smart cards, but it is evolving and will be used for many forms of biometric authentication using a person's fingerprint, retina scan, and so on.

Exam Essentials

Be able to explain factors of user authentication.   You should understand that user authentication involves a user proving their identity through network communication. This is generally accomplished by one or more of three factors — something the user knows, something the user has, or something the user is. Some protocols combine two or more of these factors.

Understand PKI.   You should understand that PKI consists of the management of certificates that contain key pairs. One key, the public key, is used to encrypt data that will be sent to the user through the network. It cannot decrypt any data. The corresponding key, the private key, is used to decrypt data that has been encrypted with the public key. Many applications use PKI in creative ways to exchange information securely.

Understand Kerberos.   You should understand that Kerberos is the default authentication protocol on the latest Microsoft and Novell server systems. It uses a series of tickets that expire after their use or after a specific period of time. It's designed especially to prevent replay attacks in which a user's credentials are recorded and played back to gain access to resources.

Understand AAA.   You should understand that AAA is a general term. Authentication is "Who are you?" Authorization is "What are you allowed to do?" Accounting is "What did you do?" Most security protocols involve one or more of these concepts.

Understand RADIUS and TACACS+.   You should know that RADIUS and TACACS are both services that provide a centralized system for AAA. A RAS acts as a go-between and actually gets its authority from an authentication server. Since every authentication request goes through the authentication server, the accounting can also be centralized.

RADIUS, the default AAA service used with Microsoft systems, uses UDP to broadcast requests between a RAS and the authentication server. TACACS works in much the same way but uses TCP to provide connection-oriented communications between the client and the RAS as well as the RAS and the authentication server. This allows for much more secure communication between the RAS and the authentication server.

Understand 802.1x.   You should understand that 802.1x is a type of network access control that is used on wireless and wired networks to improve authentication procedures and security. The client computer, or supplicant, will give its credentials to the access point, the authenticator, but does not actually perform the authentication. Instead, the access point will give the credentials to a server with a database (usually a domain controller), and that server will authenticate the request and give the "authenticator" permission to let the traffic pass through it and into the network.

Understand CHAP, MS-CHAP, and EAP.   You should understand that CHAP is a protocol that protects the secrecy of a password by not sending the password at all. Instead, a hashing algorithm is used, and the result of the hash (called a *message digest*) is sent to prove that the password is known. MS-CHAP is Microsoft's variation of CHAP that provides greater security for Microsoft clients. MS-CHAPv2 is a much stronger form of authentication that provides two-way authentication of the latest Microsoft clients and servers. Finally, you should know that EAP is an open set of standards that allows for the addition of new methods of authentication such as smart cards and various forms of biometric authentication methods.

6.5 Explain issues that affect device security

Part of maintaining device security is assuring that your servers and other network devices are physically secure so that only approved and qualified individuals can gain access to them. However, since most network devices and servers can be configured remotely, you should also assure that all methods used to configure them are secure. In the past, not all methods used to configure servers and network equipment remotely were secure. Now there are much safer methods from which you can choose. You should understand the need for device security and be able to recognize a secure method of remote configuration vs. an unsecure method. In the following sections, I'll discuss these important concepts.

Physical Security

The physical security of your network and its devices is generally accomplished by three things: locks, cameras, and intimidation. The intimidation may come from signs, login banners, and known rules of behavior. It might also come from guard dogs or even electric fences. Once when I was teaching a class at the Osan Air Force Base in South Korea, I took a wrong turn on my way back from the restroom and found myself face to face with a big guy holding an M-16 submachine gun and asking me whether I really needed to be in that hallway. They take their security seriously there!

Based on the sensitivity of the network data and devices, more or less of the aforementioned may be used. If an attacker can get physical access to servers and network equipment, then all the passwords and logical security cannot stop him from doing harm. You should also consider that an attacker could hurt you by cutting power or even damaging the air conditioning systems for the data center.

Restricting Local and Remote Access

You can restrict local access with the techniques mentioned previously, but what about remote access to devices? The biggest difference between restricting local access to devices and restricting remote access in general is that the restriction of remote access is largely accomplished by logical means such as usernames, passwords, and cryptographic systems. Many devices allow remote access including routers, switches, servers, and even clients.

Different vendors handle this in very different ways. For example, Cisco routers and switches cannot be remotely managed unless there is a virtual terminal password set on the device. In other words, they are protected from remote management by default and must be modified by assigning a password before they can be remotely managed. If you try to Telnet to a Cisco router or switch that does not have a virtual terminal password, the device will return the message "Password required but none set." On the other hand, Microsoft clients can be accessed and managed remotely if they are configured properly, without the need of a password at all. Figure 6.5 shows the remote administration settings on a Windows Vista client.

FIGURE 6.5   Remote administration settings on Windows Vista

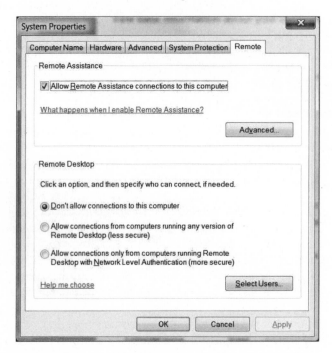

Secure Methods vs. Unsecure Methods

Since many devices in today's networks are managed remotely, it has been necessary to develop more secure remote management protocols. Some organizations still use a mixture of secure and unsecure methods of remote management. In the following sections, I will focus first on the newer and more secure methods. Then you will turn your attention to the older and less secure methods.

Secure Methods

What makes a secure method of remote management secure? Typically a method is considered secure only when authentication is required and the authentication process itself is secure from eavesdropping, tampering, and replay attacks. Many methods of remote management have been developed to meet these goals. In the following sections, I'll discuss these secure methods.

SSH

First developed by SSH Communications Security Ltd., *Secure Shell* (SSH) is a program that allows you to log in to another computer over a network, execute commands, and move files from one computer to another. SSH provides strong authentication and secure communications over unsecure channels. It protects networks from attacks such as IP spoofing, IP source routing, and DNS spoofing. The entire login session is encrypted; therefore, it is almost impossible for an outsider to collect passwords. SSH is available for Windows, Unix, Macintosh, and Linux, and it also works with RSA authentication. SSH operates at the Application and Session layers (layer 7 and layer 5) of the OSI model.

HTTPS

One of the disadvantages of using HTTP is that all the requests are sent in clear text. This means that the communication is not secure, and therefore it is unsuited for web applications such as e-commerce or the exchange of sensitive or personal information through the Web. For these applications, *Hypertext Transfer Protocol Secure* (HTTPS) is an Application layer (layer 7) protocol that provides a more secure solution. It uses Secure Sockets Layer (SSL) to encrypt information sent between the client and the server. For HTTPS to operate, both the client and the server must support it. All the most popular browsers now support HTTPS as do web server products such as Microsoft Internet Information Services (IIS), Apache, and most other web server applications. To use a URL to access a website using HTTPS and SSL, start with `https://` instead of `http://` — for example, `https://partnering.one.microsoft.com/mcp` is a secure page that is used to authenticate Microsoft Certified Professionals to Microsoft's private website.

SNMPv3

Simple Network Management Protocol (SNMP) is a protocol that has been used by network administrators for more than 20 years to get information about the devices in their network. The problem has been that the information that was being gathered for the network administrator could also be read by an attacker. *Secure Network Management Protocol version 3* (SNMPv3) was developed in December 1997 to address these security issues. It uses a secure authentication mechanism and encrypts data packets in transit. It also employs a message integrity algorithm to assure that the information that is sent to the administrator is accurate and has not been changed in transit.

SFTP

Secure File Transfer Protocol (SFTP) might at first glance sound like a revision of FTP that makes it more secure. Actually, it is a completely different protocol that is based on SSH. SFTP is much more secure than FTP because the authentication mechanisms are encrypted. It is commonly used in networks today when secure file transfer is necessary.

SCP

Secure Copy Protocol (SCP) runs at the Application layer and is used to copy files securely within a network or between networks. SCP is often used in high-security networks.

Unsecure Methods

Conversely, what makes an unsecure method unsecure is that it leaves open vulnerabilities that an attacker can exploit. Now you may wonder why someone would make a protocol like that. Well, most of these protocols were made for communication purposes only, and there were no attackers, or at least the problem was far less of a concern than it is today. The only question now is whether the protocols can still be used in some parts of your network where you are not concerned with the results of an attack. In other words, if the data or the network devices just aren't important or sensitive, then you can get away with the older and less secure methods.

These methods might also offer advantages in regard to bandwidth utilization since they require less bandwidth to operate. As you might imagine, this option is becoming less and less popular. In the following sections, I'll discuss the most common of the unsecure protocols from which you can choose.

Telnet

Telnet is a virtual terminal protocol that has been used for many years. Originally, Telnet was used to connect "dumb terminals" to mainframe computers. It was also the connection method used by earlier Unix systems. In today's networks, Telnet is sometimes used to access and control network devices such as routers and switches. It operates at the Application and Presentation layers (layer 6 and layer 7) of the OSI model.

Telnet can be used for remote control and remote configuration of servers in network environments. The main problem with Telnet for today's environment is that it is not a secure protocol; everything is transmitted in plain text. For this reason, Telnet is being replaced by more secure methods such as Secure Shell and Microsoft's Remote Desktop Connection, which provide encrypted communication.

HTTP

Hypertext Transfer Protocol (HTTP) is the Application layer (layer 7) protocol that users utilize to browse the World Wide Web. HTTP clients use a browser to make special requests from an HTTP server (web server) that contains the files that they need. The files on the HTTP server are formatted in Hypertext Markup Language (HTML) and are located using a uniform resource locator (URL). The URL contains the type of request being generated (for example, http://), the DNS name of the server to which the request is being made, and, optionally, the path to the file on the server. For example, if you type **http://micosoft.com/support** in a browser, you will be directed to the Support pages on Microsoft's servers. There are no security features on HTTP.

FTP

File Transfer Protocol (FTP), as its name indicates, provides for the transfer of files through a network environment. It can be used within an intranet or through the Internet. FTP is more than just a protocol; it is an application as well, and thus FTP works at the Application layer (layer 7) of the OSI model and uses the TCP protocol as a transport mechanism. FTP allows a user to browse a folder structure on another computer (assuming that the user has been given the permissions to authenticate to the computer) and then to download files from the folders or to upload additional files.

Many organizations use FTP to make files available to the general public and therefore allow users to log onto the FTP server anonymously. In other words, the users do not have to utilize a username and password to authenticate to the server. Since the files are there for the public, the users are allowed to access them without authenticating. Organizations also use FTP to transfer files within an organization. Typically, these servers require authentication by the user, either by supplying an additional username and password or by a pass-through authentication provided by a previous logon, such as to Active Directory. The data that they transfer is in plain text and is not encrypted.

You can use FTP through most browsers and even from a command line, but users typically purchase a third-party software program such CuteFTP or SmartFTP instead. Using FTP to transfer files allows you to transfer much larger files than are generally allowed as an email attachment by most ISPs. Using the third-party tool allows you to see that the file is transferred to the intended location. Figure 6.6 shows a connection to the FTP server at Wiley. This is one of the servers to which authors send completed work.

FIGURE 6.6 An FTP application

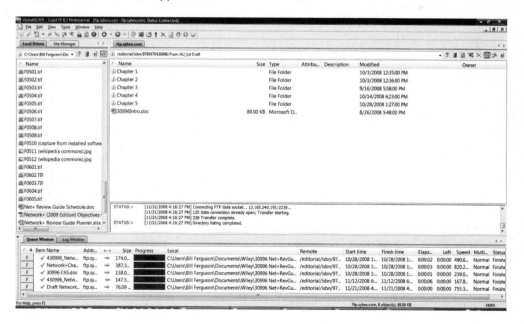

RSH

Remote Shell (RSH) is a remote control command-line program that has been used for many years. It is not secure because it sends all information unencrypted, including passwords. In fact, some versions have been used that required authentication even though the credentials were going to be sent in clear text! Because of its lack of security, RSH has been largely superseded by SSH.

RCP

Remote Copy Protocol (RCP) is a Unix command-line tool that has been used for many years to copy programs from one computer system to another. RCP is not considered secure because it copies the files using no encryption mechanisms. It can be used without authentication, and if authentication is employed, it will be sent in clear text. RCP has been largely superseded by more secure protocols such as SFTP.

SNMPv1/2

Simple Network Management Protocol versions 1 and 2, as mentioned earlier, were developed to assist network administrators in gathering information about the computers and network devices in their networks. Unfortunately, what was initially a tool for the network administrator quickly became a vulnerability to exploit for attackers. Since the network data was not encrypted, it was simple for attackers to eavesdrop on the communication between the devices and the administrator and obtain information about the network that they could use later to exploit its weaknesses.

Exam Essentials

Understand issues that affect physical device security.   You should understand that a device cannot really be secure unless it is first physically secure. Physical security is best accomplished by locks, cameras, and intimidation. Physical security must be maintained for all servers, routers, switches, and other network devices.

Understand secure protocols.   You should understand that the movement of data and the ability to make changes to device configurations should be made secure both from inside your organization and from the outside. Many protocols are available that you can use for the communication and transfer of files. Some of these protocols are secure, and some are not. Protocols that provide secure authentication such as SSH, HTTPS, SNMPv3, SFTP, and SCP are considered secure. Conversely, protocols that do not provide secure authentication and/or secure data transfer are considered unsecure protocols.

Understand unsecure protocols.   You should understand that there are many protocols that can be used to configure devices remotely and transfer data that are not considered secure because the authentication is in clear text or because the data is transferred in an unencrypted state. These protocols include Telnet, HTTP, FTP, RSH, and SNMPv1/2. Many of these protocols have been superseded by the more secure protocols discussed earlier.

6.6 Identify common security threats and mitigation techniques

Networks are created to share resources between the users and the computers that are authorized to use their resources. If networks are not configured properly, they can leave vulnerabilities that can be exploited by an attacker from outside the network or even from within the network itself. The exploitation of these vulnerabilities constitutes a threat to the network. Therefore, mitigating (defending against) these threats is one of the most important considerations for a network administrator. In the following sections, I will discuss the most common security threats and the mitigation techniques to defend against them.

Security Threats

A security threat to a network can be an attacker who attempts to gain information that they can use to exploit a network vulnerability. This type of attack is referred to as a *passive attack*. In another type of attack, the attacker is actually attempting to disrupt network communication and affect the productivity of the users of the network. This is referred to as an *active attack*. In the following sections, I will discuss the most common types of security threats.

DoS

A *denial of service* (DoS) attack overwhelms a network host with a stream of bogus data that keeps it from being able to process the data that it was designed to process. DoS attacks can be launched against computers as well as against network devices. Often a DoS attack is a security threat that indicates that a larger attack is in progress. The DoS attack is sometimes part of an attack that hijacks communication from a user who has already authenticated to a resource. While the user's computer is blocked by the DoS attack, the attacker accesses the resource and gets the information they want and then returns the control to the user who may not even know what has occurred.

Viruses

A computer *virus* is a program that can infect a computer and then copy itself without the consent of the user. Viruses began infecting computers in the early 1980s and have continued to evolve with technology ever since. Some viruses are able to change themselves after they infect a computer to attempt to "hide" from antivirus software. As viruses have changed over the years, companies such as Symantec and McAfee have specialized in software that can detect and eradicate viruses from computer systems or even keep them from infecting the computer in the first place. These programs are kept up-to-date by downloading the latest list of virus signatures that can detect the very latest viruses. There are more than 75,000 known viruses today, but most if not all of them are defeated by just keeping your antivirus software up-to-date on all servers and clients.

Worms

A *worm* is different from a virus in that it is a program and not just an "infestation." Worms use the computer network to send copies of themselves to other computers without the user's consent. Unlike viruses, worms do not need to attach themselves to an existing program but can instead work on their own. They are generally designed to cause network problems including bandwidth and resource utilization issues. Famous worms like the Mydoom and Sobig worms have affected thousands of computers and servers in the past. Worms typically spread by exploiting vulnerabilities in operating systems. You can prevent their spread by keeping clients and servers up-to-date with the latest security patches.

Attackers

It would be nice if everyone that is on your network and the networks connected to yours had good intentions. Unfortunately, this is not the case. Today's networks are under constant threats from attackers from the outside and even from the inside of their networks. These attackers may infiltrate and monitor your network if you're not careful to keep them under control. They could be someone who works for you, or they might even be someone who has been hired to get information. In any case, they must be considered in your security policy, and measures must be taken to thwart their attacks.

Man in the Middle

A *man-in-the-middle attack* occurs when a person places equipment or logical connections between two communicating parties. The two communicating parties still assume they are communicating directly to each other, but their information is actually being sent to the man in the middle who then forwards it to the intended recipient. The man-in-the-middle attack may just listen in on the communication and learn new information, or it may begin to change the communication between the parties so as to confuse or sabotage the communication. In either case, man-in-the-middle attacks are harmful to an organization. Most organizations adopt measures including strong authentication and the latest protocols such as L2TP with tunnel endpoint authentication.

Smurf

A *smurf* attack exploits a common network tool, specifically ping. As you know, when you ping a host, you will get a reply from that host. Well, let's say that you are in a network with hundreds of hosts. If you were to ping the broadcast address of your network, then all the hosts would reply to you. That means you would be flooded with replies from all over the network; however, you asked for it! Now let's say that you didn't ask for it but instead someone else pretended to be you and sent a ping using your source address to the broadcast address of the network. You would still get flooded with replies even though you didn't ping anyone. You would then be the victim of a smurf attack. To prevent this type of attack, simply install the latest security patches. One of the changes that the patches will make is to disallow any network host to ping their own broadcast address. This will put a stop to the smurf attack.

Rogue Access Points

You can control your security best if you understand your own network and if you know every piece of it. In fact, your whole security plan will likely be built around your network topology and the specific capabilities of the devices in your network. Now, suppose a user brings in their own equipment such as a wireless access point or a modem. Since you did not approve this equipment and it is not welcome on your network, it is referred to as a *rogue access point.*

The biggest problem with rogue access points is that they provide a shortcut to resources that goes around your security on the inside of your organization. They can also open a security vulnerability that would not have existed had they not been installed in your network. To prevent rogue access points from being installed, you should provide physical security and use authentication protocols between devices in the network.

Social Engineering

Social engineering attacks do not rely on protocols or technology to succeed, but instead they rely on human nature. People generally want to trust each other, and that's where social engineering attacks start. They could consist of something as simple as getting to know someone well enough to guess their password or tricking someone into giving their credentials on the phone. They could also consist of false websites that ask for information from unsuspecting web surfers. This type of attack is referred to as *phishing.* Social engineering attacks can be prevented best by simply training all users not to give out their credentials and to be very careful about anyone who asks for this information on a web page.

Mitigation Techniques

Now that I have discussed the main security threats against your network, let's look deeper into the ways that you can protect against these threats. The method you will use to mitigate a threat is largely dependent upon the type of threat. Methods from which you can choose include policies and procedures, user training, and patches and updates. In the following sections, I'll discuss each of these mitigation techniques.

Policies and Procedures

Security policies and procedures should be clearly outlined in writing in your organization. They should be written by those who know the network best and signed off on by upper management to give them authority. They should clearly define acceptable behavior on the organization's computers and networks and the consequences for violating acceptable behavior standards. Anyone who uses computers should be required to read these policies and procedures and sign a form agreeing that they have read and understood them. Finally, when someone does violate the acceptable behavior standards, the rules should be enforced to provide a deterrent to those who might "test" the policies next.

User Training

Although it may not seem to be the most convenient form of security at the time that it's done, user training is one of the most effective and least expensive mitigation techniques. The best way to keep users from making the mistakes that can lead to the success of a social engineering attack is to educate them about what to expect and how to handle it. In regard to IT personnel, the more they know about the policies, procedures, and protocols, the better they can assist you in the security of the network. In either case, training users provides a real benefit for a relatively low cost.

Patches and Updates

When an operating system or an application is released, it is typically not perfect from a security perspective. After its release, security patches and updates are also released on an ongoing basis that can be added to the software to make it more secure or give it more functionality. For example, Microsoft releases security patches on the second Tuesday of each month, "patch Tuesday," for most of its operating systems. The Windows Update system that is installed in all the latest clients, and servers can be configured to download and install these patches automatically. In addition, hotfixes may be released on other dates when there is a security reason to do so. Network administrators can also use Software Update Services (SUS) to download these patches to servers and test them before applying them to the bulk of clients on their network.

Exam Essentials

Understand the main security threats affecting networks.   You should understand the main security threats affecting networks such as DoS attacks, viruses and worms, man-in-the-middle, smurf, and social engineering attacks. You should know how each type of attack operates and how it creates a security hole.

Understand the main mitigation techniques.   You should understand what should be included in security policies and procedures and who should be involved in their creation. In addition, you should understand why training users is an effective and efficient method of guarding against social engineering threats and other network weaknesses. Finally, you should understand that security patches should be used to update your operating systems and applications.

Review Questions

1. Which type of firewall examines only the static attributes of a packet such as the IP address and protocol?

   A. Stateless

   B. IDS

   C. IPS

   D. Stateful

2. Which of the following is an advantage of signature identification? (Choose two.)

   A. The administrator's signature is required.

   B. It lets you benefit from the previous security issues of others.

   C. Signatures are identified by the vendor.

   D. It does not require programming or configuration.

3. Which of the following servers would most likely be placed in the DMZ? (Choose two.)

   A. Web

   B. FTP

   C. Domain controller

   D. DHCP

4. Which of the following are common tunneling protocols? (Choose two.)

   A. PPP

   B. VPN

   C. PPTP

   D. L2TP

5. Which of the following remote control protocols is installed by default on the latest Microsoft clients and servers?

   A. VNC

   B. TCP/IP

   C. ARP

   D. RDP

6. In PKI, which key(s) can be used to decrypt a message?

   A. Only the public key

   B. Only the private key

   C. Both the public key and the private key

   D. Neither key is used for decryption.

7. Which of the following is a remote access service that uses TCP?

   A. RADIUS

   B. WEP

   C. TACACS+

   D. WPA

8. In 802.1x, what is role of the client machine?

   A. Authenticator

   B. Authentication server

   C. Supplicant

   D. The client does not have a defined role.

9. Which of the following protocols is an open set of standards that allows the addition of new methods of authentication such as smart cards and biometric authentication?

   A. EAP

   B. CHAP

   C. MS-CHAP

   D. MS-CHAPv2

10. Which of the following is a type of social engineering attack?

   A. Man-in-the-middle

   B. Smurf

   C. DoS

   D. Phishing

Answers to Review Questions

1. A A stateless firewall examines only those static attributes of a packet such as the IP address and protocol. A stateful firewall identifies a packet stream and determines whether it is the normal stream that it should be seeing for that protocol. IDS and IPS are intrusion prevention/intrusion detection systems, which are not the same as a firewall.

2. B, C Signature identification is a method by which administrators can determine what they are filtering on a firewall. Security threats are identified with a signature ID, and the prevention technique can be deployed using the signature ID. You can also combine IDs into common groups to increase security and make sure nothing is forgotten. Since these can be programmed and don't have to be learned, it lets you benefit from the previous security issues of others.

3. A, B Servers that are likely to be used from the inside and the outside of the same organization should be placed in the DMZ. These include web, FTP, and VPN servers. Servers that are of higher security should be placed in the internal zone behind both firewalls. These include domain controllers, DHCP servers, and internal DNS servers. Servers that are used only on the outside, such as an external DNS server, may be placed in the external zone.

4. C, D The most common tunneling protocols are PPTP and L2TP. VPN is not a protocol but instead a type of network connection. PPP is used for serial point-to-point connections and for dial-up, but it is not a tunneling protocol.

5. D RDP is installed by default on all the latest Microsoft clients and servers. VNC is a remote control protocol that was developed by Oracle and since acquired by AT&T, but it is not installed by default on the latest Microsoft clients and servers. TCP/IP is an entire protocol suite and not a remote control protocol. ARP resolves IP addresses to MAC addresses and is not a remote control protocol.

6. B PKI uses key pairs such that when a message is encrypted using the public key, the only key that can decrypt the message is the private key of same key pair. The public key is never used to decrypt a message.

7. C TACACS is a remote access service developed by Cisco that centralizes authentication, authorization, and accounting (AAA). It is connection-oriented and uses TCP for communication. RADIUS is another remote access AAA service, but it uses UDP instead of TCP. WEP and WPA are wireless protocol security standards are not remote access services.

8. C 802.1x is often used for wired and wireless network access control. In 802.1x, the client is the supplicant who supplies the credentials to the authenticator and requests access. The authenticator does not authenticate the request but instead passes it to the authentication server. The authentication server authenticates the requests and gives the authenticator the permission to open the port and the client to communicate through it.

9.   A EAP is an open set of standards that allows for the addition of new methods of authentication. These may include smart cards, biometric authentication, and other forms of authentication. CHAP, MS-CHAP, and MS-CHAPv2 are challenge handshake protocols that have evolved over time. MS-CHAP and MS-CHAPv2 are proprietary to Microsoft, and the latter protocol can be used only on the latest clients and servers.

10. D A phishing attack is a type of social engineering attack because it relies on the behavior of the user who trusts a bogus website. Man-in-the-middle is a rather sophisticated attack by which the attacker places themself in the data stream between two hosts without the knowledge or consent of the users. A smurf attack uses the ICMP protocol and a bogus source address. The user is the victim and is not directly involved in the attack's success or failure. A DoS attack floods the network with useless data that takes up resources and keep systems from functioning properly.

Appendix: About the Companion CD

IN THIS APPENDIX:

✓ What you'll find on the CD

✓ System requirements

✓ Using the CD

✓ Troubleshooting

What You'll Find on the CD

The following sections are arranged by category and summarize the software and other goodies you'll find on the CD. If you need help with installing the items provided on the CD, refer to the installation instructions in the "Using the CD" section of this appendix.

Some programs on the CD might fall into one of these categories:

Shareware programs are fully functional, free, trial versions of copyrighted programs. If you like particular programs, register with their authors for a nominal fee and receive licenses, enhanced versions, and technical support.

Freeware programs are free, copyrighted games, applications, and utilities. You can copy them to as many computers as you like — for free — but they offer no technical support.

GNU software is governed by its own license, which is included inside the folder of the GNU software. There are no restrictions on distribution of GNU software. See the GNU license at the root of the CD for more details.

Trial, *demo*, or *evaluation* versions of software are usually limited either by time or by functionality (such as not letting you save a project after you create it).

Sybex Test Engine

For Windows

The CD contains the Sybex test engine, which includes two bonus exams located only on the CD.

PDF of Glossary of Terms

For Windows

We have included an electronic version of the Glossary in pdf format. You can view the electronic version of the Glossary with Adobe Reader.

Adobe Reader

For Windows

We've also included a copy of Adobe Reader so you can view PDF files that accompany the book's content. For more information on Adobe Reader or to check for a newer version, visit Adobe's website at www.adobe.com/products/reader/.

Electronic Flashcards

For PC, Pocket PC, and Palm

These handy electronic flashcards are just what they sound like. One side contains a question or fill-in-the-blank question, and the other side shows the answer.

System Requirements

Make sure your computer meets the minimum system requirements shown in the following list. If your computer doesn't match up to most of these requirements, you may have problems using the software and files on the companion CD. For the latest and greatest information, please refer to the ReadMe file located at the root of the CD-ROM.

- A PC running Microsoft Windows 98, Windows 2000, Windows NT4 (with SP4 or later), Windows Me, Windows XP, or Windows Vista
- An Internet connection
- A CD-ROM drive

Using the CD

To install the items from the CD to your hard drive, follow these steps:

1. Insert the CD into your computer's CD-ROM drive. The license agreement appears.

Windows users: The interface won't launch if you have autorun disabled. In that case, click Start ➤ Run (for Windows Vista, Start ➤ All Programs ➤ Accessories ➤ Run). In the dialog box that appears, type . (Replace D with the proper letter if your CD drive uses a different letter. If you don't know the letter, see how your CD drive is listed under My Computer.) Click OK.

2. Read the license agreement, and then click the Accept button if you want to use the CD.

The CD interface appears. The interface allows you to access the content with just one or two clicks.

Troubleshooting

Wiley has attempted to provide programs that work on most computers with the minimum system requirements. Alas, your computer may differ, and some programs may not work properly for some reason.

The two likeliest problems are that you don't have enough memory (RAM) for the programs you want to use or you have other programs running that are affecting installation or running of a program. If you get an error message such as "Not enough memory" or "Setup cannot continue," try one or more of the following suggestions and then try using the software again:

Turn off any antivirus software running on your computer. Installation programs sometimes mimic virus activity and may make your computer incorrectly believe that it's being infected by a virus.

Close all running programs. The more programs you have running, the less memory is available to other programs. Installation programs typically update files and programs; so if you keep other programs running, installation may not work properly.

Have your local computer store add more RAM to your computer. This is, admittedly, a drastic and somewhat expensive step. However, adding more memory can really help the speed of your computer and allow more programs to run at the same time.

Customer Care

If you have trouble with the book's companion CD-ROM, please call the Wiley Product Technical Support phone number at (800) 762-2974. Outside the United States, call +1(317) 572-3994. You can also contact Wiley Product Technical Support at http://sybex.custhelp.com. John Wiley & Sons will provide technical support only for installation and other general quality-control items. For technical support on the applications themselves, consult the program's vendor or author.

To place additional orders or to request information about other Wiley products, please call (877) 762-2974.°

Index

Note to the reader: Throughout this index **boldfaced** page numbers indicate primary discussions of a topic. *Italicized* page numbers indicate illustrations.

The Best CompTIA Network+ Quick Reference Book/CD Package on the Market!

Brush up on key Network+ topics with hundreds of challenging review questions!

- Two bonus exams available only on the CD. Each question includes a detailed explanation.

- 200 electronic flashcards.

- Glossary of Key Terms for instant reference.

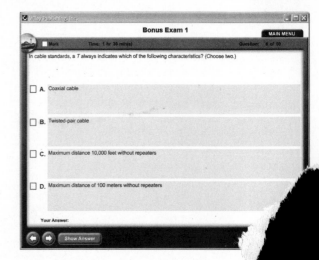

Use Glossary for instant reference

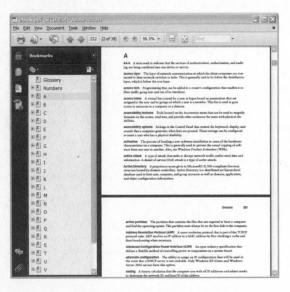

Reinforce your understanding of key concepts with flashcards for your PC, Pocket PC, or Palm handheld!

- Contains 200 flashcard questions.

- Run on multiple platforms for usability and portability.

- Quiz yourself anytime, anywhere.

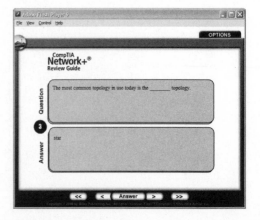